T0328987

Digital and Social Media Marketing

The second edition of *Digital and Social Media Marketing* is an up-to-date, industry-led results-driven guide to digital marketing. Mixing academic theory with practical examples from a range of different organisations worldwide, it provides insight into, and techniques to enable, the creation, development and maintenance of a successful digital presence.

This highly regarded textbook has been fully revised to bring the content up-to-date with the newest digital technologies. With topics including developing an effective digital presence, search engine optimization, and measuring brand awareness, the new edition also looks at digital ethics, General Data Protection Regulation and privacy, artificial intelligence and machine learning, and voice strategies. New international case studies are explored, including Alibaba and Amazon, as well as revised practical exercises in each chapter, enabling students to see how the concepts underpinning digital and social media marketing support business success. The book's customisable Digital Business Maturity Model, and the Buyer Persona Spring, offer organisations a clear road map for understanding their own levels of technology adoption and digital strategy development.

This accessible textbook provides a hands-on, user-friendly platform to turn skills and knowledge into strategic advantage. It is ideal for advanced undergraduate and postgraduate students of digital marketing and marketing strategy and for practitioners aiming to be at the cutting edge of digital and social media marketing.

Alongside electronic resources for each chapter, this new edition also includes digital learning materials, case studies and exercises available in a supporting online learning environment. The online materials further enhance learners' experience and support a worldwide learning community.

Aleksej Heinze is Associate Professor at KEDGE Business School, France.

Gordon Fletcher is Director of Business 4.0 at Salford Business School, University of Salford, UK.

Tahir Rashid is Senior Lecturer at the University of Salford, UK.

Ana Cruz is a Lecturer in Marketing at the University of Sheffield International Faculty, CITY College, Greece.

Digital and Social Media Marketing

A Results-Driven Approach

Second Edition

**Edited by Aleksej Heinze,
Gordon Fletcher, Tahir Rashid
and Ana Cruz**

Routledge
Taylor & Francis Group

LONDON AND NEW YORK

Second edition published 2020
by Routledge
2 Park Square, Milton Park, Abingdon, Oxon, OX14 4RN

and by Routledge
605 Third Avenue, New York, NY 10017

Routledge is an imprint of the Taylor & Francis Group, an informa business

© 2020 selection and editorial matter, Aleksej Heinze, Gordon Fletcher, Tahir Rashid and Ana Cruz; individual chapters, the contributors

First edition published by Routledge 2017

British Library Cataloguing-in-Publication Data
A catalogue record for this book is available from the British Library

Library of Congress Cataloging-in-Publication Data
Names: Heinze, Aleksej, editor. | Fletcher, Gordon, editor. | Rashid, Tahir, editor. | Cruz, Ana, editor.
Title: Digital and social media marketing : a results-driven approach / edited by Aleksej Heinze, Gordon Fletcher, Tahir Rashid and Ana Cruz.
Description: Second edition. | Milton Park, Abingdon, Oxon ; New York, NY : Routledge, 2020. | Includes bibliographical references and index.
Identifiers: LCCN 2019051095 (print) | LCCN 2019051096 (ebook) | ISBN 9780367235901 (hardback) | ISBN 9780367236021 (paperback) | ISBN 9780429280689 (ebook)
Subjects: LCSH: Internet marketing. | Internet advertising. | Electronic commerce. | Social media.
Classification: LCC HF5415.1265 .D5385 2020 (print) | LCC HF5415.1265 (ebook) | DDC 658.8/72—dc23
LC record available at https://lccn.loc.gov/2019051095
LC ebook record available at https://lccn.loc.gov/2019051096

ISBN 13: 978−0−367−23590−1 (hbk)
ISBN 13: 978−0−367−23602−1 (pbk)

Typeset in Bembo
by Apex CoVantage, LLC

Visit the companion website at www.mastersindigitalmarketing.org/book
Visit the eResources: www.routledge.com/9780367236021

We dedicate the second edition of *Digital and Social Media Marketing: A Results-Driven Approach* to our colleague Professor Rimantas Gatautis. We unexpectedly lost him on 3 March 2018, but he will continue to be with us in our memories as a valuable co-author of this book, mentor and dear friend.

Contents

Boxes

Case studies

Figures

Tables

Contributors

Alexander Christov, University of National and World Economy (UNWE), Bulgaria

Ana Cruz, University of Sheffield International Faculty, CITY College, Greece

Alex Fenton, Salford Business School, University of Salford, UK

Gordon Fletcher, Salford Business School, University of Salford, UK

Rimantas Gatautis, Kaunas University of Technology, Lithuania

Verena Hausmann, Universität Koblenz-Landau, Germany

Sayed Ali Hayder, Salford Business School, University of Salford, UK

Aleksej Heinze, KEDGE Business School, France

Sophie Iredale, Manchester Metropolitan University Business School, UK

Ashley Jones, Great Influence, UK

Stelios Karatzas, Best Plumbing and Lightning, Canada

Bartłomiej Kurzyk, University of Łódź, Poland

Mostafa Mohamad, Salford Business School, University of Salford, UK

Tahir Rashid, Salford Business School, University of Salford, UK

Milanka Slavova, University of National and World Economy (UNWE), Bulgaria

Ivan Stoychev, University of National and World Economy (UNWE), Bulgaria

Anna Tarabasz, S P Jain School of Global Management, United Arab Emirates

Elena Vitkauskaitè, Kaunas University of Technology, Lithuania

Martin J Williams, Managing Director, UKcopywriting.com, UK

Sue Williams, Universität Koblenz-Landau, Germany

Acknowledgements

We would like to thank our international advisory board members and all the contributors who have offered their feedback on the ideas of this book:

Barry Adams – Managing Director – Polemic Digital – UK
Dawn Anderson – Director – Bertey – UK
Olga Andrienko – Head of Global Marketing – SEMrush – USA
Tomasz Bartosz Kalinowski – Head of Knowbase, University of Łódź – Poland
Anjlee Bhatt – Chief Conversationalist and Caffeine Enthusiast – UK
James Bowman – Central Operations Manager – Prescribing Support Services – UK
Christina Chokoeva – Marketing Director – DINO Ltd – Bulgaria
Aisha Choudhry – Head of Search – Fast Web Media – UK
Vida Davidavičienė – Head of Department of Business Technologies – Vilnius Gediminas Technical University – Lithuania
Carla Dawson – Digital Marketing Strategist – xdawson.com – Argentina
Ian Dodson – Co-Founder and Director – Digital Marketing Institute – Ireland
Richard Dron – Lecturer in Digital Business – Salford Business School – UK
Alex Fenton – Lecturer in Digital Business – Salford Business School – UK
Joana Ferreira – Digital Marketing Consultant and Trainer – JVF Marketing – UK
Richard George – Managing Partner – Wavemaker North Manchester – UK
Briony Gunson – Consultant – Proctor Gallagher Institute – UK
Christopher Hackett – Technical Team Lead – Mporium – UK
Sophie Iredale – Manchester Metropolitan University Business School, UK
Emilis Jarockis – CEO – UAB 2066 – Lithuania
Chris Kent – Owner and Founder – 21st Century Marketing – Isle of Man
Błażej Kupaj – Sales and Marketing Director – PL Europa S.A. – Poland
Georgi Malchev – Managing Partner – Xplora.bg – Bulgaria
Cathal Melinn – Director/Founder – Digital Basics – Ireland
Susan Patch – Cofounder – Development Knowledge – Canada
Adrian Solomon – Project Manager – South East European Research Centre – Greece

Marco Schlüter – International Development Manager – Naturland – Germany

Colin Telford – Managing Partner – The Candidate Ltd – UK

Diana Tolockaite – Group Programmatic Trading Manager – Dentsu Aegis Network – UK

Jo Turnbull – Organiser – Search London – UK

Regimantas Urbanas – CMO – Tesonet – Lithuania

Rolandas Urka – Co-Founder and CEO – Sinergija verslui – Lithuania

Elena Vasilieva – Project Manager – University of Central Lancashire – UK

Marc Wilson – Head of information & security – Focus Independent Adult Social Work CIC – UK

Students

Mariam Ali – Student at Salford Business School – UK

Elsa Bota – Student at University of Sheffield International Faculty, CITY College – Greece

Cariad Fiddy – Student at Salford Business School – UK

Emily Goddard – Student at Salford Business School – UK

Nadia Latif – Student at Salford Business School – UK

Anka Gorgiev – Student at University of Sheffield International Faculty, CITY College – Greece

Anna Stavroudi – Student at University of Sheffield International Faculty, CITY College – Greece

Lia Nersisyan – Student at University of Sheffield International Faculty, CITY College – Greece

Felicia Siavalas – Student at University of Sheffield International Faculty, CITY College – Greece

Shazia Ullah – Student at Salford Business School – UK

Mohammed Waqar – Student at Salford Business School – UK

Lifelong Learning Programme

This book has been funded with support from the European Commission. This publication [communication] reflects the views only of the author, and the Commission cannot be held responsible for any use which may be made of the information contained therein.

Definitions of terms

Affiliate marketing – is a commission-based arrangement where referring websites receive a commission on sales or leads that are sent to merchants' e-commerce sites. Commissions can be fixed per lead or action or an agreed-upon percentage of the purchase.

AIDA model – Attention, Interest, Desire and Action model. This model was developed in 1893 in traditional advertising content evaluation and refined by many, including Elmo Lewis (1872–1948). It is used to evaluate the quality of marketing communication content, which should attract the Attention of the audience by focusing on the benefits of the product or service, raise the audience's Interest, offer evidence that it will meet their needs, hence raising their Desire, and finally, have a call-to-Action which could be tracked for measuring the success of content engagement.

Anchor text – text that appears as a link to a web page.

Black hat SEO – method of manipulating the search engine algorithm to achieve high search engine ranking by breaking stated search engine guidelines, for example, through buying incoming links from spam and irrelevant websites. Black hat SEO is also referred to as spamdexing, search spam, web spam, search engine spam or search engine poisoning, amongst others.

Buyer persona – is a representation of your customer that is based on your market research data or science fiction prototyping. It usually includes demographics, average order value, locations, national and regional culture, socio-economic background and decision making patterns. Central to buyer persona information are the 'pain touchpoints' and corresponding 'trust touchpoints'. It also includes the keywords they might use on search engines and social networks that they might engage with and other information that helps marketers to focus content towards buyers' needs.

Collaterals – or digital marketing collaterals are the assets that are produced for communicating messages about a product or service. This could include, for example, web pages, social media hashtags, apps, traditional print brochures, leaflets and videos.

Critical mass – the minimum number of individuals needed to sustain a community or make a community viable.

Customer – an individual who has made a purchase from you in the past if you are a business or – for a non-transactional organisation such as a health advice centre – a recorded interaction where value has been exchanged, such as advice being given or medicine prescribed.

Decision Making Unit – also DMU, a group of individuals who assume varying roles in making a purchase decision. In a family environment, a child may influence the decision while a parent undertakes the purchase. In a B2B organisational environment senior managers may influence the decision but the purchasing manager is charged with the specific task of buying.

Digital marketing strategy – sets out a long-term set of priorities (over three to five years) for an organisation using relevant channels, content and data in relation to specific buyer personas.

EEA – the European Economic Area is the largest economic marketplace in the world and creates an economic bond amongst EEA country member states.

Emergent strategy – development of a pattern of activities that start with actions and practices that over time become successful routines and are documented. This approach can be seen in contrast to a prescriptive strategy where a long-term plan is developed that then defines and informs a pattern of regular activities.

EU – the European Union unites most of the European countries in a politico-economic bond.

Fold – on a web page, an imaginary line where the screen ends and a user has to scroll (usually down) to see further content. This description is borrowed from newspapers, where usually you can only see the top section of a paper after it is folded.

Hashtag – a word or a number prefixed with a # sign which is used to develop and curate topics on social media networks. For example, the hashtag for this book is #passion4digital.

Hot touchpoint – also hot point or trust touchpoint. The 'perceived' solution to a pain touchpoint that has been identified by a buyer persona. See also 'pain point'.

HTML – Hypertext Markup Language. A standardised language that uses 'tags' to format content on web pages and facilitates the World Wide Web (WWW) in order to make it accessible to web browsers and other web content readers such as search engines.

Influencer – an individual who has enough social capital to influence the opinion of others with the result that the influenced individual changes their point of view or increases the likelihood they will purchase a reviewed product or a service.

Keyword – a significant search query of one or more words that are regularly used by search engine visitors and has been methodically identified considering the Relevance, Specificity, Popularity and Competition of the term.

Keyword map – a list of keywords systematically identified for a particular organisation, which takes into account organisational strategy as well as existing services and products that provide focus for the web properties that need to be developed.

Long tail keyword – a search term of three or more words that are used by individuals who are closer to completing their purchase decision compared to those who use a 'short tail keyword'. For example, 'Nikon D3500 Digital SLR Camera in Black' is a long tail keyword compared to 'Digital Camera'.

Metadata – a small piece of data that is used to describe larger pieces of data; for example, a book has metadata that includes a book title, the author and the year of publication. A web page metadata includes similar fields, including two very important fields for search engines – page title and page description. If a web page has metadata defined for a page title and description, these tend to be displayed on a search engine results page (SERP).

Organic SEO – also described as natural SEO, a method of improving search engine rankings that does not rely on payment for getting individual visitor clicks. The method relies on strategies such as content marketing that places emphasis on developing relevant content that attracts external links and social shares and is developed around strategic keywords.

Paid search marketing – pay-per-click or PPC is part of search engine marketing. It differs from 'organic' or 'natural' search engine optimisation (SEO), as it involves paid advertising. PPC is a text-based ad with a link to a company or product page that is displayed to a user when their keyword query matches a phrase chosen by the advertiser. The advertiser pays a fee for the predefined action undertaken by the user. Although this is usually a click on the ad, there are other charging methods, as PPC may additionally involve advertising through a display/content network of third-party sites – these are described as cost-per-click (CPC), cost-per-mille (CPM) or cost-per-action (CPA).

Pain point – also referred to as pain touchpoint, issues that are key challenges for the buyer persona in relation to obtaining our products or services. Pain may be experienced at the point of finding, ordering or delivering the product or service. See also 'hot touchpoint'.

PPC – see paid search marketing.

PPC SEO – a method of optimising paid advertising campaigns. This approach relies on strategies such as click-through optimisation, which increases the number of relevant people clicking on an ad as a reduced cost to the advertiser.

Primary keyword – a search term that is used as the focus for a particular digital profile page and describes the main aspect of the content being developed. For example, a web page should have one primary keyword and two or three secondary keywords.

Prospects – individuals who have the potential to become customers. A customer has made a purchase from you in the past whilst the prospect has not.

rel=nofollow – an HTML tag used by some search engines to determine whether a link should be used as endorsement and hence increase the ranking authority of that web page.

Science fiction prototyping – a method that uses a science fiction approach to describing the future in order to develop market leading products or services which cannot necessarily be envisaged through past data uses or current buyer persona behaviour.

Secondary keyword – a search term that is used as a supporting term on a digital profile page but unlike the primary keyword does not describe the main focus of the content.

Seed keyword – a search term that is entered into a keyword research tool with the intention of discovering related terms.

SEO – search engine optimisation. A method of improving the position of an online profile such as a website or a social media profile in SERPs for relevant keyword terms.

SERP –search engine results page – the web page that displays the results to a search query and usually lists the top ten answers. The web pages generated by a search engine are based on its index of the web at the time of a search query.

Short tail keyword – a search query term that comprises one or two words. Typically, these terms are used in the early stages of a buyer's search for information. See also 'long tail keyword'.

Sitemap – a protocol used by major search engines to interpret the structure and intended relationship of web pages on a website. The sitemaps.org website outlines the standards used: www.sitemaps.org/

SMART objective – a specific, measurable, attainable, realistic and timely statement that breaks down a broader aim. Objectives can be set out at an organisational, business or campaign level. Once objectives are set, these are reviewed on a regular basis in order to learn from them before they are revised for the next round of continuous improvement.

Spam – generally used in an email context where a large quantity of unsolicited emails is received. However, spam also occurs on online forums where repeat and often off-topic messages are posted in order to gain visibility to search engines of the outward links from a forum. In a search engine context, spam is considered to be any action that violates the fair use guidelines of a search engine and tends to include actions that are exclusively made to unfairly manipulate the search engine ranking algorithm.

Thin content – a web page that does not add any value for the visitor. Thin content tends to have display a lot of advertisements and no original content. The number of words is always a determinant factor for the thinness of a page, but web pages with a low number of words (fewer than 500) are likely to be considered thin.

UK – United Kingdom.

URL – Universal Resource Locator or web address – it is the unique address of a web page on the World Wide Web.

USA – United States of America.

Section I

Introduction

A visual introduction to digital and social media marketing

Gordon Fletcher

This book takes a practical approach. Regardless of whether you are running a flower shop in Krakow, a building contractor supplier in Glasgow, a charity in Marseille or a multinational in Thessaloniki, there will be useful lessons to be found throughout the book. At the same time as being practical, this book is 'always strategic' about digital marketing. Attention is always turned towards those who buy your goods or services and how you can have ongoing sustainable interaction with them.

The importance of marketing is significant for all facets of an organisation. In this book, we present an approach to digitally mature business that is described as 'marketing first'. For your organisation, this means placing digital marketing at the heart of everything you do and allowing it to contribute to all of the key decisions that you make. A marketing first approach within a digitally mature organisation enables rapid respond to changing business practices; global markets, including new competitors; and the increased expectations of transparency and engagement from your highly networked customers.

Digital marketing is not simply about generating a short-term boost in sales. All of the actions described in the book have an impact on the way that an organisation functions internally and, over time, contribute to a realignment of your organisation. As a business recognises the pivotal importance of data in the operation of all its functions, the business itself changes as it progresses through the Digital Business Maturity Model (Figure 0.1) – a model that we explain in detail in later chapters.

This chapter introduces the concepts of digital and social media marketing through a visual device that we describe as the 'Buyer Persona Spring' (Figure 0.2). Step by step through this chapter we will explain the value and purpose of the Spring and each of its elements with the goal of connecting you – and your organisation – in an ongoing and sustainable way with your customers.

The Spring will also guide you through the rest of this book as we explain the key concepts and activities that are currently used in digital and social media marketing. This structured explanation of the concepts will give you a clear basis for understanding and then applying the marketing actions that we recommend as world-leading practice throughout the rest of this book.

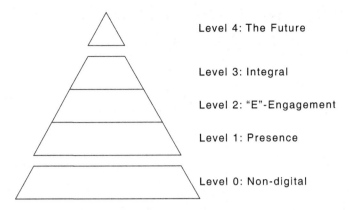

Figure 0.1 The Digital Business Maturity Model

Figure 0.2 The Buyer Persona Spring

Figure 0.3 The Buyer Persona Spring now labelled

The Spring (Figures 0.2 and 0.3) is composed of three key elements. On the left is the organisation (you) attempting to engage and interact with your customers who are represented at the right-hand side of the Buyer Persona Spring. You, your organisation and your customers are complex in their own right and composed of many parts. We will describe these parts in detail later. The device that connects you to your customers is the Spring itself, which has three loops representing the three key elements of all digital marketing strategy. These three elements are channels, content and data and distill the most important parts of the relationship between you and your buyer persona. By using the

Buyer Persona Spring to structure your thoughts, this book sets out to help you understand your own dynamic organisation and your customers as well as the complexities of maintaining communications with them in a digital era.

The starting point for understanding digital marketing is found in the answer to the question, 'What is a buyer persona?'. To understand all of your customers, we describe and speak to them collectively through the buyer persona. The buyer persona recognises that you are not just speaking on a one-to-one basis with each individual customer but instead are speaking with an archetypal representation of a group of customers who share similar qualities, attributes and attitudes. The buyer persona consolidates all your similar customers and consumers that you describe (in detail) as the target of your strategic planning.

In the era of digital communications, the buyer persona also recognises that your customers are never all the same and that their combinations of interests and motivations vary slightly, amongst themselves and over time, in relation to you and your products and services. In the unplanned rush to become digital, the era of mass-consumerism and mass-consumption has quietly disappeared and been overtaken by the rising stars of individualised e-commerce, mass-customisation and short-run (or single-run) production. Your buyer persona enjoys and appreciates being spoken to as an individual – even if they are ultimately a construct of your own market research – and responds positively to your considerations.

Making the buyer persona the focus of your attention is acknowledgement that all marketing – but especially digital marketing – is about building ongoing, long-term positive and context-driven relationships. You want your organisational brands as well as your products and services to engage with your buyer persona. Your buyer persona is a narrative about the optimal buyer, it is an identity that is recognisable to your consumers and customers, and talking to your buyer persona creates a recognisable and meaningful conversation with them.

The buyer persona is an important recognition that successful digital marketing requires you to work with all those who 'engage with' you rather than solely 'those who buy your products and services'. Through your digital marketing strategies and your engagement with your buyer persona, you are engaging with not only buyers but also potential buyers, influencers, previous buyers (who can become influencers) and potentially even competitors. In other words, while this book uses the term buyer persona consistently, it represents a potential range of personas beyond solely that of a buyer.

The buyer persona is visually represented in this book by a series of intersecting circles that describe the various roles and identities that are often used in digital marketing texts (Figure 0.4). 'Users' are the outermost wrapper category for the buyer persona. This is the most inclusive category of individuals that effectively includes everyone who can be engaged through digital channels. The implication of the label is that an individual 'uses' digital media, but their forms of engagement in the specifics will vary by context. There is also a tacit recognition that the 'digital' of digital marketing has transformed 'marketing' into a two-way conversation that diminishes the value of broadcast approaches.

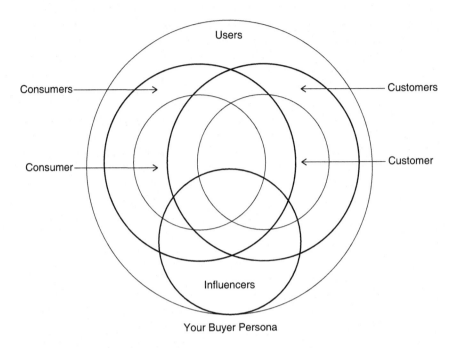

Figure 0.4 Inside the buyer persona

However, the impact of digital channels and the content they convey, as well as the importance of creating data-driven experiences, are also felt by those who do not engage regularly with digital media.

Strategic approaches to digital marketing recognise clearer differentiations that move beyond broad brush identifications of 'users'. Influencers are the individuals who influence the buying decisions for themselves and others. In the context of digital channels, influencers include product reviewers and bloggers as well as the closer and more traditional influence of, for example, friends and family. Influencers overlap with all the other categories within the buyer persona, not as a result of their comparative importance but rather because of their complex relationship with all aspects of the buyer persona. This complexity translates – in marketing terms – into the difficulty that organisations have in engaging with these individuals in a suitable manner.

Within the buyer persona are the consumers and customers. Customers are those who buy your goods and services and are distinct from consumers, who actually consume and gain benefit by realising the value of your goods and services. It is likely that in many if not most cases these two categories will overlap, but as any retailer of children's toys will recognise, these roles can often have a very significant distinction. Within the circles of the consumers and customers, two further circles represent the individual consumer and customer. These

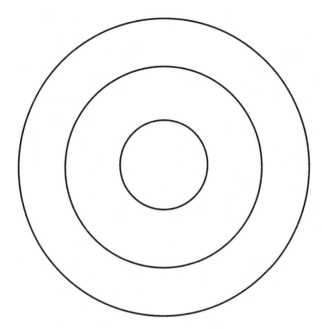

Figure 0.5 The buyer persona symbol

inner circles remind us that consumers and customers themselves are also differentiated between individuals within these categories.

Your goal in working with the buyer persona is to gain advantage through digital technologies to individually address a specific point of intersection within the circle of users that may incorporate influencers, consumers and customers and which is recognisable to those who buy and consume your goods and services. Chapter 3 defines the concept of the buyer persona in more detail, but the key point to remember is that it is a versatile concept. Successfully engaging the buyer persona might be measured by purchases in a retail sense, by an increased volume of orders in a business-to-business (B2B) context or by an increase in charitable giving for a specific cause in the non-profit sector.

We use an unlabelled symbol of the buyer persona (Figure 0.5) throughout the book to reinforce the focus of our discussions and its relationship to the other elements of the Buyer Persona Spring.

0.1 You and your buyer persona

Explaining the role of the buyer persona within the Buyer Persona Spring requires a return to the beginning. By examining and constantly reflecting on your relationship with the people who buy your goods and services – your customers – you are actively engaging with the ongoing process of defining your buyer persona.

Figure 0.6 The simplistic relationship between your organisation and the buyer

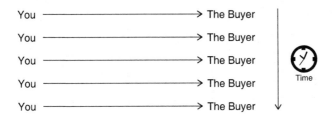

Figure 0.7 The simplistic relationship between you and the buyer persona repeated over time

The buyer persona has a more complex meaning than that of buyer, consumer or customer. In a simple world, the relationship between you and your buyers can be represented by a single straight line (Figure 0.6).

You sell goods (or services) to a buyer. This is a single transaction that is repeated with each buyer. Some buyers may return to you to buy again, but this simple relationship model only regards a return buyer as yet another (new) buyer. In this model, every transaction you have with a buyer is regarded as the same relationship repeated again and again over time (Figure 0.7). In this situation the relationship you have with the buyer never develops or progresses beyond the last transaction.

The relationship shown in Figure 0.7 is unlikely to be sustainable unless it is modelling a specific combination of circumstances. The most likely circumstance that echoes the model of Figure 0.7 will be found where you may have the privilege of being the sole supplier of goods or services as a result of location, time, convenience or the type of product or service that is being sold (Figure 0.8).

For example, a late-night store, a highly specialised B2B product or a business in a highly regulated industry could all exploit one or more parameters of being a sole supplier. However, even if this is your current business situation or you currently benefit from having multiple parameters that mean that you are in some way a sole supplier, it will not remain the case permanently. Already, in most sectors, more consumers have access to mobile commerce and global alternatives that enable far greater choice and options than ever before.

Even traditional business models, for example, taxis and bed and breakfasts, have felt the influence of digital technology through the impact of the Uber and AirBnB apps and their associated business models. With the business models of these disruptors built around the sharing economy and social networking channels, the challenge they present to other models is the way they resist being pinned down to conventional definitions or practices. All of these imminent competitors remove the privilege of assuming you will always be – in some way – a sole supplier.

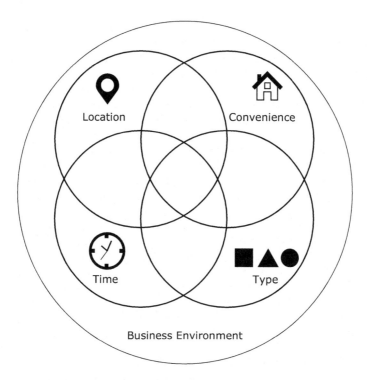

Figure 0.8 The parameters for being a sole supplier

In the competitive global environment and with the acknowledgement that your organisation must sensibly and regularly engage with the buyers of your goods or services, you are already recognising the need and importance of marketing. This recognition of need is the basis for our description of a 'marketing first' approach to digital business. The briefest of mentions in the previous paragraph to mobile commerce and global alternatives has already pointed towards a need for your marketing to be digital, as that is the direction in which your entire organisation needs to move. Digital marketing will enable this to happen proactively rather than being faced with the prospect of becoming a casualty of the change prevailing in all business sectors. A marketing first approach to becoming a more digitally mature business is the most accessible opportunity for you to be able to take on and overtake your slower-moving competitors.

To reflect the necessary two-way ongoing and communicative nature of the relationship that you build with your customers, a second arrow is added (Figure 0.9) to our original simple relationship (Figure 0.6). In traditional marketing, this extra arrow can be used to reflect a wide range of meanings. The two-way relationship reflects the influence of marketing communications on the buyer, marks the combination of push and pull factors that influence buyer

You ←⎯⎯⎯⎯⎯⎯⎯⎯⎯⎯⎯→ The Buyer

Figure 0.9 A simple communicative relationship between you and the buyer

You The Buyer

Figure 0.10 Purely tactical marketing activities

behaviour and is a recognition that it is easier to encourage return custom from previous buyers than to continuously initiate new relationships (Figure 0.7). More implicit in this two-way relationship is the recognition that you actively learn from your interactions with buyers and modify your approach as a result of reflection and learning. All of these implied understandings that are embedded in a relatively simple diagram (Figure 0.9) are already pushing you towards a continuously strategic perspective.

Of course, if this two-way diagram (Figure 0.9) represented the sum total of the relationship between a buyer and a business, then the organisation could manage the majority of its marketing activities through continuous direct conversations with each of its buyers individually. Some (very small) businesses can still continue to do this. Imagine, for example, the conversations of a local baker, the local milkman or a local retailer of high-value jewellery, who all choose to solely serve their very local community. In the most straightforward of ways the local baker in this example will receive return customers because of their conversations and interactions. However, as soon as the lines of communication become more complex or become mediated through digital technologies, the business becomes busier. If an organisation has growing ambition, then this face-to-face relationship and direct communications approach to marketing requires the support of well-planned, more wide-ranging and more strategic forms of engagement.

A common response by some organisations to the complexity of engaging with their customers and prospective customers is to try as many different activities and actions (whether they are offline or online) as possible (Figure 0.10). The ensuing whirlwind of activity may produce some positive results, but without receiving any clear feedback or verifiable measure of the results the chances of repeating or learning from these actions are incredibly small. Taking an entirely tactical approach to marketing with varying results and no reflection is what this book seeks to avoid in all sizes of organisations.

Even in the digital domain, where the measurement of activities is significantly easier and more accurate than in traditional marketing, there are numerous examples of businesses employing this 'pay, spray and pray' approach to digital marketing across a range of channels to try to communicate with an undefined audience that may or may not include their target customers. Importantly, and more specifically, the application of analogies between traditional media-oriented marketing actions and the digital domain does not hold up well.

Table 0.1 The digital marketing challenge matrix

Digital marketing challenges	Barriers (to digital marketing)	Benefits (of digital marketing)
Small business	Expense to engage	Competitive advantage
	Lack of human resources	Expand markets
	No strategic view	Diversify products/services
		Target buyers
Large business	Broadcast media perspective	Data-driven decisions
	'Lock in' with agencies	Iterative planning and learning
	Low expectation of feedback	Focus on buyer persona

However, without a clear understanding of digital marketing it is unsurprising that many large and well-established businesses have applied the (to them) familiar techniques of traditional marketing and mass-consumer advertising. False assurances are offered by internal experts and outside consultants to these businesses that maintaining old strategies is the lowest-risk strategy. Some digital channels encourage this thinking and similar levels of spending by offering what seem to be familiar sales packages.

At the same time, for many smaller organisations, the sophistication of digital marketing has resulted in many seeing their own online activities as experiments in a new and untested domain. Neither the small nor large organisational scenarios that are described here reflect a strong understanding of the benefits or differences of digital marketing. For the smaller organisation, the majority of the models and tools for strategic marketing continue to have value and meaning in a digital domain. With the addition of the digital context, an organisation's marketing function has the capacity to provide greater levels of analytical feedback and rapid responses than have ever been possible with traditional methods. The use of digital also means that data-driven feedback can have input into wider decisions in the organisation including internal process design and long-term design of their products or services. For small organisations, their marketing challenge is the same as it has always been: committing to the ongoing investment of resources that allow them to become strategic (Table 0.1).

For larger organisations with well-established approaches to their marketing, digital marketing offers the ability to be more sophisticated in addressing a more tightly defined core audience (the buyer persona) with differentiated and carefully positioned content and opportunities for conversations. This form of change also introduces the importance of data and the embedding of a learning cycle into marketing activity, which for some organisations is a major challenge to their existing practice (Table 0.1).

0.2 Your complex organisation

Your complex organisation (Figure 0.11) must interact with your buyer persona. Your buyer persona is the narrative that represents – through a single persona – the many buyers who want your products and services and who seek an association with your brand. The buyer persona is the focus of attention for your digital marketing actions, as a strategically oriented organisation, but you must also have some self-awareness of your own organisation. In the Buyer Persona Spring, your complex organisation is presented as a series of overlapping circles (Figure 0.12).

The outside circle of the organisation represents the market (or markets) within which you exist. Most organisations will recognise this in a straightforward way as being what they 'do', their profession or the things that they sell. Increasing business transparency, innovative business models and the use of sharing and crowdsourcing

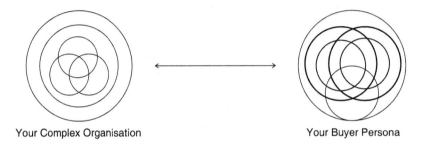

Your Complex Organisation   Your Buyer Persona

Figure 0.11 The complex organisation and the buyer persona

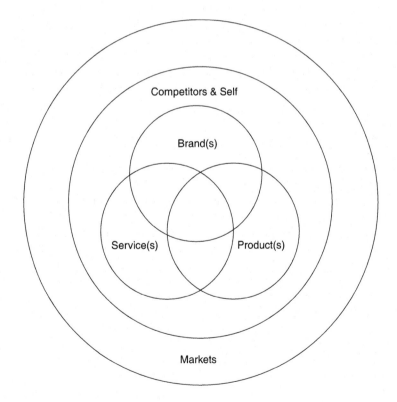

Figure 0.12 Your complex organisation

challenge existing labels and traditional definitions requiring deeper reflection and more mature responses from an organization. These particular challenges and the need for a change of perspective are for discussion in later chapters.

You and your competitors are positioned within your market. The acknowledgement here of competitors and markets is a recognition of the many external factors that have an impact upon your plans for interacting with your buyer persona. The market itself is also affected by other factors beyond just your activities and those of your competitors. An understanding of these factors can be gained through a PESTLE (political, economic, social, technical, legal, environmental and ethical) analysis of the external environment.

Both you and your competitors have a range of goods and services that you are offering to your buyer persona. If you are successful or at least sustainable as an organisation you are also meeting some specific needs of your current buyer persona. Even if you currently only offer tangible goods, the organisation diagram (Figure 0.12) does acknowledge your future as an increasingly digitally mature business with the potential for new services that are driven by data that you hold or can access. Overlapping with your goods and services is your brand (or brands). Brands can communicate with the buyer persona in a way that is distinct from the goods and services themselves. The meaning that brands convey in their presentation is an important start and end point for feeding back from the buyer persona.

Your organisation is dynamic, with a continuously shifting relationship with your buyer persona. Being strategic means that you learn from the buyer persona and respond to the changing external environment with data-driven evidence-based decisions.

We represent your organisation throughout this book with a simplified icon (Figure 0.13).

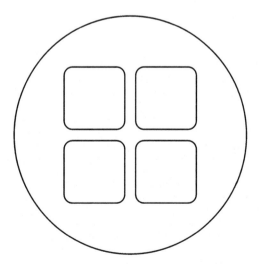

Figure 0.13 Your organisation

0.3 The Buyer Persona Spring and action-based learning

The final element of the Buyer Persona Spring is the connecting spirals – considered overall, this is the strategy that connects your organisation with your buyer persona. The iterative nature of successful strategic digital marketing means that the buyer persona as well as your tactics and techniques are all regularly reviewed. This iterative strategic approach to marketing is the key concept embedded in the Buyer Persona Spring.

Each of the spirals contained within the Buyer Persona Spring visually represents the action learning cycle (Figure 0.14). The cycle is a continuous process of planning, acting, observing and reflecting. After the completion of each cycle, the reflection and learning resulting from the process inform any changes needed for subsequent plans. The action learning cycle is a well-established and recognisable theory of learning that has direct application to organisational planning and, through this linkage, to digital marketing. The action learning cycle is generally represented with directional arrows indicating that reflection will always lead onwards to the next stage of planning.

The action learning cycle is by definition an iterative process and is never accurately conveyed as a single cycle of action. Instead, the action learning cycle should be represented as a continuous – possibly never-ending – process (Figure 0.15).

In the Buyer Persona Spring, we overlay the principles of the action learning cycle to reflect the need to plan and enact marketing activities (Figure 0.16). The Buyer Persona Spring and the action learning cycle can then be read in parallel. This continuous iterative loop of activities will also be familiar to those with experience of Agile project management, which advocates a similar iterative, continuous and consciously self-reflective strategic approach to core processes and activities. With a strategy in place to reach the buyer persona, specific plans can then be made. Planning for digital marketing sets SMART (specific, measurable, attainable, realistic and timely) objectives (discussed in Chapters 1 and 2) that will determine the outcomes necessary to measure and assess the

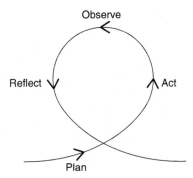

Figure 0.14 Action learning cycle

success of specific actions. Planning will start with the definition of campaigns and then, within those campaigns, the specific tactics required will be identified. The tactics and campaigns will need to be observed and monitored. At the end of the timeframe determined by the SMART objectives, there will be an opportunity to assess and reflect upon the success of the plan. This reflection will then feed back into the overall strategy and subsequent planning. In effect, at this point the next cycle has been initiated. In distinction from the action learning cycle, the cycle of activities in the Buyer Persona Spring is not always one-directional. Your assessment may require only small revisions to your tactics or campaign. In a practical sense, this involves one or two steps backwards rather than pressing onwards to a completely new iteration of your objectives. Similarly, the Buyer Persona Spring recognises that changes and alterations in your strategy may be compatible with your current campaigns and tactics, effectively creating a repeat of the same loop.

As with the action learning cycle, the Buyer Persona Spring is a continuous process (Figure 0.17). Each iteration of the spring allows an opportunity for you to revise your strategy and to accommodate changes in the buyer persona or your organisation. Within each iteration there are opportunities – upon

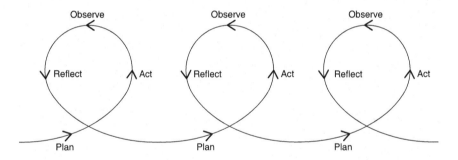

Figure 0.15 The repeating action learning cycle

Figure 0.16 An individual loop in the Buyer Persona Spring

reflection and assessment – to modify or tweak your tactics and campaign based on immediate feedback from the data that you will continuously collect.

For successful digital marketing, we identify three key elements that are each taken up by the continuous cycles of the Buyer Persona Spring. These three elements are channels, content and data (Figure 0.18). The ordering of these three elements also represents greater sophistication as your organisation moves towards higher levels of digital maturity. Channels deal with the specific channels through which your organisation represents itself. Channels include your essential website presence as well as any more specialised presence channels you might have, such as a DeviantArt account for creative businesses.

The content element decouples specific platforms from the content that your organisation produces and how it disseminates this content. The content element will inevitably overlap with the channels element, but it will also tackle other systems where your organisation may not have direct control or access.

The broader data element will take your organisation to more sophisticated levels of digital maturity through recognition of the pivotal importance of all types of data. The data element will overlap with the content element and then extend to encompass all data that can be accessed or interrogated by the organisation. The more integrated use of data throughout the organisation is the key driver to increasing digital maturity. The data element will itself directly

Figure 0.17 Iterative loops within the Buyer Persona Spring

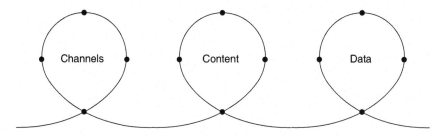

Figure 0.18 The three key elements of digital marketing

contribute to the reflective and iterative basis of the Buyer Persona Spring and inform the evolution of all three elements – as well as your overall strategy – as they engage the buyer persona.

0.4 The Buyer Persona Spring

In combination, the organisation, the buyer persona and the three elements of digital marketing strategy represent the Buyer Persona Spring (Figure 0.19). The relationship and interactions between the organisation and the buyer persona are two-way, iterative, dynamic and strategic. The specific planning, interactions and activities that are the basis for your organisation's digital marketing activities are defined and shaped by existing and relatively familiar tools of business analysis in the form of PESTLE and SWOT (strengths, weaknesses, opportunities and threats) analyses and setting SMART objectives, with success being measured through key performance indicators (KPIs).

The full model of the Buyer Persona Spring (Figure 0.20) recognises that development of each element must run in parallel (and in harmony) with the others and that each strategy is iterative and actively incorporates feedback into subsequent planning and activities. However, the Buyer Persona Spring containing a single set of loops (Figure 0.19) is used as a simpler representation of the challenges and opportunities that become available as you step through the development of a digital marketing strategy for your organisation in subsequent chapters.

Ultimately, success – measured by comparing your organisation's performance against that of your competitors and the outcomes that you will define in your marketing strategy – will conceptually draw the Buyer Persona Spring closer to your organisation. This will only be achieved with the parallel alignment of the three elements – of content, channels and data – and the alignment of the actions you implement to address these elements with your own organisation's position, your overall strategy and the relevance of your buyer persona. Symbolically, this tight alignment will contract the Buyer Persona Spring and draw your organisation closer to your buyer persona (Figure 0.21).

Figure 0.19 The Buyer Persona Spring

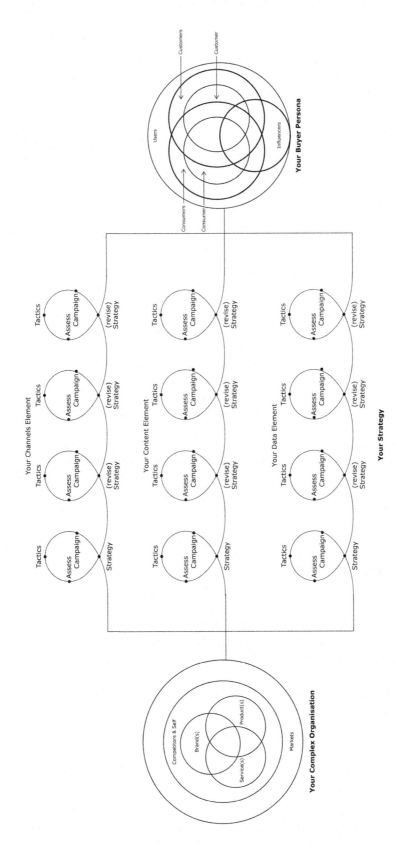

Figure 0.20 The complete Buyer Persona Spring

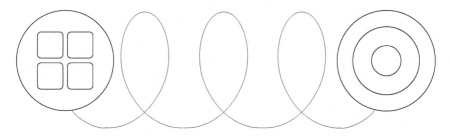

Figure 0.21 The Buyer Persona Spring – success

0.5 Book structure

- Chapter 1 describes digital marketing in terms of the concepts, key technologies, technology adoption in organisations and the recognition of success.
- Chapter 2 explains how digital technologies can be utilised in an organisational context to serve specific business needs.
- Chapter 3 explains how to understand digital consumers. Understanding consumers enables the description of the buyer persona to capture the drivers behind digital consumer decision making.
- Chapter 4 develops a digital strategy. By understanding the digital consumer, an organisation can then develop a strategy that sets objectives and uses tactics to achieve its aims.
- Chapter 5 discusses campaign planning and management as a key tactic for implementing a digital strategy.
- Chapters 6, 7, 8, 9 and 10 are interrelated chapters that provide more details on the specific actions required to implement digital campaigns.
- Chapter 6 describes the issues of digital presence.
- Chapter 7 details the practice of search engine optimisation (SEO) and explains how digital presence should be optimised to obtain strong search engine results.
- Chapter 8 focuses on social media and the behaviour of online communities.
- Chapter 9 focuses on content marketing and the importance of amplifying such content.
- Chapter 10 considers pay-per-click (PPC) advertising as a means of driving customers towards an organisation's digital presence.
- Chapter 11 incorporates the actions of mobile marketing and describes the peculiarities of working within a mobile environment.
- Chapter 12 looks at campaign evaluation, including the benefits of and cautions in using web analytics.
- Chapter 13 considers future users and future marketing issues.

Each of the chapters of the book can, in turn, be mapped to one of more of the individual elements of the Buyer Persona Spring (Figure 0.22)

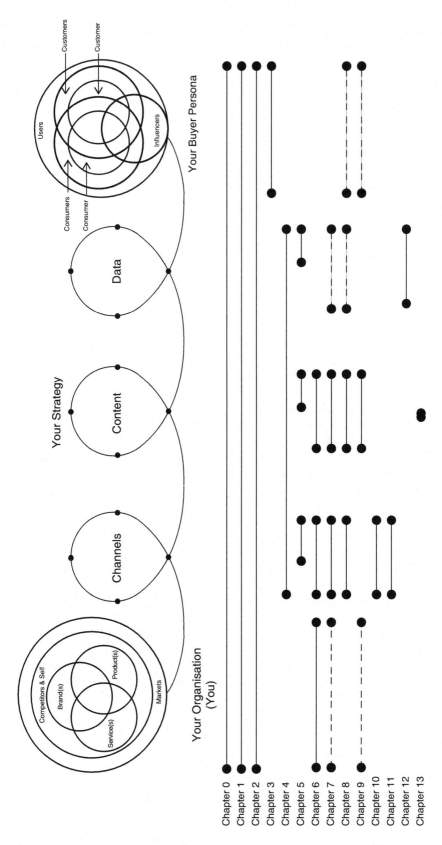

Figure 0.22 The book's chapters mapped to the Buyer Persona Spring

1 Understanding digital and social media marketing concepts

Rimantas Gatautis

1.0 Learning objectives

In this chapter you will learn how to:

- understand and use the terms and concepts relating to digital marketing;
- recognise patterns of success and failure in digital marketing;
- position individual organisations – including your own – within the Digital Business Maturity Model; and
- understand online consumer behaviour using the Zero Moment of Truth (ZMOT) model.

1.1 Understanding digital and social media marketing

This chapter introduces the key concepts that can make organisations more effective, more impactful, more sustainable and more strategic. These concepts are presented within a 'marketing first' perspective that acknowledges that the marketing function within most organisations will be the most externally facing and digitally aware of all the business functions. Marketing in this sense is presented here as the vanguard for change within the organisation as it endeavours to become more digitally mature in all of its activities and processes.

This perspective is also important as a conceptual starting point, as it recognises marketing as an integral business function and a key mechanism for driving an organisation towards being digital in outlook and perspective. The viewpoint taken by many traditional marketing texts separates out different business functions – including digital engagement – into discrete parts of an organisation with no acknowledgement of the feedback each function introduces into the organisation overall (Figure 1.1). In direct contrast, the strategic and integrated approach taken throughout this book positions the marketing function of an organisation as being intertwined with all other functions in order to achieve overall sustainable success (Figure 1.2).

The Buyer Persona Spring used throughout the book reflects the strategic perspective necessary for successful digital marketing – and for successfully improving the digital maturity of an organisation overall. The representation of

Figure 1.1 A traditional view of marketing, digital and other functions within a business

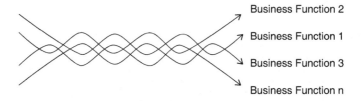

Figure 1.2 Visualising the conceptual understanding of business used in this book

the organisation in the Buyer Persona Spring acknowledges the influence of external factors, including competitors, and connects with the buyer persona itself through an iterative, self-reflective cycle of campaigns that deploy specific digital marketing tools and techniques.

The essential first step in taking a strategic 'marketing first' approach to becoming a digitally mature organisation is to demystify the current jargon used in digital and social media marketing and to link the meanings of these words with more recognisable and well-established business terms and concepts. After defining key current terminology, the chapter goes on to discuss the general principles relating to digital marketing success and failure and relates this insight to an assessment of an organisation's overall digital maturity.

This chapter builds on the visual introduction of the previous chapter, with continuing emphasis on the importance of the buyer persona for understanding the relationship of customers to the goods and services offered by your organisation. The Buyer Persona Spring is then returned to later in this chapter and throughout the rest of the book. This chapter concludes with a summary of the tools used for planning and delivering strategic digital and social media marketing. The purpose and value of these planning tools are also presented in relation to the overall Buyer Persona Spring model.

1.2 How to speak digital and social media marketing

The terms used in digital and social media marketing can have multiple and sometimes contradictory meanings. For the sake of consistency and clarity, the key terms and definitions set out in this chapter are applied throughout this book.

- *Digital technologies* describes the complex combination of different types of hardware, software, Internet access and social networks that now represent the familiar forms of computing that influence most people's everyday lives in Europe and in other advanced economies.
- *Information and communication technologies* (or *ICTs*) is a longer-standing term for digital technologies. The term is generally used more restrictively than 'digital technologies' to describe the traditional computers and sometimes the software used to store, process and share information. In this sense, the most recognisable examples of ICTs are personal computers (PCs) with familiar software installed such as word processors or spreadsheets.
- *The Internet* is the largest and most commonly used network for digitally mediated communications. The Internet is a cooperative globe-spanning network of linked digital technologies including mobile phones, computers as well as increasingly things such as domestic appliances (e.g. fridges), sensors, wearable devices and cars in a way that enables interchangeable communication. This connectivity of nontraditional but digitally enabled items is labelled the 'Internet of Things'.
- *The World Wide Web* (or *WWW*, or just *'the Web'*) is often confused with the Internet as the global network of interlinked computers providing digitally mediated communications. However, more precisely, the Web is a very specific but very popular service delivered through the infrastructure of the Internet. The simplicity of authoring a web page – creating web content – combined with the embedding of web browsers – accessing web content – on to most Internet-enabled devices makes the Web the second most popular Internet service after email.
- *Web 2.0* was a term popularised by Tim O'Reilly – the founder of the technical publishing company, now O'Reilly Media – and refers to websites and applications that allow the interactive creation and sharing of information. The importance of Web 2.0 technologies is based on the ability for anyone to create, share, collaborate and communicate through a web-based interface. This definition contrasts with Web 1.0 – a *post hoc* label that defines earlier web presence as a broadcast form of communication that enabled a website owner address an audience with limited opportunity for two-way interaction. Web 2.0 is a watershed development for digital marketing, as genuine audience interaction through a web interface allowed marketing actions to fully apply the central tenets of traditional marketing and then exceed traditional marketing's ability to measure, assess and evaluate individual actions.
- *Social media* is the collective term for digital technologies that enable communications amongst many users. It is often characterised by platforms such as Facebook or Twitter. However, the term can also be used to describe other technologies – including blogs, YouTube, Instagram and Telegram – that take advantage of the interconnectivity of the Internet and the interactivity of Web 2.0 technologies to enable creation and sharing.

- *Digital Economy* was first used by Tapscott (1995) in his book *The Digital Economy: Promise and Peril in the Age of Networked Intelligence*. The digital economy refers to the commercial opportunities facilitated through digital technologies in the widest sense. This term encompasses the entire supply chain and all the associated ancillary business services that enable transactions and actions. The Internet economy, Net economy and Web economy are also sometimes used as synonyms for digital economy.
- *Digital business, electronic business* and *e-business* variously refer to aspects of the activities an organisation undertakes using digital technologies. Electronic business or e-business first emerged in reference to isolated digital activities within more traditionally structured businesses. Digital business is a more recent term that describes an organisation which is structured largely or wholly around the use of digital tools for its internal and external activities and actions.
- *Social commerce* is a term first introduced by Yahoo! in 2005 and refers to e-commerce that uses social media channels to enable buying and selling.
- The *marketing function* is a core business function of any organisation. Marketing is the continuous and iterative process of listening to customers, understanding their needs and offering products or services that satisfy these needs.
- *Digital marketing* describes the primary use of digital technologies to support the marketing function of an organisation. In organisations that understand their marketing function, digital techniques are combined with traditional forms of marketing activity. However, in more fully digitally mature organisations, traditional activities are led by, guided by and integrated with digital techniques. Synonyms for digital marketing include electronic marketing, online marketing and Internet marketing.
- *Search engine marketing* – also referred to as search marketing or just abbreviated to SEM – is the part of digital marketing that aims to understand and guide the behaviour of prospective buyers when they use search engines. Search engine marketing then directs content development to trigger positive responses from search engine algorithms as well as engaging individuals. There are two types of search engine marketing: organic SEO or natural search and paid search engine marketing or PPC. Organisations with higher levels of digital maturity will employ a mixture of both forms of search engine marketing.
- *Social media marketing* is the aspect of digital marketing that focuses on understanding and engaging the buyer persona through social media use. Social media marketing involves activity on a carefully selected combination of social media channels that are most relevant to the defined buyer persona. Social media marketing has both organic and paid approaches. However, as more social media channels fully monetise their business models, the paid aspect of social media marketing will dominate over organic approaches.
- *Mobile marketing* describes an organisation's digital marketing activities that facilitate customer engagement through mobile devices. As business itself is

increasingly experienced through mobile interfaces, this form of marketing is more commonly part of mainstream marketing strategy.

• *Mobile commerce* describes business transactions that are transacted through mobile devices. Specific forms of commerce may be more appropriate for certain sectors or purchases, for example, food delivery, public transport tickets and access to physical tourist and public attractions. Mobile commerce is growing at a significantly faster pace than other forms of ecommerce.

These terms are clearly interrelated concepts that cannot be read in isolation from the overall activities, strategy or vision of any organisation. Figure 1.3 maps the close connection and interrelationships of these terms.

1.3 Success and failure in digital marketing

Through a combination of continuous external change, the introduction of new technologies, and the current immaturity of existing technologies, the adoption of search engine and social media activity into an organisation's marketing mix has not always been successfully realised. The Buyer Persona Spring is a dynamic model that delivers success and manages potential failure by minimising any detrimental impact on the organisation. Recognising the hallmarks of success and failure in all types of organisations is an instructive process in developing your own organisation's digital strategy.

During the period of the so-called *dot-com bubble*, between 1997 and 2000, thousands of Internet-based companies failed. This period of recent history is an ever-present warning to all businesses about the importance of using, and actively engaging in, robust business planning and management techniques irrespective of whether they are being applied to a traditional or digital business.

Recognising patterns of failure

An instructive failure during the dot-com bubble was Boo.com. Boo.com aimed to create a global online fashion store and brand that served the needs of contemporary consumers. However, having spent $US 188 million in six months, it was declared bankrupt in May 2000. The key factors in Boo.com's rapid failure was its over-ambition – in a relatively unknown market, the lack of sufficient capital to sustain it through its establishment period and most significantly the degree to which it failed to exert clear managerial control. The company planned to reach $US 100 million in sales in the first year, but did not consider the sheer number of customers it would need in order to realise this volume of sales as well as factoring in the cost of attracting each new consumer and the average cost of each transaction.

The company's attempt to use the most innovative and sophisticated technological solutions was a high-risk strategy that also contributed to its failure. Boo.com offered each customer the ability to virtually model the items

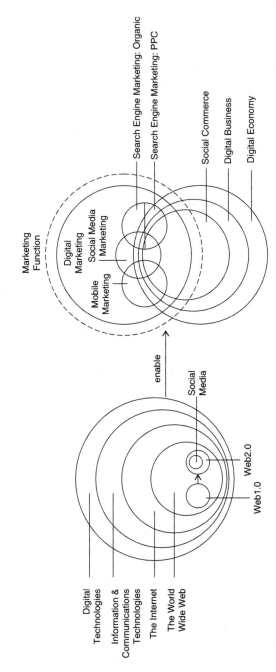

Digital
Technologies

Information &
Communications
Technologies

The Internet

The World
Wide Web

Web1.0

Web2.0

Social
Media

enable

Marketing
Function

Digital
Marketing

Mobile
Marketing

Social Media
Marketing

Search Engine Marketing: Organic

Search Engine Marketing: PPC

Social Commerce

Digital Business

Digital Economy

Figure 1.3 A visualisation of the interrelationships amongst the key terms used in this book of clothing they were considering buying. The technology behind the virtual showroom was resource-intensive and required high-speed Internet connectivity, which – in 2000 – was not widely available. Boo.com was also overly ambitious in developing its international reach. The company tried to start up simultaneously in 18 countries – a task that was at the same time beyond the capabilities of the infant Amazon or Google. A further impact on Boo.com's chances of success was a six-month technical delay in the development of the online platform. During this initial delay the company simultaneously committed to maintaining significant stock levels and paying its employees' salaries. As a fashion retailer, the stock quickly became dated and the staff could not do any meaningful work that contributed to company revenues while the platform was unavailable. Boo.com went into receivership with $US 25 million of debt.

There are many other possible case studies of failed Internet ventures. Some of these failures were based on managerial or financial factors; others related to poor marketing decisions or a lack of understanding regarding their specifically targeted buyer personas. Pets.com, Startups.com and Lastminute.com all faced similar challenges to Boo.com and, in turn, each organisation failed to successfully exploit the available digital technologies in ways that were relevant or that realised genuine additional value for their buyer personas.

More recent examples of poor decision making in social media are Belvedere, a French vodka company that posted corporate messages on its Facebook and Twitter pages promoting the company's products. Unfortunately, the message included a scene of simulated sexual assault and resulted in significant negative feedback from Belvedere community members. Following the initial reaction of users, Belvedere removed the advertisement and posted a lightly worded apology, which stated:

> *We apologize to any of our fans who were offended by our recent tweet. We continue to be an advocate of safe and responsible drinking.*

However, this statement was seen by some users as being too weak to be a genuine apology. The former senior editor of *The Atlantic*, Megan McArdle, summarised the community's concerns very clearly in a single tweet:

> *Fascinated by Belvedere Vodka's non-apology apology, which seems to assume that most of their customers think rape is awesome.*

The examples of Belvedere and Boo.com provide some initial guidance for planning your own organisation's strategy. Both examples reveal the close and constant interplay between technology and people. In digital marketing, people and their opinions, emotions, ethics and attitudes inevitably win over the capabilities over the most recently introduced technology – no matter how advanced or simple it is to use. The experiences of these organisations can be summarised as the five signals for imminent strategic failure (Table 1.1). Your organisation needs to consciously avoid these signals.

Table 1.1 Signals of failure for a digital strategy

Signals to avoid	Response and remedy
1. Lack of a digital strategy or operational plan	Primarily characterised by impulsive digital marketing actions with no assessment of the costs or risks. For example, a website requires continuous maintenance to keep the content relevant and the site secure, and each social media profile must be constantly monitored.
2. Lack of sufficient skilled staff for digital activities	Digitally mature marketing and business is a constantly changing field. There is a need for continuous learning and a holistic understanding of an organisation's digital activities in relation to the buyer persona.
3. Lack of high-level organisational sponsorship	The senior leadership responsible for driving the vision and mission of the organisation can undervalue the role of digital technology within the business. Digital developments extend beyond the marketing or IT function. In order to set the right strategic aims and to support the creation of effective digital strategies, new organisational structures as well as infrastructures are needed. The structures will necessarily incorporate multidisciplinary teams to understand the buyer persona and respond with the most appropriate solutions.
4. Lack of originality	Often the organisational approach to the use of digital is one of 'me too'. Time and effort must be dedicated to understanding the buyer persona and how an organisation's goods and services can be most effectively presented.
5. Lack of agility	Digital technologies and the buyer persona can both change rapidly. Organisations must be proactive to prevailing market conditions through their use of technology in order to continue to deliver unique value to their buyer persona.

Recognising patterns of success

The adoption of social media has created hype similar to that seen in the dot-com boom of the late 1990s. Advocates for the primacy of social media have claimed that these networks are more important than an organisation's website. The challenge set by this form of 'social media first' advocacy is an atmosphere of continuous catch-up. Every time a new social media network becomes popular, without strategic awareness of the buyer persona or the audience of the new channel, the organisation is necessarily forced to add another line of communications. The human and financial effort invested into building an individual social media profile is also subsequently lost when a network becomes less relevant to the target customers. Avoiding the dangers of overhyped new media is part of an organisation's sustainable strategy for digital business in general and social media specifically.

The majority of sustainable digital strategies will usually include investment in a website and a blog and the repurposing of this content for amplification on the most relevant social media platforms. As your organisation moves towards

Table 1.2 The seven steps towards improving digital engagements

Stage	Actions
Plan	Activities should be planned as campaigns that are implemented, tracked and evaluated so that future activities benefit and build upon the lessons learned.
Budget	Budget to establish and support the ongoing technical operation of the organisation's digital environments. Budget to ensure ongoing security and correct functionality.
Manage	Day-to-day content management of an organisation's digital assets does not require major technical knowledge but it must be managed.
Buyer Persona	The initial buyer persona should focus on local users. But remember that there are no geographical limits and your content also has a global reach.
Share	Content, including the organisation's website, must share information about the organisation's mission and vision, its products and its services.
Engage	Use a relevant mix of content and engagement, including the Web, as well as social networks, and review sites that are used by the buyer persona. Attract, inform and persuade. Create a community for the buyer persona.
Align	Online and offline marketing and engagement actions should all be aligned.

data-driven decision making, social media network activity and engagement will both become good indicators of the trust that is extended towards your organisation. High levels of trust require a sustained investment of time and effort by your organisation, with the risk that a single wrong action has the potential to seriously damage all your previous positive efforts.

Learning from previous mistakes in social media communication, including those of Belvedere Vodka and Boo.com and more recognisable global brands that successfully utilise digital marketing, highlights five rules for social media success:

1   The buyer persona can be accurately targeted using social media channels.
2   The buyer persona expects sincere two-way communication with 'their' brands.
3   The buyer persona will immediately react to poor messages that denigrate 'their' brand – including messages from the brand itself.
4   The buyer persona will quickly spread negative word of mouth about 'their' brand if they are mistreated.
5   The buyer persona will resist the most blatant and untargeted advertising messages on social media.

The range of online activities available to brands highlights seven important considerations for organisations evolving to become digitally mature businesses (Table 1.2).

A McKinsey report (Hirt and Willmott, 2014) outlines seven traits for organisations doing digital marketing successfully that should inform the development of your own strategy.

1   Be unreasonably aspirational. Many organisations treat digital activities as an extension to their existing business. Be aspirational in the use of digital channels and respect these as value creation channels.

2   Acquire new capabilities. You do not necessarily need to concentrate on developing digital talents internally. As an alternative, attract digital talent from other industries or through crowdsourcing.

3   'Ring fence' and cultivate talent. Digital talents need 'space for creativity'. If your talent is buried in daily updates, development documentation or uninspired corporate communications, they will 'wither'.

4   Challenge everything. Being successful means critically questioning every assumption – goals, situation, solution, means and platform. Successful organisations generate unique value for the buyer persona by stepping away from historical norms.

5   Be quick and data-driven. The digital environment is a rapidly changing environment; however, it is also a data-rich environment. Always endeavour to make decisions that are based on evidence from existing data. If the data is unavailable, then question its absence.

6   Follow the money. Digital transformation doesn't always mean investing in new revenue streams. You can also save money. Functional integration, sharing, process merging, co-creation and crowdsourcing may all generate more efficient ways of working.

7   Be obsessed with your buyer persona. Your buyer persona has constantly expanding expectations. The good service you previously offered may now be the 'norm' or even below average for the sector.

All of these traits of successful digital business can be summarised by the simple statement: 'Be Strategic'. As a supporting statement, 'Be Holistic' emphasises the need to consider all of your organisation's activities in your drive to become a sustainable 'marketing first' digitally mature organisation.

1.4 The Digital Business Maturity Model

The history of digital and social media marketing to date can be categorised into four distinct phases. These phases also reflect the continuous shifting definition of what constitutes a digitally mature organisation. Each phase can be hallmarked by the principal and leading technologies that were used to deliver marketing messages and the relationship of these technologies to the overall development and popularity of the Internet. The quickest method for identifying the developing digital sophistication of a business overall can be discerned in the look, feel and user interactions of their web pages.

•   Phase one: Brochureware

    This initial phase of development introduced the first websites. The model for marketing activity at this stage was to create the digital twins of printed brochures. Early restrictions on commercial activity through some networks meant that even brochureware could be seen as a risky activity. Some organisations still retain this mindset and take a largely broadcast-based approach to their digital marketing messages that offers no form of two-way communication with customers.

- Phase two: Tradigital

  Tuten and Solomon (2017) label the second period of digital marketing as being 'Tradigital'. This phase is based around the concepts of push marketing that were already well established long before the rising importance of digital technologies. Tradigital used new tools to share content that are similar in style and intent to television and direct mail marketing campaigns. This period is characterised as one of digitally enabled mass and targeted marketing activities, such as banner advertising, microsites, email campaigns and search marketing.

- Phase three: Social media marketing

  The development of social technologies – often described as Web 2.0 – brought marketing actions based around a pull approach, with organisations utilising, for example, social networks and the capability to encourage sharing, rating and reviewing to enhance other digital marketing activities (Pomirleanu et al., 2013).

- Phase four: Engagement marketing

  Engagement marketing is characterised by the development of engaging content and the use of tools and techniques that bring prospects into deep contact with the organisation. These engagements can include augmented reality, gamification and 'smart-everything' through the use of Internet of Things sensors and devices such as voice assistants. New technologies that rely on ubiquitous mobile Internet connections, including wearables and drones, open up the prospects for further digital marketing techniques to develop.

Through the phases of this evolution, content has become more customised and interactive as well as increasingly immersive. Irrespective of the increased technical capabilities required by new marketing techniques – such as customised video content – the aim of each marketing action still remains to capture and engage the attention of the buyer persona.

The changes in approach and perspective, brought about through increasingly sophisticated forms of digital marketing, also mean that organisations are becoming more digitally mature overall. With increasing digital marketing activity there is an opportunity to recognise the pivotal role that data plays in the overall management of an organisation. The self-aware and digitally mature business is then able to rapidly and proactively respond, through data-driven decision making, to the ever-changing circumstances of the buyer persona.

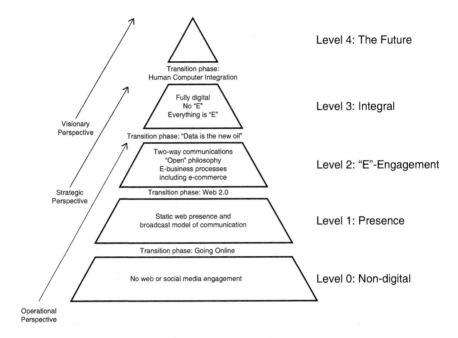

Figure 1.4 The Digital Business Maturity Model

The uptake of practices that requires digital technologies includes the measurement of business performance and consequently produces organisational change. The Digital Business Maturity Model (Figure 1.4 and Table 1.3) presents broad phases of development without proposing a single deterministic route or process of adoption. Many external influences act upon the development of individual digital business maturity, including existing policy frameworks, industry sector levels of competitiveness and business collaboration, relative levels and quality of education and training, the presence of an entrepreneurial and fail-fast startup culture and the robustness of national and regional ICT infrastructures. This means that your individual steps as an organisation towards full digital maturity will vary in the specifics of its implementation and order of development. However, the most ready route to digital maturity for a small or medium sized organisations is achieved through a 'marketing first' approach.

The majority of organisations currently conduct their digital marketing activities within Level 1 and Level 2 of the Digital Business Maturity Model. More highly developed stages of the model move your organisation towards becoming a fully digitally mature organisation, a situation that will become increasingly important in order to remain competitive. Constant experimentation and evaluation are crucial for successful digital marketing, as there is an external backdrop of new tools and techniques that are continuously becoming available to all organisations, including your competitors. Until each new tool

Table 1.3 A description of the Digital Business Maturity Model

Phase	Description of phase
Level 0 – Non-digital	'Traditional' organisations. These businesses are not online in any meaningful way. Any presence may have been created robotically by one of the many online business directories that pollute Google and the other search engine results pages (SERPs). However, a business owner has no control over or input into the information being presented about their own organisation.
Level 1 – Presence	The presence level of digital maturity uses digital technologies to broadcast untargeted messages to a still ill-defined audience. No active interaction or two-way communication can be observed at this level.
Level 2 – 'E'-engagement	An organisation has an operational information system that allows some reporting and integration of activities between multiple channels. Increasing efforts to achieve operational efficiencies and to gain competitive advantage through the analysis and interpretation of data.
Level 3 – Integral	Most of the organisation's functions are digital. Decision making in these digital businesses is data-driven and value is being created through the use and reuse of the organisation's digital assets.
Level 4 – The future	A fully integrated data-driven digital business with day-to-day functions being driven by predefined business rules and potentially decision making being guided by the application of artificial intelligence.

or technique is tried, experimented with and documented, there is no evidence to understand the individual use case or the prospective specific benefits to your organisation. Knowing when to stop using a tool or a technique is equally important, as digital marketing becomes increasingly sophisticated and integrated within the overall operations of a more fully digitally mature organisation. All of these decisions should also be incorporated within your long-term strategic thinking and planning rather than being undertaken as 'gut' reactions to immediate change in the external environment including the use of new tools or the deployment of new actions by your competitors.

1.5 Online customer journey

As digital environments create ever more opportunities for marketing, it is increasingly important for your organisation to understand your buyer persona. All organisations aim to achieve favourable behaviours from their intended consumers and customers. These behaviours can vary from heightened awareness to a purchase decision and repeat custom. Understanding and responding to these behaviour patterns and the decision making journey is how you create new opportunities for your organisation. We represent these opportunities in the

Figure 1.5 Traditional buyer persona decision making process

Buyer Persona Spring as the focus and drive of your activities. The buyer persona builds on the research and writings of a range of different authors who have all tackled the question of understanding consumer decision making and the journey that consumers take towards a positive outcome for your organisation.

The classic marketing approach defines the consumer journey or consumer decision making activities as a linear process undertaken over several stages (Figure 1.5).

However, several alternatives to this model have been proposed to identify consumer behaviour within digital environments. Marsden (2011) supports the classical approach but suggests that the behaviour is more cyclical and that it iterates over three phases.

According to Marsden (2011), the journey starts from the recognition of a problem and is followed by a consideration set or a dynamic decision loop. Consideration leads to purchase and post-purchase decisions that form a loyalty loop. Marsden (2011) builds his proposition on Edelman (2010) and McKinsey's research by defining a shift from the traditional linear approach to a more complex consumer decision making journey that emphasises the cyclical nature of consumer decisions.

Owyang (2012) also supports a cyclical representation of the consumer journey and sees the journey as dynamic and being influenced by a number of factors, including:

- recent development and advancement in technology deployment;
- change of media use and consumption; and
- increasing power of word of mouth in its velocity, veracity, volume and variety.

This cyclical process is further supported by the view on the future of retailing (Grewal et al., 2017; Pantano et al., 2018). A digitally transformed cyclical consumer journey is based on the ZMOT (Zero Moment of Truth) (Lecinski, 2011) theory developed by Google and Shopper Sciences research.

According to the ZMOT perspective, the buyer persona journey is emotional and triggered by various factors, including advertising, friends' comments

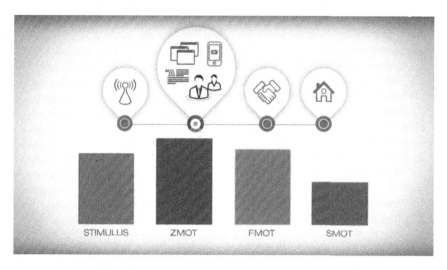

Figure 1.6 The Zero Moment of Truth (ZMOT) – digital decision making process. Google and Shopper Sciences (2011).

Source: Google

and word of mouth. This positions digital and social media marketing actions as having an important role in the initiation and leading of consumers through the entire journey. The initial stage of the buyer persona journey is referred to as a "Stimulus".

The ZMOT is illustrated by Figure 1.6. The image also suggests the importance of individual stages of this process, indicating that ZMOT is the second most important stage after the First Moment of Truth (FMOT) and the Stimulus stages. The Second Moment of Truth (SMOT) is also important, since it feeds the ZMOT for the future buyer persona interaction, as illustrated in Figure 1.7.

The digital decision making process affects almost all areas of buyer persona's life. Although the study was conducted by Google and Shoppers Science in 2011, it is still an accurate reflection of buyer persona behaviour over a decade later. The study marked a significant development of digital marketing ideas in comparison to the traditional marketing approach. It is important that it changed the understanding of the process from linear to circular. Figure 1.7 illustrates the link between the SMOT and the ZMOT for the next buyer persona. There are a number of versions of this model. For example, some of them develop a more elaborate stage for the second moment of truth by adding customer advocacy– and retention-related stages. However, the core idea summarises the key issue highlighted in this work, and we prefer to use these four stages for the digital marketing strategy building blocks. This application of this process is illustrated in the consumer journey touchpoints analysis in Chapter 3.

Figure 1.7 ZMOT showing the link of the Second Moment of Truth (SMOT) to the ZMOT.
Source: Google

The stimulus stage is followed by a consideration moment or the ZMOT. The consideration moment relates to the information search that is required to make the purchase decisions. At this point, a consumer will deploy search engines, social networks and their own personal networks in order to obtain this information. It is also important to note that with the increase in Internet penetration rates offering better access to more resources, this stage is regularly undertaken in the digital realm. In the past it was only friends and family who an individual would have access to. Now, online communities, bloggers and influencers around the world will share their views on pretty much everything in ways that are readily accessible for free. Reviews of past consumers and star ratings are used as filters for product searches, and not being mentioned at all in a review also sends negative signals to the buyer persona.

Once the research is concluded, a purchase decision is taken and the time of making the purchase is referred to as the FMOT. The actual purchase decision can take in person offline or online. Increasingly brands combine offline and online experience to allow customers flexibility. Some customers still prefer to have the instant gratification of purchasing and using a good or service and choose to make the actual purchase in person.

The stage of unwrapping the item and sharing the experience of having it is called the SMOT. It is the stage when consumers start consuming the product or service and then start to form their own opinion. The SMOT may then also very likely serve as the Stimulus or ZMOT for another consumer. This relation of the SMOT to ZMOT offers a clear explanation for the proliferation of influencers sharing their 'unboxing' experience through YouTube or other streaming services. This is influencing at its coarsest level.

The ZMOT and the SMOT are very important from a digital marketing perspective. These two stages are now more evident than in a traditional customer journey and this empowers more digitally mature buyer personas. The buyer personas can either become your brand advocates and become loyal users by sharing publicly positive feedback or become brand adversaries and share complaints about their experience received. Customer feedback should always be encouraged and if it is positive, amplified where possible and if negative, addressed with a swift, justified and reasonable response.

An alternative approach to understanding the consumer journey is to consider how consumers behave within online ecosystems. Online ecosystems describe a consumer's behaviour or movement amongst search engines, media sites, other intermediaries and competitors. All of these approaches attempt to systematise the relationship you have with your customers. By systematising the relationship, it becomes more manageable and as a result can be better controlled.

The challenge for your organisation is to understand what influences individuals to show interest in your goods and services. Who is buying your goods and services? Who is using them? Who are the influencers that bring customers (back) to you?

Understanding this combination of behaviours means developing and then understanding your buyer persona. The buyer persona is your own description of your ideal customer and consumer. This account of the buyer persona is descriptive and detailed. It will include a description of the preferences, interests and background of your ideal customer. The buyer persona recognises the situation in which this customer is positioned in terms of demographics, location, situation and aspirations. The account must be fact-based and should draw heavily on evidence from your own organisational experience as well as relevant details gathered from external sources. While the majority of your customers, consumers and influencers will never completely align with your buyer persona, by consistently addressing the buyer persona you will create a genuine rapport with a range of customers and consumers who recognise and identify with the buyer persona you have defined, and this will, in turn, build a meaningful trust-based engagement with them that persists over time.

1.6 Summary

This chapter outlines the key concepts and marketing actions that can make organisations more effective, more impactful, more sustainable and more strategic within a 'marketing first' digitally mature organisation. Digital technologies are becoming an integral part of an organisation's activities as well as of modern consumer life. Many organisations face significant challenges and are seeking the best opportunities to utilise the benefits of digital technologies.

The key lesson of this chapter is that there is no 'one size fits all' approach when it comes to developing a digital marketing strategy. Indeed, a number of factors determined by your buyer persona need to be considered over the long term. This perspective is itself an important conceptual starting point, as it recognises marketing as an integral business function and a key mechanism that drives an organisation towards becoming fully digital mature.

Digital approaches to business remain challenging and must compete with the opportunities in the physical world. Therefore, organisations must clearly demonstrate the value of their digital offerings to consumers and select appropriate metrics to understand when and whether these efforts are returning benefits to the organisation. A strategic, iterative and reflective approach is the only way to reduce risk and to keep digital marketing innovations relevant to any organisation. This is the focus of the next chapter.

1.7 References

Edelman, D. C. (2010) Branding in the digital age. *Harvard Business Review*, 88(12), 14–18. Palgrave Macmillan. doi: 10.1108/eb040166.

Grewal, D., Roggeveen, A. L. and Nordfält, J. (2017) The future of retailing. *Journal of Retailing*, 93(1), 1–6.

Hirt, M. and Willmott, P. (2014) Strategic principles for competing in the digital age. *McKinsey Quarterly* (May), 1–13.

Lecinski, J. (2011) *Winning the zero moment of truth eBook*. www.thinkwithgoogle.com/marketing-resources/micro-moments/2011-winning-zmot-ebook/

Marsden, P. (2011) *F-commerce. Selling on Facebook: The opportunities for consumer brands*. London: Syzygy Group.

Owyang, J. (2012) *Strategy: Lead the dynamic consumer decision journey*. www.altimetergroup.com

Pantano, E., Priporas, C.V. and Dennis, C. (2018) A new approach to retailing for successful competition in the new smart scenario. *International Journal of Retail & Distribution Management*, 46(3), 264–282.

Pomirleanu, N., Schibrowsky, J. A., Peltier, J. and Nill, A. (2013) A review of Internet marketing research over the past 20 years and future research direction. *Journal of Research in Interactive Marketing*, 7(3), 166–181.

Tapscott, D. (1995) *The digital economy: Promise and peril in the age of networked intelligence*. New York: McGraw Hill.

Tuten, T. L. and Solomon, M. R. (2017) *Social media marketing*. Los Angeles, CA: Sage.

2 Identifying business needs

Milanka Slavova

2.0 Learning objectives

In this chapter you will learn how to:

- recognise external factors that have an impact on your digital marketing strategy;
- recognise internal factors that may influence your digital marketing activities;
- translate the aspirations of your long-term plans into practical projects;
- develop an organisational culture of continuous improvement; and
- re-evaluate your current business model from a buyer persona perspective.

2.1 Digital marketing strategy

A long-term strategic marketing plan is essential to the success of your digital business. A strategic perspective (three to five years) ensures that your organisation does not become solely reactive to the decisions of your competitors or the introduction of unexpected technologies or tools. A good strategy – for any purpose – will be sufficiently robust to resist the short-term impact of external changes in the market. At the same time, your strategy should be sufficiently flexible to enable a planned, considered response to external changes that can bring additional benefit and value. The dynamic pace of change brought by digital technologies means that organisations, customers and the external environment will not remain static over a three-year period.

Before you can implement a digital marketing strategy, you need to identify your organisational needs. Understanding these needs will then shape the actions you implement, while ensuring that they are precisely suited to your organisation and meet the needs of your buyer persona. The Buyer Persona Spring recognises that both your organisation and your buyer persona are complex. As a result, the relationship that you build between the two must be sufficiently flexible.

You must first analyse the external situation and the internal environment of your organisation (Figure 2.1). With this insight you can then identify your

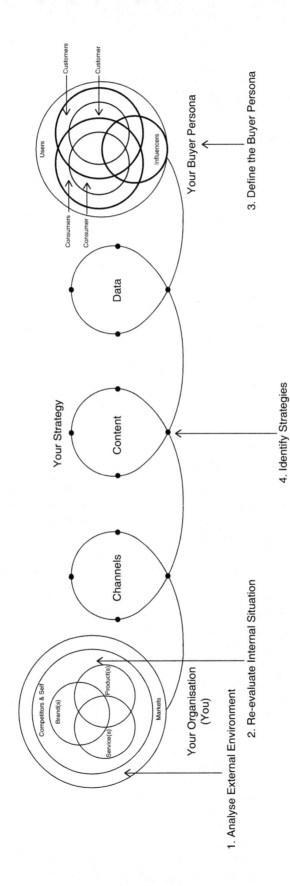

Figure 2.1 Creating a digital marketing strategy

buyer persona, including the products and services that are wanted and needed, and align it with organisational vision and mission. Once you have an understanding of the buyer persona and your own organisation in place you can define strategies for bringing the two together. By completing this series of actions, you will have placed your organisation in a strong position to use digital marketing successfully.

2.2 Analysing the external environment

The external environment includes all the external forces that influence your organisation and its activities. While these external forces cannot be directly controlled, they can be identified and analysed. By doing this analysis, you will understand what influences your customers' changing needs, be able to take advantage of new opportunities before your competitors and anticipate problems in advance. For example, when the demand for online shopping began to grow, direct selling companies had to respond in ways that minimised negative impact on sales in physical stores. In some of these types of organisations the solution was to offer different product lines for e-commerce than those available in stores.

Deeper understanding of the external environment can be gained through detailed examination of both macro and micro factors (Kotler et al., 2018). The broad macro-environmental factors include demographics, economics, technology, political and legal forces and social factors, while the more specific micro-environmental factors include suppliers, resellers, customers, competition and the general public.

Analysing the macro-environment

The tool most often used to explore the macro-business environment is labelled PESTLE and evaluates the large external forces. Traditionally these forces are recognised as political, economic, social, technological, legal and environmental. Reflecting changing consumer attitudes and perspectives means that more contemporary versions of PESTLE now recognise the additional force of ethical.

The demographic environment

People are your market, and they adjust their attitudes, perspectives, ethical position and worldviews constantly. Whether it is caused by changing age structures, improving levels of education, newly acquired digital skills, shifting opinions about ethical behaviours or increasing population diversity, your market is always in flux.

A key force in the macro-environment that has significant impact for digital marketing is generational difference. Currently at one end of the consumer generational spectrum are the group described as Millennials or 'Generation Y'. According to most marketing analysts, Millennials are generally regarded as born-to-digital customers who expect more of everything, including greater control over their experience with products and services. At the other end of the spectrum, the requirements of an aging population for digital products and services are different again. For some markets, at the other end of the generational spectrum, the 'silver surfers' are an important growing demographic who are affluent and digitally connected but with distinct needs and preferences from other younger generations.

There are also those who are excluded from the digital world through a lack of skills and limited means to access online networks. This lack of access and skills may be a result of disadvantages including poor levels of education, unemployment as well as other forms of economic or social inequality.

Understanding how your target audiences are engaging with your products is essential. It allows you to adapt your offering accordingly and informs the construction of your buyer persona. This approach to market research is called *user experience testing and observation*.

One example of this research approach is the way that the Royal College of Art in the UK worked with Samsung to help older people set up a smartphone. Their design solution emerged from co-creation sessions with older people and resulted in the use of a hardback 'storybook' containing the SIM card and battery within its pages, which guided the user through an understandable narrative to set up their phone (Myerson, 2014).

The potential to draw an aging population into the digital economy sees organisations designing their digital services to correspond with the perspectives and thinking of older generations. If you can understand how your market is engaging with your organisation and its products and services, you are in an ideal position to better meet their needs.

The political environment

The political situation in your target market plays a role in shaping your buyer persona. The European Union (EU) has attempted to harmonise national practices to encourage trade within Europe, but every country still has issues that require specific consideration.

From legal regulations, such as safety, tax laws, social security expenses and retirement age, to aspects such as privacy laws, you need to know the rules of each country where you operate. For digital and social media marketing, the most significant rules and regulations are connected with issues of privacy, data collection and how customer information is used.

For example:

- In the USA, the Federal Trade Commission requires Internet businesses to post a privacy policy that explains how the company uses any collected personal information.
- In the UK, the Committee of Advertising Practice is regulated by the Advertising Standards Authority, which includes general rules that state

advertising must be responsible, and must not mislead or offend, and has specific rules that cover advertising to children and ads for specific sectors like alcohol, gambling, motoring, health and financial products.

- The EU Consumer Rights Directive (European Commission, 2014) is designed to protect consumers when shopping online. Prices have to be clearly displayed and businesses have to explicitly disclose the total cost of the product or service as well as any extra fees or delivery charges.

The political decisions of governments can also influence the access that customers in each country have to individual digital channels. These are decisions are often the result of social unrest or dissent. For example, in 2015 Turkey banned user access to Twitter and YouTube after users published images of a prosecutor held hostage by far-left militants.

The economic environment

Consideration of the economic environment includes rates of growth, inflation, interest rates, exchange rates and the level of unemployment. Generally, during periods of economic growth, the demand for an organisation's products and services will expand. Similarly, during periods of economic decline, sales will generally decrease primarily because consumer income shrinks. Lower income levels are also a hallmark for wider economic downturns.

Understanding the economic environment enables an organisation to position itself, in relation to their buyer persona, with accuracy and to maximum effect. The global scope of digital marketing tools enables an organisation to address a changing economic situation with immediate beneficial impact. For example, a florist based in Poland, when the economy is in a downturn, might consider targeting the wedding market in Germany, where the economy may be growing or at least experiencing a lesser downturn than that in Poland.

An important reason for doing an economic analysis is to understand the impact of these forces on consumer purchasing power and the ways in which different groups of buyers consume. A major trend in the post-2008 economic crisis was price-conscious purchasing. Digital technologies, including the introduction of fully digital supply chain management, allow dynamic pricing based on current availability and quantity. This is a practice already used by most airlines as well as many hotel chains and is also a key reason for the successful business model implementations found with price comparison websites. During the same period, similar price-conscious purchasing was felt in high street stores although in different ways. In the high street stores customers are freely offered an opportunity to see the goods and try them out. The rise of 'showrooming' means that once a customer has identified the product they want they can then go online and place an order for the same item with a cheaper online retailer before even leaving the physical premises. Attracting and retaining the price-conscious customer requires pricing strategies that bring them longer-term economic benefits. This may come in the form of, for example, rewarding the return visitor, offering monthly payment schemes, 24-hour sales or discount codes. Understanding these types of economic influences shapes your buyer persona.

The technological environment

Consideration of the external technical environment is a key factor for digital marketing. In markets where digital penetration is high, consumers spend more time online and willingly engage in a wide variety of activities, including the creation of content. Consumers are generally more immersed in social networks that, in turn, influence their purchasing behaviour. Mobile devices also allow consumers to communicate from everywhere and to access content in a variety of formats – video, audio, images and text. Physical location is no longer a constraint on consuming – and online communities increasingly make a greater impact on consumer decision making than any physical influencers.

To speak to the customer in a digital world, you need to bring value to them in new ways, engage them with your brand and your organisation and increase the immediacy of the exchange (see Case Study 2.1).

Case Study 2.1   Chobolabs targets hard-core gamers using mobile devices

Established in 2011 by Bulgarians Deyan Vitanov and Petar Dobrev after selling a successful philanthropic start-up (Vitanov, 2019).

The goal of Chobolabs was to create a platform that would keep hard-core gamers 'on the edge of their seat'. Passionate gamers, Vitanov and Dobrev were frustrated by the lack of apps for their favourite games and believed that competitive multiplayer games could become a reality on mobile devices. Their aim was to create a 'unicorn' in Silicon Valley – an innovative start-up with a market value of over $US 1 billion dollars.

Vitanov and Dobrev developed a game engine that works on all platforms – iOS, Android, Windows and the Web. Unlike their competitors, the young entrepreneurs did not copy game designs from PCs or consoles. Their approach was based on the idea that 'mobile demands original thinking' because the display is smaller and customers are accustomed to using a touch screen. Aware that many hard-core gamers did not trust the mobile multiplayer games, Vitanov and Dobrev were convinced that mobility was a major advantage because it allows playing everywhere.

In 2014 Chobolabs attracted investors after demonstrating their idea and a rough prototype. The company successfully completed a $US 1.3 million round of funding to finance its first game. Chobolabs then sought out engineering talents from all over the world, intending to create a team of 15 developers in Bulgaria and 10 in the USA.

Chobolabs have developed the game *Mayhem* on top of their cross-platform *ChoboEngine*, which is built around a business model that generates revenue through the sale of additional in-game items such as weapons and clothes. The organisation is now exploring the highly profitable esports industry and plans to use *ChoboEngine* to enter this new expanding sector.

Sources: www.chobolabs.com and Vitanov (2019)

Digital technologies enable you to quickly and continuously connect, collaborate and conduct business with your customers. To get the most out of them, you need to understand the technological environment within which your organisation and in which your buyer persona operate. You need to understand how your customers access the Internet, how, what and when they purchase and the type of online experience they desire.

What works for one organisation will not necessarily work for another. For example, apps work well for companies that have a lot of repeat business. A florist specialising in weddings is likely to only encounter their customers once or twice in a lifetime. An app will bring little additional value to this small number of transactions. In contrast, a florist dealing regularly with wedding planners might find that an app can add significant value. Connecting the technological environment with the specifics of your organisation and the development of your buyer persona will contribute, in turn, to the strategies that you employ to bring your organisation and buyer persona closer together through the Buyer Persona Spring.

The variety of opportunities that digital technologies enable will only continue to further empower the customers by allowing the individualisation of offerings on a global scale. This form and level of engagement will also increasingly become the expected norm. By learning your customers' online habits, your buyer persona will become more detailed and this will, in turn, let your organisation find new methods for appropriate engagement.

Environmental factors

Environmental factors include issues and phenomena such as climate crisis, natural resources depletion, pollution control and the generation of renewable energy.

Many organisations already use digital marketing to encourage environmentally friendly behaviour and to promote their own environmental efforts. For example, in May 2014 Unilever officially launched a digital marketing platform to promote its environmental protection efforts in China (Yining, 2014). The 'Small Action, Big Difference' campaign encouraged Chinese consumers to reduce energy consumption by turning off lights and printing documents on both sides of the paper. Consumers could access their profile and see their contributions on the popular social networks Weibo and WeChat as well as the campaign's official website (Yining, 2014). Glenmorangie Whiskey in Dornoch, Scotland, sponsored a programme to regenerate a reef near its distillery by adding 20,000 oysters to an area that had been overfished. By contributing to improving the local environment, the regenerated reef will also help to clean and filter waste water from the distillery itself, creating an alignment of benefit and need for the business and the local community.

Changes in ethical, social and cultural aspects

New social and cultural trends need to be continuously scanned to align digital marketing with the current behaviours and expectations of consumers. Social and cultural changes can create shifts in consumer attitudes that can become opportunities, threats or both. There are many tools to help you systematically assess ethical, social and cultural changes, including analysis services such as Think with Google, Google Trends and SocialBakers as well as digital marketing communities such as #passion4digital and businessculture.org.

Although these aspects of the external environment are closely related and generally change at a slow pace, they are each distinct and should be considered separately within your external analysis. Social aspects relate to the structures that guide our day-to-day lives including our education system, management of an organisation and the availability of public health care. Cultural aspects relate to the common shared experiences, practices and knowledge amongst a group of people. In traditional cultures, we describe these specific shared elements as customs or traditions. In contemporary culture, we might similarly share a love of football (irrespective of the team we support).

Ethical aspects of the external environment relate to the boundaries that we collectively believe are acceptable, both socially – such as being late for a meeting – and culturally – such as overly sharing about our personal life at a party. Ethical boundaries shift continuously, even when social and cultural norms may remain relatively static.

The most evident shift in ethical perspectives from a digital marketing perspective can be seen in the increasingly open default policies relating to the sharing of personal information through social media channels such as Facebook. The default privacy settings are a matter of company policy that reflect current strategy, commercial agendas and social understandings of being a digitally mature business. The willingness to accept these terms by the users of a social network reflects prevailing ethical and cultural attitudes towards sharing personal information. Tension, complaints or resistance all reflect the boundaries of what is generally regarded as ethical behaviour. When legislation has been implemented or advocated around issues of data privacy and sharing, this is a social control introduced to match the boundaries of generally accepted ethical behaviour and to restrict commercial activities that exceed these boundaries.

Understanding the social, cultural and ethical environment in which you are working will also help to define and state your own organisation's ethical world-view. This is an increasingly necessary expectation made by customers and is a direct result of the increased transparency created by digital communications.

Analysing the micro-environment

Micro-environment analysis involves examining those forces that are closer to the organisation and have a direct impact on creating and delivering value to the customers. The micro-environment is generally easier to identify and respond to as an organisation. A popular model for studying these forces and their impact on organisational strategies is Michael Porter's five forces and stakeholder analysis.

The five forces model is a framework for industry analysis that explores the impact of 1) current competition, 2) new entrants, 3) substitutes, 4) buyers and 5) suppliers. Examining the five forces allows an organisation to clearly define its strengths and weaknesses and to choose an appropriate strategic direction that will lead to new positioning or the utilisation of industry change. The impact of digital technologies can be integrated into all aspects of this classic model (Figure 2.2).

Rivalry amongst existing competitors

As the most powerful of the five competitive forces, rivalry has a big impact on the attractiveness and profitability of your organisation. The digital economy

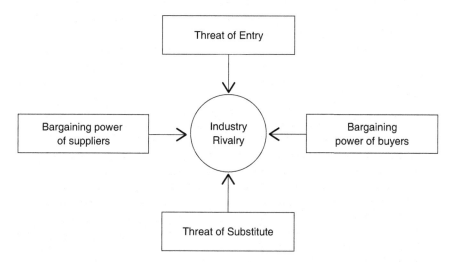

Figure 2.2 Industry analysis model

Source: adapted from Porter (1979)

tends to accelerate rivalry but simultaneously offers ways of gaining a competitive advantage through differentiation, tailored offerings and individual customisation. By understanding the strengths and weaknesses of your major competitors, you also learn how your organisation can gain a competitive advantage.

A well-known example of this assessment and response to rivalry is AirBnB. AirBnB offers an accommodation service by building a 'platform of trust' that allows property owners to rent out spare rooms, homes, castles or yurts. Technology – in the form of the organisation's app and website – connects prospective renters to every property owner directly. AirBnB's founders realised that if the system is trusted, it will match accommodation needs and opportunities in a way previously only possible through family and friends and on a scale not possible without digital technologies.

The example of AirBnB takes advantage of holiday accommodation provided by 'friends and family' to the next level by using digital channels and, as a result, introduces a significant rivalry to the traditional hospitality industry. One of the major successes for the organisation occurred during the 2014 World Cup, when 120,000 people stayed in Brazilian homes by using AirBnB instead of using conventional hotels. A similar business model could be implemented in a variety of situations, including the childcare example of Yoopies (Case Study 2.2).

Case Study 2.2   Yoopies. Digital intermediary for quality childcare

Established in 2012, Yoopies is a social platform that allows parents to easily find a babysitter, tutoring, house keeping, pet sitting and senior care. It was created by Benjamin Suchar after he saw the problems his sisters and friends were experiencing finding a reliable babysitter.

Yoopies promotes its services through social networks, search engine optimisation (SEO) and search engine marketing (SEM) and word of mouth. The target market for the company is urban parents. According to its founder, the major differentiators between Yoopies and its competitors are the quality of profiles and the parents' network.

Yoopies enables parents to find the perfect babysitter according to 50 criteria including availability, distance, experience and qualifications. The company certifies babysitters by checking their ID and their qualifications and by conducting a personal interview with every babysitter that is certified. Parents can search for recommendations and reviews of trustworthy babysitters in their network of friends and family. By linking their Facebook account to their Yoopies account, parents can develop their network and receive more feedback and comments on babysitters (Cymerman and Suchar, 2013).

Yoopies' business model requires parents to subscribe to the website. The first contact with a babysitter is free. The subscription starts at €4.90 per month for an annual subscription and €9.90 for a monthly subscription to access all contacts in unlimited ways. The company offers preferential rates on products, services and activities related to children for their premium subscribers (https://yoopies.fr/).

After only 18 months, Yoopies became the leading childcare provider in France, with a double-digit monthly growth. In four years, it had expanded to eight European countries (France, Spain, Italy, Belgium, Switzerland, Australia, Germany and the UK), and by the end of 2015 the company had ten employees.

The goal of Yoopies is to become the European leader in linking home services that are based on trust (Boogar, 2014). In 2014 the company acquired Yokoro, a marketplace for homecare services including babysitting, cleaning, tutoring and personal assistance.

Source: Boogar, 2014

The threat of new entrants

The threat of new organisations entering the industry is high when the barriers to entry are low. This is especially relevant when digital technologies can constantly disrupt established business models by allowing new types of competitors to appear. The example of AirBnB is only one example of many organisations that have successfully entered a new market where the barrier to entry was low.

An example of a disruptive technology-based 'new entrant' is the Estonian peer-to-peer money transfer service TransferWise. Regarded as one of Europe's digital icons, the company built a web platform that lets customers transfer money quickly and at less cost than any of its traditional competitors, particularly high street banks.

The threat of substitute products and services

A substitute has the same, or very similar, function to your existing product or service but it is presented or performed in a different way. The readiness of customers to buy substitutes on the basis of a benefit or quality-to-price ratio determines the degree of risk posed to your own products and services. It is easy to overlook the threat of substitutes when they appear from a different industry or when the threat is based on a new technology. Many large organisations have fallen victim to substitutions that have emerged from new business models that are built on digital technologies. A relevant example is the interrelated functions of smartphones and cameras. Smartphones decrease the appeal of low-end digital cameras and cheap video cameras. However, at the prestige end of the market, high-end digital SLR cameras still attract consumers who are eager to capture professional-quality images and video not possible on consumer-grade mobile phones.

The substitution to the photography industry is a result of mobiles being – as the MIT Technology Review says – 'the Swiss Army knives of consumer electronics' that perform decently on many tasks. The ubiquity, ease of use and extensibility – through the use of apps – of smartphones offered a substitute product for low-end cameras that effectively destroyed the market for these single-purpose devices.

The bargaining power of suppliers

Suppliers are an essential contributor to the success of your organisation. A supplier's power can manifest itself through access to limited resources or through the capital requirements and ongoing costs of switching to another supplier. In the digital economy, the power of many traditional suppliers decreases as new options emerge and as supply requirements change. Suppliers also appear that offer new but essential goods and services, such as providers of the data storage, connectivity, sensors and embedded operating systems that all form the potential basis for new data-driven services for your organisation or for your customers and their product experience.

As a contemporary example, in the search industry, Google now dominates the supply of website visitors through the provision of search results. The relationships with end users and their knowledge of consumers' product usage are the basis for their business power (Porter and Heppelmann, 2014).

Another recent example of a change in suppliers' services are massive open online courses (MOOCs), which offer global access to university courses for a virtually unlimited number of students. Traditionally and in contrast, the choice of a higher education provider is geographically constrained, except for the most wealthy.

The bargaining power of buyers

Buyers can exert influence and control over an industry when there is little product differentiation and substitutes can be easily found. This circumstance particularly applies to products and services when buyers are price-sensitive and where switching does not result in significant cost to the customer. Digital technologies have the capacity to increase or decrease the bargaining power of buyers.

Digital technologies empower customers by making them more informed, allowing them to easily compare the benefits and prices of products and services, communicate through different channels, share information and participate together in company processes like new product development (see Case Study 2.3). Digital technologies also allow producers to 'disintermediate' – to remove intermediaries who increase the price of a product or a service as a result of increased transaction costs. Reducing the length of supply chains and precisely targeting the buyer persona are key strategies of a digitally mature business that are bringing major change within most industries (Gielens and Steenkamp, 2019).

Case Study 2.3   LEGO®. Ideas innovation and crowdsourcing re-energised the company

In the 1990s and early 2000s, as children started to prefer video games and computers to plastic blocks, LEGO was close to bankruptcy.

Their solution was the implementation of open innovation and crowdsourcing. In 2008 LEGO launched the online platform LEGO Cuusoo, allowing LEGO fans to become actively involved in the new product development process, both in the idea generation and the screening.

With LEGO Cuusoo, users could produce a page describing their new concept and then share it with others to elicit their reactions. LEGO fans could collaborate with others on LEGO projects. The LEGO Review Board, composed of designers, product managers and other key team members, would evaluate projects that reached 10,000 supporters for playability, safety and fit with the LEGO brand, and winners would receive 1 per cent of the total net sales of the product.

One of the first products based on this open innovation and crowdsourcing was the Hayabusa 369-piece building set, a model of the world's first mission probe to collect samples from the surface of an asteroid and return them to Earth.

At the end of April 2014, LEGO renamed the platform LEGO Ideas and continues to encourage fans to submit 'projects'.

Between 2011 and 2019 LEGO Ideas has released 26 sets with a further 29 sets announced. The majority of the released sets relate to television or film franchises including *Doctor Who*, *Ghostbusters*, *Adventure Time* and *Tron*. LEGO has subsequently cross-licensed the released sets to populate its toys-to-life platform game LEGO Dimensions.

Sources: Mejia (2014) and Ideaconnection (2013)

By understanding the external and internal situation of your organisation, you have already filled in some key aspects of your Buyer Persona Spring (Figure 2.3). With this recognition, you are also in a position to recognise external organisations that can support the development and achievement of your strategy.

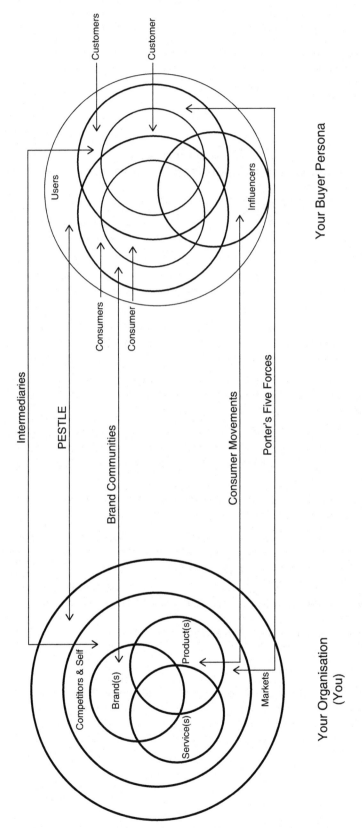

Figure 2.3 The Buyer Persona Spring in relation to existing models, tools and potential sources of support

Marketing intermediaries

Marketing intermediaries include resellers, physical distribution firms, marketing services agencies and financial intermediaries. Intermediaries help your organisation research the market and promote, sell and distribute your products and services to your buyer persona.

Financial intermediaries include banks and insurance companies. Increasingly, services and interactions in this sector are mediated through digital technologies (see Case Study 2.4).

Intermediaries reduce the need for your organisation to try to do everything. The disruptive organisational environment enabled by the digital economy requires new technologies to be implemented quickly and demands new types of business service providers. Most organisations do not have sufficient internal resources to manage the demands of rapid change.

When a business is actively investing in building its necessary digital capabilities and skills, it also runs the risk of wasting its investment when it tries to accomplish everything by itself (May and Fersht, 2014). To avoid this, large companies like Procter & Gamble, Mondelez and Unilever use mobile and social start-ups as well as technology vendors to enrich their marketing strategies with creative energy.

Case Study 2.4   Talkwalker. Marketing intermediary

Luxembourg-based Talkwalker is a marketing intermediary that helps companies track and optimise their social performance.

Established in 2009 by young engineers, Talkwalker is an easy-to-use, powerful social media search, analytics, measurement and monitoring engine. According to its Twitter certification page, Talkwalker is used by companies 'to find key influencers, top conversations, trending topics, for risk management, business intelligence and measuring the effectiveness of social campaigns and presence (187 languages)'. Talkwalker currently has over 200 employees and offices in Luxembourg, New York, San Francisco, Singapore and Frankfurt.

The company offers a platform for a variety of analytical insights online (www.talkwalker.com). Its search index covers 150 million sources. The algorithm makes it possible to analyse and interpret any website. Carson (2014) explains that Talkwalker can pull in information from customer reviews on Amazon even though the structure of the website is quite complex. The services of this intermediary include listening, sentiment analysis, analytics and insight, mention alerts and many other features that allow companies to get a full picture of the brand and its competitors online. The analysis offered by Talkwalker even covers less popular social networks. The company integrates these results and then makes the results available to all clients.

The company received buzz in the marketspace for Talkwalker Alerts, which allow a high level of customisation and which are fast emerging as a reliable alternative to Google Alerts.

The approach the company has chosen is to keep the simplicity of the platform while adding features. The approach has been recognised through awards including "Best Use of AI in Marketing Technology" and "Best in Innovation" at the 2018 Social Tools Summit.

Sources: Carson (2014), Price (2013) and Talkwalker (2014, 2019)

Utilising marketing intermediaries is also your route to apply the advice and guidance found in this book from a do-it-yourself 'kitchen table' approach to being a professional service. The principles and concepts outlined in all of the chapters can be applied directly by your own organisation – if you are small or if you have your own marketing department – or separately – under your instruction – by a marketing company, once you have grown big enough.

Consumer movements

Consumer movements unite consumers to protect their rights. Digital technologies are democratising consumer movements by blurring the difference between an expert and an ordinary consumer with in-depth knowledge. Digital technologies allow individual consumers to communicate with any organisation and enables them to have continuous access to company information. Marketing management increasingly requires recognition that the power held by consumer movements and online brand communities is an opportunity to create new product offerings to meet the needs of what can become emerging market segments (Jobber and Ellis-Chadwick, 2012).

2.3 The practicalities: identifying micro- and macro-conditions

After exploring the external environment, it will be clear that there are many opportunities for your organisation. Determining what your next steps will be requires an internal analysis of your organisation, to connect the potentials of external opportunities with the existing strengths of your organisation.

Internal analysis

Right now, your organisation has both tangible and intangible assets that you can apply to digital solutions. Your tangible assets might include equipment, cash availability and human resources each with their own particular knowledge and skills. Your intangible resources might include intellectual property rights, tacit embedded knowledge, brand equity or reputation.

When your resources are integrated and organised to perform effectively and efficiently, they become capabilities. Your core capabilities will be unique and will differentiate your organisation from your competitors.

To start your internal analysis, you need to identify the strengths and weaknesses of your current business model and business strategy and then decide what needs to be adjusted or changed to align with the identified opportunities and threats.

Business model and business strategy

The terms 'business model' and 'business strategy' are often used interchangeably without distinction. Your business model is the way your organisation creates and offers value to your customers. Your business strategy represents all the methods your organisation uses to realise that business model. There are many organisations that operate the same business model but their strategies vary significantly.

An example in the digital domain is the difference amongst VKontakte, WeChat and Facebook. Each organisation employs the same business model – they are social network brokers that facilitate personal connections amongst users. The major source of revenue for these brokers is the sale of advertising space targeted to users' interests.

However, the strategic approach each company took was different. Facebook started with a US-based university audience and then opened its membership to everyone, offering flexibility for the users to define their own communities. Facebook became a leading global network in the English-speaking world. In contrast, VKontakte in Russia and WeChat in China focused on a sense of identity offered by specific language communities. WeChat had a further advantage of being available inside China's censorship wall and focused on the specific needs of the Chinese social networking community.

Digital health check

A digital health check determines how effectively your organisation is using digital technology. The health check consists of a list of questions concerning digital business and marketing performance:

- Digital thinking – What managerial support is in place to increase the digital maturity of the organisation? To what extent is digital technology an aspect of daily work? Where and to what extent is digital technology used in marketing communications channels?

- Digital infrastructure – What hardware and software are in place? Are there organisational guidelines, policies and processes to support digital projects? Does your organisation have a digital strategy?
- Digital tools – What provision is there to create and support digital teams, projects and training?
- Digital decision investment – How much investment is required for your organisation's digital and social media marketing to achieve its objectives?

A digital health check can tell you which level of the Digital Business Maturity Model your company is at currently and also what is needed to achieve the next level (Fletcher, 2014). A marketing-led approach to increasing digital maturity will take your organisation towards a wider and more complete business transformation.

There are two major characteristics which organisations that have transformed and reached high levels of digital maturity have in common: a preparedness to invest in digital initiatives and senior leadership with a clear vision that engages the whole organisation and sustains the transformation.

High-tech companies are some of the most mature digital companies, while others such as the pharmaceutical, healthcare and hospitality industries are just beginning their journey towards digital maturity (Westerman et al., 2013).

Value stream mapping

Value stream mapping is a diagnostic tool for analysing the value created by an organisation and how it delivers value to customers. Traditionally, this is a technique used in manufacturing facilities and supply chains, but it is now increasingly applied more widely across the service industries.

To begin, the organisation selects a process and breaks it down into a series of discrete steps. Within every process there are some steps that add value and some that do not. Both cost money and time. The steps that produce waste or do not add value are then examined in order to make improvements.

Value stream mapping conducted by the Boston Consulting Group on digital advertising agencies found that 80 per cent of the time was spent on non-productive activities, while only the remaining 20 per cent was spent on activities that were seen as adding value, such as strategic targeting, data-driven innovation and performance optimisation. In response to these results, organisations involved in the study deployed a unified technology platform that provided a single user interface that assisted in eliminating wasteful processes.

Collaborations and partnerships with technology providers, advertisers and media owners can similarly decrease unproductive internal activities.

Strengths, weaknesses, opportunities and threats (SWOT) analysis

External and internal data can be used to conduct a SWOT analysis (Table 2.1).

The opportunities presented through digital technologies can be overwhelming for many organisations. A SWOT analysis can manage overall digital transformation as a prioritised list of discrete projects.

A SWOT analysis enables you to make a comprehensive list of all the internal strengths and weaknesses in conjunction with external opportunities and threats. This enables your strategic planning to be based on informed decisions that increase your strengths, reduce your weaknesses, capitalise on opportunities and mitigate threats.

For example, the strengths of your organisation may include your brand value, highly qualified digital marketing staff, excellent quality of products and services, large followings on social media channels and a diverse range of buyer personas. Weaknesses may include small followings on targeted social media platforms such as Facebook, inconsistent use of Instagram, poor user experience on your website with a related high bounce rate, poor customer reviews on social media, products that do not deliver value for money and don't align with the needs of your buyer personas or content marketing that is not suitable for the buyer persona being targeted. Opportunities may include partnerships with other organisations, social media channels that are not currently being utilised, new products that can deliver high levels of customer service and integrated social communications that streamline the buyer persona's experience. Threats may come from competitors using apps and technologies that are superior to your own, content marketing from competitors that is more engaging, lower-priced products and negative customer reviews on social media channels (Table 2.2)

Responses to your SWOT are developed through specific projects or campaigns that address each identified challenge. For example, if there is a new technology identified as an opportunity, its implementation within your organisation would become a project commencing with feasibility testing. A SWOT analysis can also be undertaken on competitors to identify areas where your organisation could gain further competitive advantage (Table 2.3).

With a completed SWOT analysis, you have the basis for the development of a digital strategy. A successful digital strategy will not solely be the implementation of a set of digital tools working in isolation from one another, but

Table 2.1 The SWOT matrix

SWOT analysis	Positive factors	Negative factors
Internal factors	**Strengths**	**Weaknesses**
External factors	**Opportunities**	**Threats**

Table 2.2 A digital marketing SWOT analysis

Strengths	Weaknesses
• Brand value • Highly qualified digital marketing staff • Excellent quality of products and services • Large followings on social media channels • A diverse range of buyer personas	• Small followings on targeted social media platforms such as Facebook • Inconsistent use of Instagram • Poor user experience on website with a related high bounce rate • Poor customer reviews on social media • Products do not deliver value for money • Products don't align with the needs of buyer personas • Content marketing is not suitable for the buyer persona being targeted
Opportunities	Threats
• Partnerships with other organisations • Social media channels that are not currently being utilised • New products that can deliver high levels of customer service • Integrated social communications that streamline the buyer persona's experience	• Competitors using apps and technologies that are superior to own • Content marketing from competitors that is more engaging • Lower-priced products • Negative customer reviews on social media channels

Table 2.3 Simplified SWOT analysis of an e-commerce website

SWOT analysis	Positive factors	Negative factors
Internal factors	**High-quality content**	**Not mobile-friendly**
External factors	**New markets**	**New e-commerce technology**

rather a set of processes, tools and communications that work towards common organisational objectives.

Combining these elements of your SWOT analysis, some strategic options might be to improve market penetration by implementing full mobile support for the current customers or to enter new markets with customised content and easier checkout processes.

After having completed and interpreted your SWOT analysis, your organisation needs to determine a digital marketing strategy. One way of planning this is to use the Business Model Canvas, which will emphasise how to best take advantage of the business environment.

Ansoff matrix

Analysis of your own organisation's current situation, and the impact of the ever-changing external environment, provides the foundation for developing your own organisation's digital maturity. Both the PESTLE analysis and the

Table 2.4 The Ansoff matrix

Ansoff matrix	Existing products	New products
Existing markets	Market penetration	Product development
New markets	Market development	Diversity

SWOT analysis let you examine the opportunities and prospective future direction for your organisation. Arguably, the most widely used strategic framework for assessing new opportunities is the Ansoff matrix (Ansoff, 1957) (Table 2.4). The Ansoff matrix is based on identification of product and market opportunities that are both existing and new. The Ansoff matrix produces a visual assessment of the four possible combinations that can then be used to determine potential strategic directions for the organisation.

Each quadrant in the Ansoff matrix provides direct guidance for subsequent strategic decision making:

- Market penetration decision – continue to perform in an existing market with an existing product, e.g. opening e-commerce channels to sell existing products.
- Market development decision – access new market segments with existing products, e.g. localised e-commerce website delivered in several languages to reach consumers in other countries or using other platforms such as eBay or Amazon to offer products through other channels.
- Product development decision – establish new products or services and offer them to an existing market, e.g. create a product information service for your specific market sector that provides answers in real time.
- Diversification decision – create new products that are offered to new markets, e.g. a customised market comparison service for new international markets.

The Ansoff matrix guides organisational strategic planning and decision making by disentangling the complexity of prospective future business directions in a highly structured way. The Ansoff matrix, however, provides no further guidance as to how to set out your objectives or to measure the success of your strategic decisions. To capture these aspects of your planning, a continuous process of planning, action, monitoring and evaluation is required and is explained in Section 2.4 of this chapter.

Business Model Canvas

Digitally mature business models challenge more traditional business models in three ways: 'ownership' of the consumer experience; business process consistency across all channels; and the use of customer data across the entire

Figure 2.4 Business Model Canvas adapted after Osterwalder and Pigneur, 2010

organisation (Weill and Woerner, 2013). New business models focus on three core principles:

- The content – what product, for which market, with what technologies.
- The experience – empowered customers can co-create products, sharing information while also requiring more of everything.
- The platform – the technologies that enable access to each of your products and services.

One of the most popular contemporary frameworks for the development of a business model is Osterwalder's Business Model Canvas (Osterwalder and Pigneur, 2010), which helps your organisation align activities and to look for new areas of growth. Osterwalder's Business Model Canvas consists of nine building blocks that produce a snapshot of the business model in a single artefact and focuses on interactions rather than a specific product or service (Figure 2.4).

The nine building blocks for Osterwalder's Business Model Canvas are:

- *Customer segments.* Who are the individuals and the organisations for which you create value?
- *Value proposition for the customer segments.* What are the products and services that you offer to those customers? Which problem does your product

solve? What benefits are provided? What is the minimum viable product – the core features that allow the product to be deployed?

- *Channels through which the organisation reaches its customers.* What are the touchpoints through which your organisation interacts with customers? What kind of channels does your organisation use? Which are the best and the most cost-efficient ones? Do these channels correspond to customer needs?
- *Customer relationships.* In what ways do you acquire customers? What is the cost for your organisation to get and keep customers?
- *Revenue streams.* How does your organisation capture value? What is your pricing strategy?
- *Key resources needed.* What infrastructure allows your company to develop, deliver and capture value? What are the key resources needed for your distribution channels, customer relationships and revenue streams?
- *Key activities.* Which activities allow your organisation to create value? What are your key activities within distribution channels, customer relationships and revenue streams?
- *Key partners.* Who helps your organisation? Which partners and suppliers provide resources and activities that are important for your organisation?
- *The cost structure of the business.* Which cost elements in your organisation are connected with activities and resources? Which resources or activities are the most expensive?

The building blocks of your Business Model Canvas are the synthesis of your previous analysis of external and internal factors. Completing the canvas will engage many people in your organisation (or all of them if you are a small organisation) and will be a dynamic process. A completed Business Model Canvas also provides key information for identifying the elements in your Buyer Persona Spring (Figure 2.5).

2.4 Digital marketing and action learning

This book applies the well-established concepts of action learning to understand digital marketing as a business activity that must be constantly evaluated and maintained. Using an iterative cycle of activity is a principle that is tightly embedded in the Buyer Persona Spring. This means that your organisation's digital marketing plans can be strategically committed to and then broken down into discrete time-constrained campaigns. Each of these campaigns is a project that has its own indicators of success. The four stages of action learning allow you to systematically undertake your digital activities in a way that can be managed and assessed. These are the four stages of planning, action, monitoring and evaluation:

1 Planning – at the outset, your organisation uses market research to inform the structure and purpose of a campaign and plan a start and end date. Key activities are defined, including the channels that will be used, and

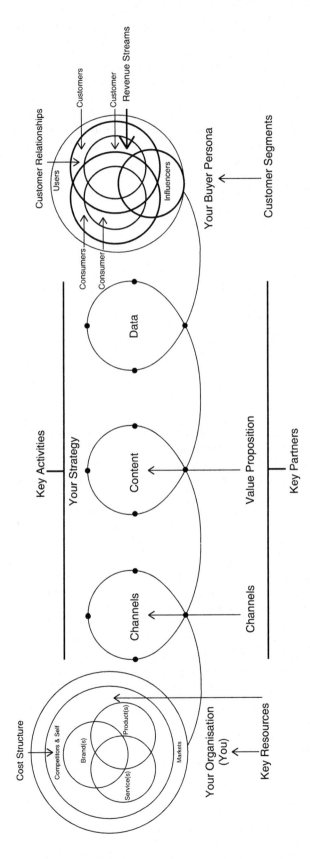

Figure 2.5 Elements of the Business Model Canvas in relation to the Buyer Persona Spring

how these activities will be tracked is set out. The objectives of the campaign are specified, and the manner by which these will be measured and evaluated is identified at the same time. How campaign success will be evidenced is made clear with the definition of key performance indicators (KPIs).

2   Action – the activities are implemented based on the plan.

3   Monitoring – feedback from the action is captured. The already defined indicators of success are observed for the campaign. These indicators could take many forms, for example, the total number of visitors, completed actions or closed sales. Other indicators might include positive or negative comments from buyers and visitors.

4   Evaluation – based on the agreed KPIs and the feedback data that has been captured, consideration is then given to what should be stopped, modified, amplified or continued as an activity.

This cycle of planning, action, monitoring and evaluation is repeated continuously. The process is systematic, with the primary objective of improving the engagement, communication and interaction with the buyer persona. The activity that is undertaken to achieve this objective is done in ways that can be evidenced, are measurable and most importantly are positive and that produce value for the organisation and the consumer.

2.5 Summary

Identifying the long-term vision of where you want your organisation to be and breaking down this vision into manageable projects allows you to create a managed pathway to long-term success. Continuously using market research and staying updated on the shifting external environment will enable your organisation to create a productive internal learning culture that encourages proactive relevant and sustainable innovation. The methodical approaches to planning and organising described in this chapter make it is easier for multiple stakeholders in your organisation to share a consistent vision and to achieve clearly defined strategic goals.

Techniques such as value stream mapping allow an organisation to evaluate the day-to-day operation of an organisation from a customer perspective. With this technique, you can identify the individual activities that add value, for which customers, and see how these activities could be improved.

While digital technologies offer you a confusing multitude of ways in which you can engage with your customers, the opportunity to use these technologies alone is not enough justification to deploy them in your organisation. Only by identifying the overall key priorities for your organisation are you able to prioritise investment in individual technologies. By taking a continuously iterative action research approach to planning and evaluating your organisation's activities, you will succeed (Figure 2.6).

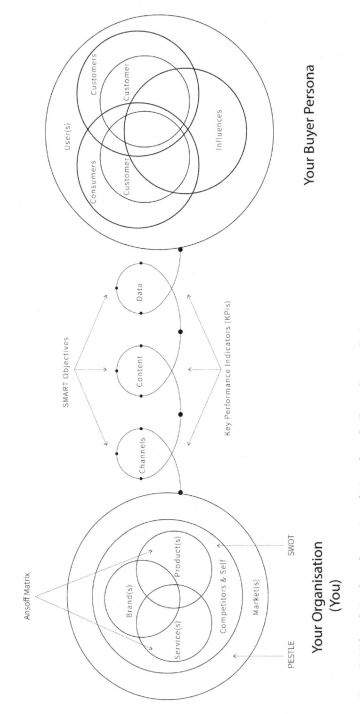

Figure 2.6 The relationship of strategic analysis tools to the Buyer Persona Spring

2.6 References

Ansoff, H. I. (1957) Strategies for diversification. *Harvard Business Review*, 35(5), 113–124.

Boogar, L. (2014) *European babysitter marketplace Yoopies acquires Yokoro to expand into homecare.* www.rudebaguette.com/2014/03/20/european-online-babysitter-platform-yoopies-acquires-yokoro-expand-homecare-marketplace/

Carson, E. (2014) *Talkwalker: Delivering extensive social media analytics to Europe and beyond.* www.techrepublic.com/article/talkwalker-delivering-extensive-social-media-analytics-to-europe-and-beyond/

Cymerman, J. and Suchar, B. (2013) *J'aime les startups.* www.jaimelesstartups.fr/yoopies/; https://yoopies.fr/

European Commission (2014) *The directive on consumer rights.* ec.europa.eu/justice/consumer-marketing/rights-contracts/directive/index_en.htm

Fletcher, G. (2014) *Digital business maturity model: The future of #Digital Business.* http://blogs.salford.ac.uk/business-school/digital-business-maturity-model/

Gielens, K. and Steenkamp, J. B. E. (2019) Branding in the era of digital (dis)intermediation. *International Journal of Research in Marketing.* www.sciencedirect.com/science/article/abs/pii/S0167811619300059

Ideaconnection (2013) *LEGO Cuusoo: Innovating with the crowd.* www.ideaconnection.com/open-innovation-success/Lego-Cuusoo-Innovating-with-the-Crowd-00376.html

Jobber, David and Ellis-Chadwick, Fiona (eds.) (2012) *Principles and practice of marketing.* Maidenhead: McGraw-Hill Education.

Kotler, P., Armstrong, G. and Opresnik, O. (2018) *Principles of marketing.* Harlow: Pearson Education.

May, N. and Fersht, P. (2014) Disrupt or be disrupted: The impact of digital technologies on business services. A study of digital's impact on business services. www.horsesforsources.com/wp-content/uploads/2015/02/The-Impact-of-Digital-Technologies-on-Business-Services.pdf

Mejia, L. (2014) *Turn your LEGO fantasies into reality with LEGO Cuusoo.* readwrite.com/2014/02/11/lego-cuusoo-dream-projects

Myerson, J. (2014) *Inclusive design: Royal College of Art research creates significant, far-reaching impact in design, industry and education.* impact.ref.ac.uk/casestudies/CaseStudy.aspx?Id=44131

Osterwalder, A. and Pigneur, Y. (2010) *Business model generation: A handbook for visionaries, game changers, and challengers.* Hoboken, NJ: John Wiley & Sons.

Porter, M. (1979) How competitive forces shape strategy. *Harvard Business Review*, 57, 86–93.

Porter, M. and Heppelmann, J. (2014) *How smart, connected products are transforming competition.* hbr.org/2014/11/how-smart-connected-products-are-transforming-competition

Price, G. (2013) *Need a Google alerts replacement? Meet Talkwalker.* searchengineland.com/talkwalker-google-alerts-replacement-153305

Talkwalker (2014) *Twitter for business.* biz.twitter.com/partners/certified-products/talkwalker

Talkwalker (2019) *Launch on Twitter.* marketing.twitter.com/na/en

Vitanov, D. (2019) *My story.* deyanvitanov.com/about/my-story/

Weill, P. and Woerner, S. (2013) Is your organization ready for total digitization? *Harvard Business Review* (24 July). hbr.org/2013/07/is-your-organization-ready-for

Westerman, G., Tannou, M., Bonnet, D., Ferrais, P. and McAfee, A. (2013) *The digital advantage. How digital leaders outperform their peers in every industry.* ebooks.capgemini-consulting.com/The-Digital-Advantage/#/21/zoomed

Yining, D. (2014) *Unilever promotes environmental protection efforts.* www.shanghaidaily.com/business/consumer/Unilever-promotes-environmental-protection-efforts/shdaily.shtml

Section II

Building your digital marketing strategy

3 Understanding your buyer persona

Ana Cruz and Stelios Karatzas

3.0 Learning objectives

In this chapter you will learn how to:

- identify online consumer behaviour;
- develop a buyer persona for a variety of sectors;
- map a customer journey through to online purchase;
- find digital 'trust touchpoints' and 'pain touchpoints'; and
- recognise the importance of ethically and morally driven consumer behaviour.

3.1 Understanding the buyer persona

The theory, application and development of a buyer persona will be covered in depth in this chapter. It will provide you with the insight and practical tools needed to develop robust buyer personas that achieve organizational objectives in a variety of sectors.

The buyer persona is a representation of your customer that is based on your market research data or science fiction prototyping. It conventionally includes demographics, locations, national and regional culture, socio-economic background, average order value, decision making patterns, their 'pain touchpoints' and corresponding 'trust touchpoints', the keywords they might use on search engines and social networks that they might engage with, and other information that assists in focus content towards their needs.

The buyer persona is also referred to as a marketing, user, customer or audience persona. The development of buyer personas guides decisions about product offering, value proposition, service, interaction and the customer's journey towards purchase (or repeat purchases). Market research and data about existing customers provide useful insight, but this data is usually abstract, in that it identifies key demographic attributes such as age, gender and location. The use of buyer personas goes further by placing a personal and human story around the individuals you are aiming to engage with and influence. These could be customers, potential donors or sponsors. This provides a focus for defining the

Table 3.1 Examples of sectors where buyer personas can be applied

Sector	Definition and differences	Examples
C2C	Individuals connect to do business with one another. Main forms of C2C platforms are classified ads and auctions.	eBay, Etsy, Amazon
B2C	Organisations selling or offering products and services directly to consumers.	Nike, Coca-Cola, Apple, Amazon, a florist shop
B2B	Selling products and services to other businesses. The decision making process can be more complex, of higher value and may take more time than in B2C sectors.	Herman Miller (office furniture), Mailchimp (marketing automation platform), Buro Happold (engineering services)
Non-profit	Revenues are used to pursue the organisation's objectives and to keep it running. Not all non-profits are charities.	Metropolitan Museum of Art, TED, The Red Cross, Creative Commons, UNICEF, United Nations Human Rights
Charity	Organisation with philanthropic goals that aims to improve the quality of life for its community of interest and beyond. All charities are non-profits.	Breast Cancer Research Foundation, Save the Children, The Rotary Foundation

Sources: Investopedia (2019); Rivera (2019); Forester (2019); Top Non Profits (2019)

marketing content that is required, as well as the tone, style and delivery (or channel) strategy for that content.

Building a buyer persona is key to designing your digital marketing strategy so that you can efficiently reach those who are most receptive and more likely to become long-term customers, advocates and influencers. The buyer personas developed here are versatile and can be applied in a wide variety of contexts including consumer-to-consumer (C2C), business-to-consumer (B2C) and business-to-business (B2B). It also applies to sectors where buying or profit motives may not be the ultimate goals e.g. non-profit, charity or behavioral change campaigns. Some of these sectors have key perspective differences (Table 3.1). However, defining relevant buyer personas still applies when developing effective digital marketing strategies.

Behavioural change campaigns are not a sector in the same sense but are an area where buyer personas can also be effectively applied to influence behaviour. These types of campaigns aim to prompt "ordinary people", as well as those in positions of authority, to improve their knowledge, change their attitudes and improve their practice related to a particular issue (UN Women, 2019). Examples include stopping smoking, wearing seat belts, recycling more and wasting fewer resources. Specific recent campaigns in the UK include, for example, Love Food Hate Waste, Love Your Clothes and Recycle Now (WRAP, 2019) (Figure 3.1).

Figure 3.1 Behavioural campaign examples
Source: Waste Resource and Action Programme (WRAP, 2019)

3.2 Building buyer personas

A marketing first approach to digital marketing requires a strong understanding of your target audience. The target audience could be direct customers, supporters, donors or groups of individuals who you are aiming to influence. The buyer persona recognizes that you are not just speaking on a one-to-one individual basis with each individual but instead are speaking to a broader grouping of people who share similar qualities, attributes and attitudes. From this point of view, building a buyer persona needs market segmentation. The process of segmentation involves dividing a market into groups who based on similar characteristics. Market segmentation lets you identify the most valuable groups and aids in better understanding your target audience's needs and motivations (Table 3.2).

By being specific about the categories that you want to work with, you can then focus on defining your primary target market through the creation of a buyer persona.

Table 3.2 Market segmentation variables

	Category	Description	Examples
Consumer markets	Demographics	Segmentation based on the characteristics of the population	Age Gender Social class Ethnic group Generation Income Family life cycle (e.g. married with no children)
	Geographic	Segmentation based on the geographical location of the population	Region: by country, continent, state Population density: urban, suburban, rural
	Psychological	Group segments according to their lifestyle, activities, interests and opinions	Lifestyle Activities, interests, opinions Personality
	Behavioural	Segmentation based on actual consumer behaviour towards products and brands	Benefits sought Brand loyalty Usage (light vs heavy) User status (potential, first time, regular) Readiness to buy
B2B markets	Geographic	Segmentation based on the location. Important, as shipping costs may have an impact on pricing and purchasing behaviour	Cluster geographically as companies may have similar needs
	Company type	Segmentation based on factors with potential impact on purchasing behaviour	Company size (turnover and headcount) Industry (e.g. services) Decision making unit (people involved in purchasing and decision making) Purchasing criteria
	Behavioural	Similar to consumer behavioural segmentation in consumer markets. Purchasing procedures may also be worth considering	Usage (light vs heavy) User status (potential, first time, regular) Readiness to buy Purchasing procedures (e.g. tenders, negotiations)

There are a variety of approaches to developing buyer personas including science fiction prototyping and data-driven. The most commonly used and evidenced approach is data-driven – it is based on market research and real data drawn from your customers. Factual information that will help to develop your buyer persona can be found through analysing Google Trends,

Google Analytics Audience data, CRM data or other platforms such as Followerwonk. Users of Chinese search engines can be profiled through Baidu and popular social networks such as WeChat. This factual information defines the most measurable aspects of your buyer persona including age, gender and geographic location. By conducting market research such as focus groups and interviews with your existing customers, more qualitative and subjective details can also be added to the story of your buyer persona, including aspects of their behaviour.

A science fiction prototyping approach to buyer persona development is based on the idea that some services and products cannot be solely predicted by evaluation of past behaviours. Many science fiction stories and films have influenced the technology that we now take for granted. *Star Trek* presented the communicator as inspiration for the smartphone that became a mini computer that manages half of your life and occasionally takes phone calls too. If your brand wants to lead in a new market or entirely disrupt an existing market, a science fiction prototyping–based buyer persona develops this opportunity. Companies such as Intel and Autodesk use science fiction prototyping to predict what their future could be, and this has helped their developers to produce solutions that are not found with their competitors.

Development of your buyer persona is an iterative process. As each new detail is added to the story, new questions raise the need for further details to ensure that the overall story remains coherent and consistent. As you bring the elements of the story of your buyer persona together, it may also become necessary to bridge the gaps of your current knowledge. Linking the details together will help everyone in your organisation understand and recognise the buyer persona. Even if these linkages must contain elements of fiction, they should be informed by insight and data based on a 'best guess' of your buyer persona that comes from knowledge of your existing customers and not be built on an unrealistic fantasy customer or internal assumptions. For the data-driven buyer persona, the process of creation might involve an annual customer profiling survey to see whether the pain and trust touchpoints have evolved, how and, if possible, why.

Data and market insight gives shape to your buyer persona. The details to consider to define your buyer persona can be categorised systematically (Table 3.3)

Creating a buyer persona allows you to think about your target audience as real people by presenting a more personal dimension. This can be further enhanced with a visual representation of the buyer persona (Figure 3.2). A London-based florist might identify Shanghai-based Nigel Bloom as a buyer persona. This buyer persona is built around a target of gaining new consumers globally (B2C).

For the same florist, creating a B2B buyer persona also benefits from a similar attention to detail (Figure 3.3). Lucy Bels is a wedding planner sourcing wedding flowers. Comparing the information and channels of the B2C and B2B shows that the two buyer personas are different and will require different kinds

Table 3.3 Defining your buyer persona

Element	Content
Who	A short biography of your ideal buyer persona, including where they work, their personality, their responsibilities, what they are motivated by and their commitments to family and friends. For B2B relationships, this includes identification of all the stakeholders involved in making the collective purchase decisions for procurement related to your brand.
What	Buyer persona's goals in relation to the products or services they are looking for
Where	Places where buyer persona spends their time both online and offline
Content	Types of content that your buyer persona prefers and what their key influencers could be in these areas
Channels	Social networks and other channels that your buyer persona prefers to access and uses regularly
Pain touchpoints	The problems that the buyer persona faces, which some of your brands' products and services can resolve
Trust touchpoints	These are the **perceived** solutions for each pain touchpoint. These are defined by the buyer persona and are not necessarily the correct or the best solution. These are the **perceived** solutions that the buyer persona trusts.
Role	Identify the role of your buyer persona in a decision making unit (DMU) if this is relevant or as a purchaser, user, customer, consumer, influencer or a combination.
'They say'	Use quotes from your buyer persona to make them come alive.
'We say'	Use sample quotes of the messages that you might send to your buyer persona in your communications.
Keywords	What are the keywords and phrases that you will associate with your buyer persona?
Average order value	Total revenue divided by the number of orders. This indicates the potential ROI (return on investment) for each individual engagement.

of messages to be conveyed by the florist through different channels. The average order value will be different and allows the organisation to set their priorities based on expected (or needed) ROI. For example, as a B2B buyer persona Lucy Bels will be more likely to place orders more regularly that each will be of a higher value than any single direct consumer order. However, on balance, there will be many more orders from many different individual consumers generated through the B2C buyer persona.

Several websites and apps such as Xtensio and Hubspot provide buyer persona templates that can be tailored with the dimensions suggested in Table 3.2 to provide a compact visualisation of your buyer persona. Alternatively, you can also create a visual representation as a simple Microsoft PowerPoint slide. The technology that is used is trivial; the important point is to maintain sight on your buyer persona when creating content and selecting relevant channels. Some creative agencies go so far as to print their buyer persona visualisations

NIGEL BLOOM

« Flowers speak a secret language »

Preferred channels

Google reviews
Website
WeChat
YouTube
Instagram
Email

PAIN POINTS:

FLOWERS THAT DO NOT LAST A LONG TIME

BOUQUETS THAT DO NOT LOOK LIKE THE IMAGE ON THE WEBSITE OF THE FLORIST STORE

DELIVERY TIMES THAT ARE NOT CONVENIENT

Bio: Nigel is a romantic who is deeply in love with his current girlfriend. He is a British ex-pat who lives in Shanghai but his girlfriend is in London.

He works for one of the international consulting firm and has to travel for work a lot of times but likes to remind his girlfriend of his affection using flowers. His average budget is £30 and he is happy to invest more into flowers for special occasions.

He is looking for flowers that are fresh and last a long time when delivered. He is also not always able to pick them up himself so relies on florists that manage the delivery process and offer high quality flowers as well cs delivery at times when his girlfriend is able to receive them.

TRUST POINTS:

WELL CHOSEN FRESHLY CUT AND CONDITIONED FLOWERS

A PHOTO CONFIRMATION OF THE BOUQUET BEING BOUGHT

FLEXIBLE DELIVERY, WHERE TIME AND LOCATION CAN BE SPECIFIED AND CHANGED AS REQUIRED

KEYWORDS

SAME DAY FLOWER DELIVERY LONDON

LUXURY FLOWER DELIVERY LONDON

FLOWER SHOP LONDON

KEY INFLUENCERS:

INTERFLORA

TIME OUT LONDON

RICHARD BRANSON

ALAN SUGAR

DECISION MAKING UNIT ROLES

INITIATOR, GATEKEEPER, DECIDER, BUYER, INFLUENCER

MOTIVATED BY:

Fear

Incentives

Achievement

Social

PERSONALITY

Introvert	X	Extravert
Analytical	X	Creative
Conservative		X Liberal
Passive	X	Active

Figure 3.2 Buyer persona example – B2C – Nigel Bloom

LUCY BELS

« Flowers make a wedding perfect »

Preferred channels

Face to face
Phone
Email
Website
LinkedIn
WhatsApp

PAIN POINTS:

FINDING NEW IDEAS FOR FASCINATING DEMANDING CLIENTS

NO WEDDING IS SAME AND ALL REQUIRE HIGH DEGREE OF FLEXIBILITY AND LAST MINUTE ADJUSTMENTS

WEDDING FLOWERS THAT ARE WASTED AFTER THE MAIN CEREMONY

Bio: Lucy is an MBA educated wedding planner in who has been co-running a wedding planning business for 5 years from London, UK. The annual business turnover is £ 3 million and average budget for wedding flowers is £ 1 500.

She is interested to always find new suppliers to surprise her customers with innovative ideas and competitively priced wedding planning packages. She wants to have the reputation of the best wedding planner in London.

She works in partnership with three other business partners and therefore all new major investment decisions are reviewed on quarterly basis at the board meeting. She prefers the initial business contact in person but is happy to use technology for placing the order and for accounts management.

TRUST POINTS:

FLORISTS WHO LOOK FOR LATEST FASHIONS AND REVIEW THEIR OFFERS

FLEXIBLE ARRANGEMENT AND ABILITY TO REACT FAST TO LAST MINUTE ADJUSTMENTS AS NEEDED

ARRANGEMENTS WHICH CAN BE RE-USED IN MANY WAYS AFTER THE INITIAL CEREMONY TO BENEFIT THE CLIENTS

KEYWORDS

WEDDING FLOWERS
WEDDING BOUQUETS
BRIDESMAID BOUQUETS
WEDDING FLORAL ARRANGEMENTS
WEDDING TABLE FLOWERS
FLORAL ARCH

KEY INFLUENCERS:

YOU & YOUR WEDDING
PERFECT WEDDING
COSMOPOLITAN BRIDE
WEDDING IDEAS
BRIDES MAGAZINE

DECISION MAKING UNIT ROLES

INITIATOR, GATEKEEPER, DECIDER, BUYER, USER, INFLUENCER

MOTIVATED BY:

Fear
Incentives
Achievement
Social

PERSONALITY

Introvert	X	Extravert
Analytical		Creative
Conservative	X	Liberal
Passive	X	Active

Figure 3.3 Buyer persona example – B2B – Lucy Bels

into full-sized person cardboard cutouts and have them handy when they are selecting channels and creating content.

3.3 Buyer persona's roles

In the Buyer Persona Spring, there is an emphasis on identifying the roles that your buyer persona plays in relation to your organisation and your products and services. There is a complex interaction amongst being a consumer, a buyer or customer and an influencer for products and services. Your buyer persona is a user of the Internet, with all of the competing opportunities that this access brings, as well as the potential for being an influencer to other consumers and customers for your brand, for example, by recommending to others through positive online reviews. This complexity of personal circumstances is what you are navigating in creating a comprehensive description of your buyer persona (Figure 3.4).

It may appear sensible to shape the story of a single buyer persona who is located right at the centre of this complexity (Figure 3.5). This most obvious target for your attention is not always directly identifiable and may not always bring the best return on your investment. Your organisation must then recognise the need for two or more buyer personas that specifically speak to different combinations of this intersecting complexity (Figure 3.6).

Your Buyer Persona

Figure 3.4 The buyer persona

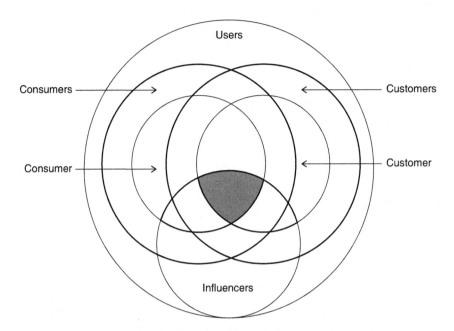

Figure 3.5 The single cover-all buyer persona at the intersection of users, influencers, consumers and customers

The earlier example of a London-based florist uses two buyer personas: one focusing on consumers (Nigel Bloom) and one focusing on a B2B relationship (Lucy Bels – wedding planner). The example of Help Scout shows how a software company might use two buyer personas to target their marketing actions more effectively (Case 3.1).

Case Study 3.1   Help Scout gets to know its buyer personas

Software company Help Scout has two different buyer personas that it addresses.

1 Growth Graham

Who: Graham is the founder of a small business and he has signed up for Help Scout because he's curious. He cares most about scale, price and providing outstanding, personalised support

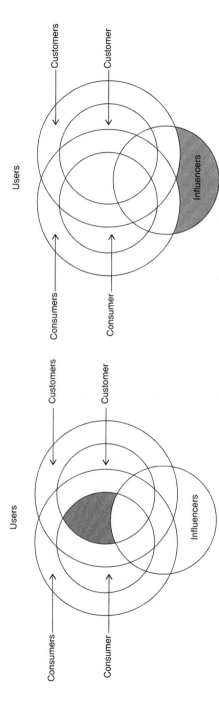

Figure 3.6 Multiple buyer personas addressing different roles (representing a customer who is also a consumer but not an influencer and one influencer who is neither a consumer nor a customer)

Figure 3.7 Growth Graham's vision

for customers. His organisation has about 30 employees but is growing.

Role in purchase process: Decision maker.

Trust touchpoints: Growth and delivering excellent customer service. Graham is utilising a free product.

Pain touchpoints: He doesn't want to give up the personal touch of email, but his team is overstretched by their current workflow.

Channels: Graham gets what it means to love customers. He's held on to using email (Gmail primarily) for a long time because he loves how personal it is, but his business is growing fast and he needs something that scales better.

Quotes (They say messages): "Great customer service is everything to us, so we need a tool that is personalised, yet scales to meet the needs of our business."

In the process of identifying user goals for the buyer persona, Help Scout identified three key questions that need to be answered:

1   What description would this customer use to identify their current problem?
2   What is their greatest hesitation in trying out our offering?
3   What is the best way to engage with this customer?

Understanding the buyer persona's goals, current problems and the ways they describe them will provide insights into how to write and communicate in relevant and persuasive ways.

Quotes (We say messages): Help Scout knows that Growth Graham is concerned about emails slipping through the cracks in his overcrowded Gmail account (Figure 3.8).

Figure 3.8 Growth Graham strategy

Figure 3.9 Growth Graham tips

In response to this, the copy on its 'Our email page' is written specifically to address those issues (Figure 3.9).

Help Scout recognises the need for multiple buyer personas and has shaped further descriptions based on their existing knowledge of how their software is used and in what type of organisations.

2 Help Desk Heidi

Who: Heidi is the lead customer support manager for a large organisation, and she has been given the task of finding a new help desk solution.

Trust touchpoints: Heidi wants a product that makes her a better, more efficient manager.

Pain touchpoints: Heidi is most concerned about agent productivity, reporting and team collaboration.

Figure 3.10 Help Desk Heidi example

Source: www.convinceandconvert.com/social-media-strategy/how-to-create-customer-profiles-to-reach-your-target-audience/

The examples of buyer personas from Help Scout show the ways in which two different buyer personas can benefit from an organisation's offering, even though each buyer persona has very different motives. Heidi needs in-depth, data-driven customer service resources while Graham's interests focus on what integration solutions are available. Understanding the needs and motivations of your buyer personas are important because:

- a customer's needs define the interest they will show in you;
- a customer's motivations define how they respond to your goods and services; and
- a customer's perception of your offerings and brand will shape their opinions of your organisation.

In website design, this principle would be applied to the 'About' section, where a description of what you offer must fit the buyer persona's needs and motivations (Chapter 6). The case of Help Scout also illustrates how a robustly developed buyer persona enables you to create content that is relevant, useful and persuasive to create customers and brand advocates.

3.4 Buyer personas and decision making units (DMUs)

In many cases purchase decisions, behavioural changes or charitable giving decisions are made by one buyer persona (e.g. Nigel Bloom) who occupies multiple roles (user, buyer, donor, supporter, consumer, customer and influencer). However, in some cases, decisions involve a number of people with different roles in relation to the decision making process. These are the decision making unit (DMU). DMUs are the group of individuals who all contribute to the decision making process.

Table 3.4 Individual roles within a DMU

Key player role	Definition	Example: Family DMU involved in a toy-based B2C relationship
Initiator	Recognises that there is a need, a want or a "problem" to be solved	The child
Gatekeeper	Responsible for the information provision. Determines the type of information that will be delivered and considered	The parents
Decider	Responsible for choosing the supplier, product or service	The parents
Buyer	Actual purchaser	One of the parents
User/consumer	Person or people who are going to benefit from the purchased product or services	The child who will play with the purchased toy
Influencer	Has a persuasive role in relation to the choices made by the decider	The child, TV, Internet, other children, family members, social media

In B2C relationships, a family might be seen as a DMU where individual buyer personas each occupy and overlap across different roles. In any DMU, there are a series of individual roles that are assumed by the members of the DMU: initiator, gatekeeper, buyer, decider, user and influencer (Table 3.4). Each role may be occupied by more than one member of the DMU and each member of the DMU may occupy more than one role. The structure of the DMU and the roles that members individually assume will shift from decision to decision. For example, the participants and roles assumed in a family DMU undertaking a private health insurance decision will be dramatically different from a toy-oriented decision.

The multiple roles within a DMU will inform the number of buyer personas your organization may require. For example, LeapFrog, the educational games and devices company for children, might define two buyer personas: one occupies the role of purchaser and one represents the user. The purchaser buyer persona will describe the parents purchasing the devices, whereas the user buyer persona will focus on defining a child but could also include the parents (Douglas, 2019). The child is not a buyer but they will exert influence over the purchaser (the parents).

Ryan ToysReview – a YouTube channel with over 21 million subscribers – illustrates the importance of understanding the multiple roles of that a buyer persona can take as user, consumer and influencer. Ryan is a charismatic child who reviews toys. According to *Forbes* (2019), he is the youngest of the highest-earning YouTube influencers. With over 26 billion views, his audience is mainly made up of children his age who do not purchase the products but influence the buyers (generally their parents) (Chapter 8).

Table 3.5 Roles and stakeholder relationships in a construction DMU

DMU Role	Stakeholder	Responsibility
Initiator	Client Architect	Commissions the building
Influencer		Specifies building materials required
Gatekeeper	Architect	Searches for information and delivers recommendations
Decider	Contractor	for Deciders
		Chooses the suppliers and services. Often the purchasing director
Buyer	Contractor	Makes the final deal or decision and places the order. Usually have a brief with criteria to judge potential products or services and the suppliers. They tend to be responsible for sourcing and negotiation
User and influencer	Subcontractor	Puts the service or product into operation. Has an influencer role as they are heavily involved in the post-purchase evaluation phase
Other influencers	Other architects, industry experts, industry bodies, building regulations	

When developing B2B-oriented buyer personas, it is important to identify who will usually contribute to the purchase decisions related to your brand. Define B2B buyer personas with an awareness of the wider DMU of which they are only one of the role-holders. Understanding the relationship your buyer persona has within their own DMU and the role they assume lets you customise your communications to support your buyer persona in their DMU role. Since you are seeking the best ROI, prioritise your buyer persona development towards the role in the DMU that can produce the most value. With this understanding you can focus on the most relevant content, channels and data to target the most relevant buyer persona.

In the B2B sector, DMUs are more complex. Table 3.5 provides an example in the design and build construction industry. In large construction projects for specialized and usually high-value purchases, the DMU players tend to include the client, the architect, the main contractor and the subcontractors.

The relationship of the DMUs role-holders will be different in every organisation, each sector and for every purchase situation. An iterative learning approach within your marketing strategy and activities will support decisions about the number of buyer personas that should be defined. Understanding when decisions relating to your own goods or services are made individually or within a DMU also supports the broader development of an effective digital marketing strategy.

3.5 Characteristics of ethical, moral and green consumer behaviour within digital environments

Increasingly, your organisation must cater to the new dimension of the online consumer: the ethical online consumer. This consumer is highly conscious and vocally aware of issues ranging from the climate crisis, environmental degradation, animal welfare, working conditions, local origins, organic ingredients and eco-friendly materials to the political affiliation of brands. These consumers make their voices heard by buying products that clearly reflect their own ethical position.

You may or may not choose to cater directly to these consumers, but you cannot ignore their presence, as ethical consumers are also influencers. In terms of developing a buyer persona, the ethical consumer may represent a core feature or necessitate the development of an additional buyer persona (Figure 3.4). Some organisations have been quick to capitalise on the ethical consumer movement by offering easy-to-find local products and by providing the ability to sell second-hand products, as the consumer demand for both is rising. The online sustainable toilet roll manufacturer whogivesacrap.com is an example of a disintermediated e-commerce that has directly picked up on this environmental consciousness to offer a market alternative to the established multinational retailers.

There are now numerous blogs, websites and ethical community groups that rate or discuss which brands are acting ethically and which ones are not, making consumer choice incredibly straightforward. For example, ethicalconsumer. org ranks brands in a table, based on the sustainability of their products and how they affect the environment, animals, people and politics, so that consumers can see where their favourite brands rank and can then decide whether they should continue buying from them. This requires brands to become more transparent in how they operate, where they operate and what they produce.

With the ethical consumer movement, even brands generally regarded as ethical can come under scrutiny when their ethical standards are seen to slip. This was the case when ethically prized brand Stella McCartney started to collaborate with brands like Target and Adidas, both of which have poor environmental standards and manufacture in under-developed economies (Ethical Fashion, 2012). This confirms the need for your organisation to do-as-you-say in a world where all our actions are visible and where consumers will actively communicate disquiet when they identify actions they regard as unethical.

Alignment with the ethical consumer requires change in practices and mindset at an organisational level as well as specifically in the products and services your offer (Lewis, 2015). The shift to ethical consumption and corporate responsibility should be genuine and undertaken because you and your organisation recognise and prioritise the importance of creating a sustainable society, not because it simply brings new customers. A cynical ethical offering will equally be called out by engaged and concerned influencers and consumers.

- Find out what your customer cares about and align your efforts with the cause.
- Embrace the cause into your organisational culture and showcase this throughout your communications.
- Tell your customers how buying from you will make a difference, and educate them.

- Make sure all your touchpoints promote your cause; consumers need to see it to believe it.
- Make your cause worth talking about so others will share your story and build credibility; do not ignore negative PR.
- Legitimise your efforts with the transparency of your ethical efforts, use authentic ethical labelling, display third-party ethical certifications, provide ethical leadership and training for your employees and create an ethical code of conduct (Delmas and Burbano, 2011).

Case Study 3.2   Kipato Unbranded creates a platform of fashionable empowerment

Ethical consumption is not a movement exclusive to the developed economies. The ethical consciousness of consumers has no boundaries and is emerging worldwide. Kipato Unbranded has found a successful way to empower their suppliers and offer unique products to their ethically minded consumers. Africa is well-known as a continent for their excellence in cultural artisanal goods. Kipato has harnessed this awareness by presenting handmade, eco-friendly jewellery, where the artists themselves benefit through higher wages and access to larger markets. Even the use of the name "Unbranded" is to suggest it is not about the brand, but about the artists who commit their hearts and souls into the creation of the jewellery.

Like many ethical brands, Kipato Unbranded does not want to be known solely for the ethical realm of its products. They also want to make a fashion statement. From the first impression made by the website's landing page, inspiring images predominate supported by taglines like: "Jewelry by Everyday People for Everyday People." (Figure 3.11). The feeling is one of indulging in the brand and standing out from the crowd, while being proud of the product's provenance. The brand draws together being ethical with being fashionable with a sense of fun.

A part of any effective brand communications strategy is the ability to successfully tell a story to your consumer. Kipato Unbranded uses the website's 'About Us' page to share their story as well as the story of some of their artisans (combined with vibrant images and video) and how the income from the company has helped artisans support their families. By doing so, they bring their brand to life and create a real connection amongst brand, artisans and consumers. The intimacy of the story creates a sense of trust, so that consumers more readily believe

Figure 3.11 Kipato Unbranded example

the jewellery they are consuming is truly coming from a place of beauty and empowerment.

In essence, Kipato Unbranded has realised that the ethical consumer not only wants to feel good about their consumption but wants to look good as well. Brands wishing to enter this type of ethically and fashion-conscious market must find a way to confidently communicate both aspects to their consumer.

Source: www.kipatounbranded.com

3.6 Privacy and data protection

Consumers with a conscience are not solely concerned about the ethical implications of your product or service; they also care about how you market it to them. These concerns also extend beyond this type of consumer and is present in the minds of all consumers to some degree. With recent privacy issues going public with such large firms like Facebook, or online customer profiles (including banking information) being compromised in even the largest hotel chains in the world, consumers are becoming less likely to want to share their information online and are losing trust in online channels that are not transparent, for example, about their data handling.

With growing consumer concerns, there are now new laws protecting these concerns. In the European Union, the General Data Protection Regulation is a legal framework that requires any website, no matter where it is based, to allow users to opt in when the website is collecting data cookies. The law also states that websites must inform users of any breach in their system in a timely manner and to disclose all security measures in place to protect their data. Other laws such as Canada's Anti-Spam Law empower consumers to even sue organizations and their employees (up to $10,000,000 CAD) for not receiving consent prior to sending electronic communications (emails and text) to them.

It is imperative to know the legal environment in which your target market exists (Chapter 2). A rule of thumb is to endeavour to comply with all of these requirements; this avoids major adjustments for your organisation when it targets new geographic areas. The main concerns for consumers are that you may be handing off their data to third parties or that your web server is not secure, which leaves their data open to be compromised. It is crucial to communicate trust with your consumer by, for example, showing the use of the most up-to-date security software and that you explicitly ask for permission when obtaining the right to use cookies. You can also give the ability for customers to make purchases on your online platform without the need to create a profile or to store vital personal information (let them check out as a guest user). Giving users the option to check out using trusted third-party platforms such as PayPal all support increasing levels of trust in your organisation and its operations.

3.7 The buying journey

Once your buyer persona is defined, it is important to describe a buying journey that will lead the buyer persona through to the full completion of an action. This exercise needs to be kept simple, it should be done from the buyer persona point-of-view and, where possible, it should use actual customer feedback to define the path. The ultimate aim for your organisation is to identify areas for improvement and where you can influence the journey. You are attempting to capture your buyer persona's journey from, for example, seeking information through to their decision to buy and onwards to the actual purchasing process. In building the buying journey and thinking about the Buyer Persona Spring, consider the three key building blocks that link your organisation with the buyer persona, namely content, channels and data.

Mapping the journey allows you to visualise current and planned buying journeys and to document the touchpoints across multiple channels. Each of your touchpoints is a single point of contact, the interface between people and products, services or brands before, during and after an individual interaction. Your buying journey should map all the relevant touchpoints. The buyer journey can be mapped in four steps:

1   *Understanding the customer touchpoints and channels*

Identify the core purchase channels. Depending on your type of organisation it could cover the store, website or call centre, and can be expanded to your marketing channels (email, postal, Facebook), order fulfilment (delivery and payment) and research channels (website customer services). Direct and indirect contacts such as social sites and customer reviews should also be considered as touchpoints.

2   *Identifying the buyer journey activities/actions*

The touchpoints, actions and activities of your buyer persona will differ according to which industry you operate in. When mapping an existing customer journey or designing a new one, it is vital that you consider the Zero Moment of Truth (ZMOT) (Chapter 1). The ZMOT refers to the stage in the buying process when the consumer is in the active stage of researching a product or service prior to the purchase. It is that moment of searching when your buyer persona grabs the laptop or mobile phone or uses their own personal networks and starts learning about a product or service they are thinking about trying or buying (Lecinski, 2011).

Overall, the activities of the buyer persona journey can be grouped into awareness (stimulus), consideration (ZMOT), purchase (First Moment of Truth – FMOT), and experience (Second Moment of Truth – SMOT). The SMOT also ideally results in retention through high levels of customer satisfaction. It happens when the buyer persona's expectations have been met or been exceeded after using the product or service. After post-purchase evaluation, the buyer persona decides whether to buy again and recommend. The use of the product or service could also be a stimulus for related purchase. The latter is the starting point for other buyer persona's ZMOT (consideration). Retention and recommendation are not an automatic outcome of a customer journey. These are outcomes that need to be planned by your organisation, encouraged through high levels of customer satisfaction and directly communicated with your buyer persona. Integrating a customer satisfaction survey as an email or phone call, where possible, will help to get information of any new pain touchpoints or trust touchpoints discovered by your buyer persona. If retention is not achieved, then optimal customer lifetime value cannot be realised. The identified pain touchpoints need to be identified and corrected. On the other hand, for those customers who are highly satisfied, encouraging them to share their experience with the public can be a great stimulus for newly defined buyer personas.

3   *Mapping the journey*

Once the touchpoints and activities are listed, they can be plotted visually or in a table following the ZMOT's four stages (Table 3.6).

Table 3.6 Customer journey map – Nigel Bloom's buyer persona

Touch points	Stimulus	ZMOT	FMOT	SMOT
Google My Business		Reviews of the best florists in London		Writes a five star review on Google My Business
Website		Search on Google for "flower shop London" "valentines day flowers London" "same day flower delivery London" "luxury flower delivery London"	Purchases the flowers online and arranges delivery date and location	
Email			Confirmation of payment and delivery details	Receives a confirmation of delivery with a picture of actual flowers bought. 5% discount from next purchase within 3 months and review request for Google My Business listing
WeChat	Valentines day romantic presents inspiration			Private message from his girlfriend thanking him about the lovely rose bouquet
YouTube	Valentines day romantic presents inspiration			
Instagram	Valentines day romantic presents inspiration. Instagram			Girlfriend shares her flowers with her followers and tags Nigel and the florist adding #ValentinesDay

4   *Using the buyer persona journey*

Having built an understanding of your buyer persona's journey, you can now set about improving it. More buyers can be retained by understanding their steps through their individual journeys. Your task is to optimise the interactions your organisation has with the buyer persona on their buying journey. You will also be able to identify communications gaps, where conflicting messages are being sent or where replies are not being received.

Pain touchpoints

Pain touchpoints were identified when the buyer persona was developed. Removing or adjusting the pain touchpoints can improve your offering and design a superior customer journey (Box 3.1).

Pain touchpoints can also be identified in different areas of your website, as well as blockages that may impede the customer journey. Once these are identified, a solution can be developed with an optimisation strategy for improving the buyer persona's experience. For example, an online classified ad site wanted to encourage visitors to sign up for email alerts when they were exhibiting behaviour indicating that they were about to leave the site. Using the buyer journey map and optimisation techniques, the company identified that a prompt at 1 minute after entering the website gave visibility, but it was a prompt at 6 minutes that led to the highest completion rates and the greatest level of returns to the site.

Touchpoints that are not optimised successfully for your buyer can rapidly become pain touchpoints. Your task is to discover where these potential pain touchpoints are located. Use 'blog patrols' to periodically peruse blogs that deal with similar products or services that you are connected with, and update your pain touchpoints based on what users are saying about your service,

---

Box 3.1   Turning pain into trust touchpoints

In the case of Nigel Bloom's customer journey (Table 3.6), one of his pain touchpoints are that the bouquets he orders do not look like the images on the website. By recognising this issue, the florist can turn this pain into a trust touchpoint by emailing him a photo of the actual bouquet delivered along with a 5 per cent discount voucher for the next purchase within three months and a request for a Google My Business listing. In this example, a pain touchpoint has been converted into a trust touchpoint. At the same time, the buyer persona has been provided with a compelling reason to do a repeat purchase (brand loyalty) and to recommend (ZMOT).

reliability and quality. You then have a core set of issues that can be addressed. Take this examination further and analyse the reviews of your competitors to identify sector-wide sets of pain touchpoints and speak to those people who deal directly with your buyers for more details about other potential pain touchpoints. Pain touchpoints push the buyer persona away from your organisation, while trust touchpoints draw the buyer persona closer to you and your organisation. See Figure 3.12.

Visitor tracking tools such as Google Analytics can identify how and whether your products and services are being searched for and how readily customers are able to find you. Finally, constantly review and track the journey that your buyers take and recognise the points at which they turn away from completing a purchase. Inward emails, online surveys and live chats will all point you towards those touchpoints that create the most pain. After having identified the main pain touchpoints for your buyers, you must act to reduce that pain. For some buyers, the main source of pain is the need to pay large amounts of money up front. One solution to this is to offer different payment options. Another common source of pain focuses on the buyer's concerns about being charged for returning an item. A solution for this particular problem might be to integrate services within your offering to minimise this pain. Options for integration include providing prepaid return pickup and allowing the buyer to organise a return through different channels including phone, email and live chat. Other buyers worry about not being able to track their purchases. This concern can be eased by providing an order number and confirmation email with meaningful information, including a tracking number. Buyers can then check on the progress of their order at any time.

Out-of-stock items also create pain touchpoints, but this can be mitigated by letting your potential buyer leave their email address so that they can be contacted when their item is back in stock. Similarly, not being able to try on clothing items that are bought online is a common source of pain for buyers. Offering third-party reviews, comprehensive details of the product (measurements, materials used, product origin and distinctive features) and free returns could resolve this pain touchpoint. Some brands take pain touchpoints and – by applying the theory of constraints – turn these into a feature of the buying process. For example, personalising a shoe would traditionally have been regarded as a source of pain, but Nike I.D. now makes personalisation a feature with minimal steps and an easy-to-follow customisation process.

Trust touchpoints

When mapping or designing a new customer journey, it is important to integrate the buyer persona's trust touchpoints. Your buyer persona is constantly 'in touch' with all types of brands through their own individual touchpoints. Each of these touchpoints can influence, either positively or negatively, a consumer's trust in a brand. Trust points are the perceived solution for each pain touchpoint. These are defined by the buyer persona and are not necessarily

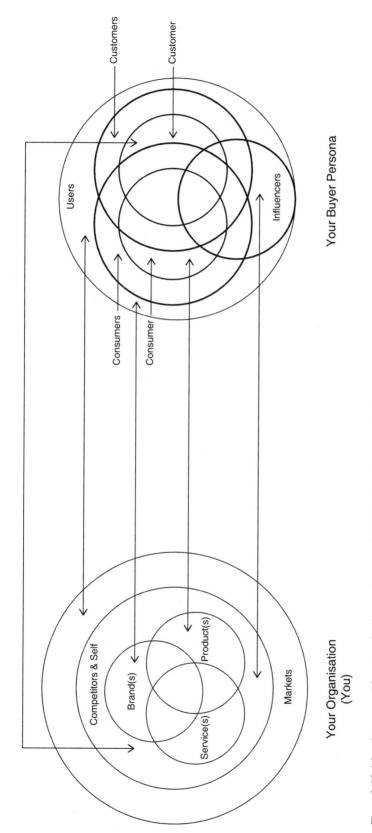

Figure 3.12 Mapping potential trust and pain touchpoints within the Buyer Persona Spring

the correct or the best solution. These are the perceived solutions the buyer persona trusts. Building trust with buyers is paramount as an incentive to purchase a product or service and create brand loyalty. Some organisations are more sensitive to trust issues, such as banking, but any business that incorporates a financial transaction with their buyers shares aspects of this sensitivity. As a consequence, it is important for you to understand the trust touchpoints that engage your buyers. Buyers legitimately worry that brands may misuse personal and financial information, or, indeed, that a website might be entirely fraudulent.

Trust in social media has declined in recent years due to privacy concerns and fake news (Vranika, 2019). In nine countries (UK, France, Germany, Canada, the USA, Brazil, United Arab Emirates, China and India), the Edelman Trust Barometer found that globally trust in traditional media (66 per cent) and search engines (63 per cent) is much higher than in social media (40 per cent). The latter is more trusted in developing economies, but in most Western economies trust has dropped. In the UK, for example, levels of trust were recorded at just 24 per cent. Only 41 per cent of respondents believed what the company was saying in advertising. This reinforces the fifth of the five rules for social media success (Chapter 1): "The buyer persona will resist the most blatant advertising messages on social media". On the positive side, 59 per cent of respondents considered an organisation more credible when it was communicating directly to them (Edelman, 2018). According to Nielsen, buyers trust branded websites more than traditional touchpoints such as ads in newspapers or on TV, or brand sponsorships (Nielsen, 2013, 2015). Thus, it is important to identify and deploy trust touchpoints when developing your buyer persona and mapping the customer journey and throughout the development of your digital strategy.

Touchpoints are moving targets. You must constantly evaluate at which touchpoints your buyers find the most trust and which touchpoints are regarded as completely untrustworthy or significantly lacking in trust. Even the most trustworthy touchpoint will still compare unfavourably with the trust that is built through personal recommendations and reviews or testimonials. Independent third-party touchpoints are trusted by 88 per cent of buyers (Anderson, 2014) and still remain a strong source of trusted information. In the US, 86per cent of consumers read reviews for local businesses (including 95 per cent of people aged 18 to 34) and 57 per cent will only use a business if it has four or more stars (Bright Local, 2018).

In the Buyer Persona Spring, knowing both trust and pain touchpoints is an integral consideration in assessing the success of campaigns and how well the application of specific tactics for each campaign has achieved the planned outcomes. Your goal is to maximise the positive consequences and reduce/ eliminate negative consequences. This will help you create a competitive advantage by providing a product and service experience that is superior to the ones offered by competitors. Channels, content and data in the Buyer Persona Spring interact with touchpoints in different ways (Table 3.7).

Table 3.7 Using the building blocks of the Buyer Persona Spring to increase trust touchpoints and reduce pain touchpoints

Channel	Trust	Pain
Increase	Utilise channels that are respected by the buyer persona Genuine engagement with a specialist channel for the buyer persona (positive consequences)	Require a sign-in or the use of an unfamiliar or unattractive channel for the buyer persona Introduce the use of a new channel into the buyer journey (negative consequences)
Decrease	Use material from individual users on a respected channel without attribution or recognition (negative consequences)	Offer options that allows the buyer persona to choose the channel they prefer – e.g. Google, Twitter and Facebook sign-in options (positive consequences)

Content	Trust	Pain
Increase	Users rather than copywriters produce brand content (positive consequences)	Vague, onerous or overly long conditions and disclaimers attached to content Media mismatch, e.g. text when video is expected or vice versa (negative consequences)
Decrease	Veiled editorial content, blatantly copywritten items or content that is inappropriate for the buyer persona (negative consequences)	Reduction of content repetition, e.g. the online catalogue is also the shopping cart (positive consequences)

Data	Trust	Pain
Increase	Transparent matching of the buyer persona with further relevant content and goods and services (positive consequences)	Sign-in systems that mistrust all users rather than helping legitimate users to verify their identity (negative consequences)
Decrease	Poor algorithmic matching of keywords in content with the intent of the buyer persona, e.g. Private Eye's *Malgorithms* column regularly documents these failures (negative consequences)	Checkout systems that remember preferences Systems that respond 'naturally' to the expected actions of the buyer persona (positive consequences)

With a workable buyer persona developed, your organisation can now consistently address and engage with a specific target for your attention. However, this process is not at an end. Your buyer persona should also be part of a continuous process of learning from your customers and their feedback and be subject to ongoing refinement and evolution.

3.8 Summary

In this chapter, you have seen how to create your buyer persona. Mapping their buying journey is vital to understanding the touchpoints that build trust and offer a positive brand experience. Likewise, determining your customer's trust and pain touchpoints ensures that the buyer persona feels connected and can enjoy the experience of engaging with your organisation. Having well-defined buyer personas is paramount to using content, channels and data that are relevant to them. The creation and use of multiple buyer personas and their role within DMUs provides further refinement to accurately defining who your organisation engages with – or wants to engage with. Building robust buyer personas provides the foundation for the design of an effective digital strategy that delivers results, which is developed further in the next chapter.

3.9 References

Anderson, M. (2014) *88% of consumers trust online reviews as much as personal recommendations.*searchengineland.com/88-consumers-trust-online-reviews-much-personal-recom mendations-195803

Bright Local (2018) *Local consumer review survey | Online reviews statistics & trends.* www. brightlocal.com/research/local-consumer-review-survey/?SSAID=314743&SSCID=31 k3_6lp2d#local-business-review-habits

Delmas, M. A. and Burbano, V. C. (2011) The drivers of greenwashing. *California Management Review,* 54(1), 64–87.

Douglas, S. (2019) *UX personas vs. marketing personas: What's the difference?* www.justinmind. com/blog/ux-personas-vs-marketing-personas-whats-the-difference/

Edelman (2018) Edelman Trust Barometer Global Report. www.edelman.com/sites/g/files/ aatuss191/files/2018-10/2018_Edelman_Trust_Barometer_Global_Report_FEB.pdf

Ethical Fashion (2012) *Behind the label: Is Stella McCartney a sustainable brand?* stellamccartney ethicalfashion.wordpress.com/2012/11/16/behind-the-label-is-stella-mccartney-a-sustainable-brand/

Forester, D. (2019) *What is the difference between a nonprofit organization and a charity?* www. score.org/resource/what-difference-between-nonprofit-organization-and-charity

Investopedia (2019) *Business to business (B2B).* www.investopedia.com/terms/b/btob.asp

Lecinski, J. (2011) *Winning the zero moment of truth.* www.thinkwithgoogle.com/marketing-resources/micro-moments/2011-winning-zmot-ebook/

Lewis, K. (2015) *6 secrets to marketing to ethical consumers.* www.imediaconnection.com/articles/ ported-articles/red-dot-articles/2015/sep/6-secrets-to-marketing-to-ethical-consumers/

Nielsen (2013) *Under the influence: Consumer trust in advertising.* www.nielsen.com/us/en/ insights/news/2013/under-the-influence-consumer-trust-in-advertising.html

Nielsen (2015) *Global trust in advertising report.* www.nielsen.com/wp-content/uploads/ sites/3/2019/04/global-trust-in-advertising-report-sept-2015-1.pdf

Rivera, A. (2019) What is C2C? *Business News Daily.* www.businessnewsdaily.com/5084-what-is-c2c.html

Top Non Profits (2019) *Top 100 nonprofits on the web*.topnonprofits.com/lists/best-nonprofits-on-the-web/

UN Women (2019) *Campaigns for behaviour change.* www.endvawnow.org/en/articles/
1192-campaigns-for-behaviour-change.html

Vranika, S. (2019) *Trust in social media falls – Raising concerns for marketers.* www.wsj.com/
articles/trust-in-social-media-fallsraising-concerns-for-marketers-1529312580

WRAP (2019) *Improving recycling through effective communications.* www.wrap.org.uk/content/
campaign-activities-0

4 Digital and social media marketing strategy

Ivan Stoychev

4.0 Learning objectives

In this chapter you will learn how to:

- create a digital marketing strategy and use a strategy development cycle;
- align your digital marketing strategy with your buyer persona;
- set appropriate goals; and
- monitor and update your strategy.

4.1 What is a digital marketing strategy?

Whatever your organisation, you need to adopt a long-term (3 to 5 years) strategic perspective. A strategy will emphasise the most advantageous direction for your organisation in terms of connecting the buyer persona with your business objectives. The key elements of the digital marketing strategy are represented by the Buyer Persona Spring, and these are objectives, channels, content (including keywords), data and the buyer persona. The digital marketing strategy will then help to guide you towards the most suitable tactics and activities that should be used to create the elements of the Buyer Persona Spring. Before moving forward with digital marketing, your organisation should first determine what it wants to accomplish.

Characteristics of digital marketing strategy

A digital strategy can be seen as a road map that helps you to maximise the impact you get from channels, content and data in order to support your organisation's mission, vision and goals. Your digital strategy should build awareness and promote your organisation, your brands and your products and services (Figure 4.1). This is an interactive and iterative process. Since the Internet allows for immediate feedback on your actions and the ability for significant and focused data gathering, you will be constantly optimising and improving your marketing efforts.

Digital marketing focuses on the use of specific content delivered through specific channels. The range of channels and opportunities includes possibilities

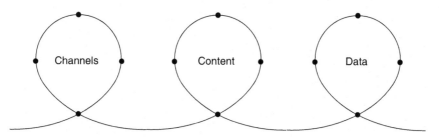

Figure 4.1 Strategy within the Buyer Persona Spring

for email, online video advertising, banner advertisements, product placement and search engine activities. The rising importance of digital channels and the direct feedback available through these channels also means that increasingly digital organisations are using their digital marketing activities to influence and shape their presence in offline channels including TV and radio.

For the Buyer Persona Spring, your starting point is to know your buyer persona. The two ways to develop a buyer persona are data-driven or using science fiction prototyping. A data-driven buyer persona will be based on your knowledge and research of your consumers, customers and influencers, drawing upon qualitative and quantitative data blended together with a mix of reporting and storytelling. The science fiction prototyping buyer persona is based on your imagination of the future needs of the buyer persona and how they could interact with your product or service. In conjunction with the discussion in Chapter 3, Table 3.2 can also act as a template for developing your own buyer persona.

Within the Buyer Persona Spring, three key building blocks are identified to draw the buyer persona closer to your organisation. The three are content, channel and data. Each building block is closely interrelated with the other, but each represents a different level of engagement with the buyer persona. Content focuses on the specific conversations that you initiate and engage with your buyer persona. The content is documented by the topics and keywords. Keywords would be identified as part of search engine optimisation. A clear commitment to keywords within a content building block enables you to focus on producing a consistent message. The channels focus on where this content is positioned (or not positioned) and relates directly to the 'usual' locations of your buyer persona. The data tracks the interaction with the buyer persona, other consumers and open sources to inform your further planning and to develop and extend your organisation's activities.

Your channels will change over time as you draw in new channels and retire less effective channels (including more traditional channels). The channels will be influenced heavily by technology developments that offer alternatives to existing traditional and digital channels. Your choice of channels will also be influenced by the reporting and analytics capability available through each channel. The aspect of your choice of channels will be determined in part by your data.

By planning and thinking strategically, whilst leaving room to be flexible and dynamic, you will be able to take advantage of new technology, resist purely reactive responses to the actions of competitors and achieve your overall goals as an organisation. The attitude of

"Fail fast, fail often"

is particularly suitable for digital marketing strategy implementation. The ongoing access to data to see trends and impact generated can help to determine whether a certain project was successful or not. Being ready to accept that some of the decisions can lead to failure is a mind-set that allows experimentation and iteration that allows learning and understanding your buyer persona and the market in general.

Digital marketing planning cycle

Experienced marketers constantly monitor the progress of their strategies by monitoring the outcomes of and responses to specific marketing activities; they will test alternative approaches and adjust their plans based on the evidence of their observations. The Buyer Persona Spring references the four-step action learning cycle (Figure 4.2), a well-tested model found especially in the context of education. The action learning cycle is significant for its iterative perspective and the degree to which it advocates continuous improvements.

The Buyer Persona Spring adapts the action learning cycle to a strategic marketing perspective (Figure 4.3). The cycle within the Buyer Persona Spring takes you from the broadest strategy and planning through to a specific campaign that then implements appropriate tactics. As these tactics are undertaken, they are constantly assessed using the evidence that is drawn from available analytics. The tactics may be adjusted as a result (by taking a step backwards in the activity loop), or if the response is failing to address the buyer persona effectively, then the campaign may need to be significantly modified or completely suspended (and necessitate the initiation of a new loop of activity). Assessment will initially encourage small revisions in the current cycle of activity but will ultimately reach a point at which it informs further refinement of your strategy, which, in turn, commences a new loop of activity that will more effectively reach your buyer persona.

A **situation analysis** and background research are the first steps in creating your strategy. From Chapter 3 you have learned that, in order to do this, the best way is to start by understanding your current customers and your ideal customer. Listening to what the customers, consumers, influencers and users of your buyer persona are saying enables your organisation to comparatively assess the situation in relation to competitors and the industry in general. Both the SWOT analysis and PESTLE analysis provide frameworks that guide and structure your strategic thinking. The insight gained from this research can then

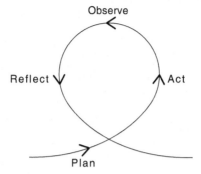

Figure 4.2 The action learning cycle

Figure 4.3 The action learning cycle within the Buyer Persona Spring

shape the setting of objectives and the key performance indicators (KPIs) that will indicate the success of your strategy.

It is critical for your organisation to discover what people are talking about before becoming part of the conversation. This lets you gauge the tone and activities of the communities that your buyer persona is part of.

Result of stage 1 – Identify the main current issues and key competitor activities, and define your buyer persona.

Objective setting is done by considering the location, behaviour, tastes and needs of your buyer persona and is informed by your external and internal analyses. You can then set objectives that set out to satisfy the needs and desires of your buyer persona in ways that capitalise on the unique strengths of your organisation while mitigating your organisational weaknesses and external threats (Figure 4.4). Your objectives should be specific, measurable, attainable, realistic and timely (or SMART).

Figure 4.4 Strategy stage

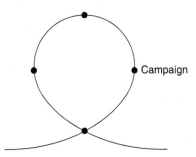

Figure 4.5 Campaign stage

Result of stage 2 – SMART objectives are set.

Campaigns turn strategy into a plan of action so that you can create a dialogue with your buyer persona that aims to hit your SMART objectives and supports the overall mission of your organisation. Campaign planning includes the practicalities of budgeting and planning the deployment of people within your organisation (Figure 4.5). Your plans should separately consider the content you will utilise, the channels that you will focus upon and the data you will collect and analyse as part of the campaigns. While content, channels and data interrelate, they should all be considered as separate parts of your overall strategy and are the key mechanisms for connecting your organisation with your buyer persona.

Result of stage 3 – Timelines, resource allocation, external support and agencies, content, channel and data plans.

Tactics turn the overall plan of action within your campaign into specific actions (Figure 4.6). Your tactics include selecting the tools to target your buyer

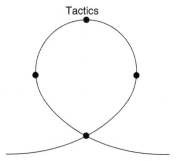

Figure 4.6 Tactics stage

Table 4.1 Tools to convert your campaign into specific activities

	Tools
Content	Curating, workflow management, editing, graphics, crisis management
Channels	Posting, monitoring, interaction, mobile control, access control
Data	Measurement, tracking, analytics, demographics, location, collecting

persona and focusing the available resources in your organisation towards implementation of the campaign (Table 4.1).

Result of stage 4 – Concrete list of activities to implement with specific tools.

Assessing allows you to optimise your campaigns, objectives and strategy. The feedback provided by assessing enables you to maintain **control** that optimises objectives, campaigns and tactics (Figure 4.7). Monitoring is the process of tracking, measuring and evaluating an organisation's social media marketing initiatives. Your buyer persona will comment on, react to and interact with your campaigns. Your purpose in assessing is to ensure that the two-way conversation is in place and that it is producing positive responses that reflect your defined objectives.

Result of stage 5 – Measurement through web analytics, conversion optimisation and other techniques that allow assessment in relation to your strategic objectives.

Updating is the constant and continuous process of adjusting and improving the elements of the plan to maximise the chances of success. Fine-tune your strategy until the results not just meet but exceed your objectives (Figure 4.8). The Buyer Persona Spring is centred on a fluid cycle of activities.

Figure 4.7 Assess stage

Figure 4.8 Updating (Evolving Strategy) stage

Your organisation should keep its action flexible and adaptive in order to be in constant conversation with your buyer persona.

Result of stage 6 – After assessing your results, your strategy will evolve and initiate a new cycle of activity (and learning).

4.2 Aligning your strategy with your buyer persona

Analysis of your existing audiences will drive an understanding of the behaviours of your customers. From this understanding, you can recognise a range of characteristics that can be represented within your buyer persona. Your buyer persona enables your organisation to focus its marketing strategy on effectively reaching those who are most receptive and most likely to become customers, influencers and even brand advocates. By addressing your buyer persona, you are effectively speaking to a range of individuals who share and recognise the values, sentiments, opinions and lifestyle of your buyer persona.

By creating an insightful buyer persona, you create for your organisation a decision tool that will shape your strategies first and then inform your campaigns

Table 4.2 The benefits of content, channels and data strategies to your buyer persona

	Benefits to the buyer persona
Content	Relevant and meaningful in ways that it answers their trust touchpoints, addresses their pain touchpoints and encourages sharing. For example, a buyer persona identifies a detailed product description that explains all the benefits in a language that they prefer and understand well.
Channel	Familiar spaces, and the site of communities for like-minded individuals includes channels to drive your buyer persona to (discovery) channels where they already congregate (centrality). For example, they encounter your product on their preferred social media channel whilst conversing with others on this topic. The content is delivered at the time and place where they feel comfortable and familiar with the channel use.
Data	Offers value back to the buyer persona in the form of summary and aggregation of actions, personalisation based on data insights and recommendations based on prior actions. For example, reviews and recommendations from other purchasers in the form of a star rating or indication that a certain product video has been seen by a high number of other viewers who left positive comments, etc.

and tactics. Your buyer persona will tell you what your core customers and consumers do, how they do it, why they do it and how they think. Speaking to your buyer persona aligns your organisation's brands, products and services through consciously created content that is delivered on relevant channels, with a suitable feedback loop to ensure that you collect data. The collected data will let you know the response to your actions and over time will drive your organisation towards becoming a fully digital business. Your buyer persona turns the complexity of qualitative and quantitative data into insight and understanding of your customers and consumers within the external environment. By endeavouring to connect your organisation to your buyer persona through the Buyer Persona Spring, your content, channel and data should return clear benefits directly back to the buyer persona (Table 4.2). If the benefits for your buyer persona of your marketing actions are not evident to the buyer persona themselves, then your conversation is not transparent, one sided and unsustainable.

Case Study 4.1 Famish'd Salad Bar: knowing your customer brings results

Georgia Samuel used to work as a corporate lawyer, but now she is the sole owner of the very successful Famish'd Salad Bar in Melbourne, Australia. It is serving soups, gourmet salads and spuds to up to 800 of downtown's business crowd each day. Georgia credits much of her success to her previous corporate role.

'The customer I'm targeting is who I was for six years – the corporate customer. I know how precious time is and how long they are prepared to wait and I know how easy it is for them to go somewhere else if the quality and customer service isn't there'.

Georgia opened the business with a very clear marketing strategy in mind – she would not engage in paid advertising, which she felt would devalue her brand. Instead, Georgia relied upon cost-effective social media networks such as Twitter and Facebook to grow the business.

'Marketing that works for hospitality and food is generally word-of-mouth style marketing. If a business is offering a quality product, it will get people talking, so naturally this is the best form of marketing'.

Georgia has stuck to her plan, using social media platforms to engage with the various different audiences who are interested in her food. She uses Facebook and Twitter to promote the daily menu to her followers, who include industry professionals.

'Social networking is all about generating talk,' says Georgia. Last winter, interest on Twitter led to a double-page write-up in the *Herald Sun* about Famish'd's soups. Since then, Famish'd has been voted best for soups and salads in town on a number of different blogs.

Recently, Georgia has had the Facebook and Twitter logos printed on all Famish'd packaging. 'Since we added the logos, we've noticed a marked increase in the number of followers on both Twitter and Facebook'.

Famish'd has never limited its social media engagement through a rigid strategy, and in some respects that is a strategy in itself. Georgia is, however, very aware of her own personal boundaries around tweeting and posting under the company's profiles. 'We are pretty liberal in what we post; that said, we rarely post anything about our private lives. I make sure that I reply to most tweets we receive'.

According to Georgia, it's also very important to try to make your posts creative and fun to read. 'We often post photos because they generate greater interest from our followers and we try to be creative; we only post what we as customers would like to read'. Georgia and the team at Famish'd are careful to remember, too, that social media isn't just a marketing tool; it's a way of engaging the public with the business and its staff.

'I see Twitter as a way of creating a personality for the business; it's about letting the customer see behind the scenes'.

Georgia's top tip: be transparent and don't be afraid to let people know about your muck-ups; it helps to give them a realistic insight into your business. 'Around 80 per cent of our new followers on Face-book and Twitter are generated from the new social media logos on our packaging'.

Unlike some innovations, it's difficult to measure the level of return generated from social media engagement. 'We do know we're generating talk', says Georgia, 'which can only be generating sales'. Georgia only spends around 5 minutes a day updating the company's Facebook pro-file or sending tweets. 'We only post as many tweets as we would like to see as customers; sometimes it's only one or two a day and sometimes we don't do any'.

Following the marketing success Famish'd has experienced with its online presence, Georgia has vowed to continue investing the business resources and increasing its social media activity in the future.

Aligning your content, channels and data with your buyer persona

The buying journey is the sequence of steps and decisions that your buyer persona takes from first contact through to the first and subsequent purchases. The channels you use should align with your buyer persona and the experiences they enjoy on their journey. The data analytics provided by most channels – or through third-party tools – allow you to build a solid picture of how people behave on your website and other channels you have decided to use before converting to customers and completed sales. Tying this together, your content must be appropriate for the channels you are using.

Listening to and viewing channels should be a key aspect of your assessment of tactics and campaigns, but this listening should also incorporate a range of channels that reach beyond the ones you or your buyer persona regularly use. This approach can eventually become horizon scanning and prospecting in each new iteration of your strategy informing your choice of channels, the forms of content that you use and how you gather data. Time spent listening and observing will benefit your strategy and enable it to dynamically respond to changes in the market as well as the behaviours of your buyer persona. Balancing the best choices of content, channels and data use will draw your brands, products and services into closer communication with your buyer persona (Table 4.3).

A strong strategy starts with the development of your buyer persona. Then you can figure out your big idea, define your objectives and set the timeline. Reaching people effectively is achieved if the channel supports the content and vice versa. Social media, email marketing, mobile marketing and video mar-keting are just some disciplines that will form part of your marketing strategy creation arsenal.

Table 4.3 Channels, content and data advice for maximising engagement with your buyer persona

---

1 **Create content that answers your buyer persona's biggest questions.** If you can answer those questions you will attract potential customers and you'll also make some seriously loyal fans.

2 **Use formats for your content that fit your buyer persona's preferences.** Ensure that your content is easily digested and enjoyed. Ensure that your content is in a format that is widely shareable.

3 **Use channels that your buyer persona prefers to use.** Promote your best content through your best channels.

4 **Measure** how much traffic and leads are generated by each channel.

5 **Learn to speak the language of your buyer persona.** Use this language appropriately in the content directed at your buyer persona.

6 **Post content on the right channels at times when your buyer persona is most engaged.** There will be times when your buyer persona uses specific channels. Identify the schedule and continuously adapt your tactics to meet these patterns.

7 **Present your content through the channels that your buyer persona respects the most.** Where possible, build closer relationships with the channels that most appeal to your buyer persona.

8 **As much as possible, customise content to conclude with clear calls-to-action that are based on your buyer persona's needs and goals.** This approach is especially helpful if your organisation has multiple buyer personas.

Source: (adapted from Corliss, 2012)

4.3 Setting objectives

The key to defining strategic objectives is to link the overall mission of your organisation with the practicalities of completing sales actions. Your objectives should include but not be limited to the following:

- **Build your brand:** One of the most important tasks for marketing is to establish your brand. You want your buyer persona to be talking about your brand and to be sharing their enthusiasm for your brand with others.

- **Create new products:** By opening up a conversation with your buyer persona, you can draw together your data-driven understanding with their creativity to co-create new products.

- **Drive customer satisfaction:** Continuously talking to your buyer persona enables nagging concerns to be addressed immediately and before they become complaints. Small concerns can be turned around and potentially become the basis for product improvement or evolving your content building block of your digital marketing strategy.

- **Increase word-of-mouth recommendations:** Encouraging your buyer persona to share their positive comments and reviews will increase the range of your products and services through genuine enthusiasm for what you offer.

- **Generate leads:** Increasing the range of types of content can produce wider interest at varying points in the buying journey. By enabling a new

Table 4.4 All your objectives must be SMART

Specific	Clear and detailed, rather than vague and general
Measurable	So that you can gauge whether you are attaining the desired outcome
Attainable	Something that is possible for your brand to achieve, based on available resources
Realistic	Sensible and based on data and trends; don't exaggerate or overestimate what can be achieved
Timely	Linked to a specific timeframe

conversation with your buyer persona, you can acquire new data from them, including email addresses and mobile numbers. Each new piece of data from your buyer persona is a new opportunity for conversation that drives them towards completion of a sale.

- **Managing reputation:** Your marketing strategy should include provision for crisis communication management. Your content should be able to respond to crises with targeted messages through appropriate channels and be customised based on the data you have that connects the crisis with your buyer persona.
- **Integrated marketing, public relations and advertising:** Your strategy should not artificially distinguish amongst these categories of activity. Good content that is well placed on the right channels and customised based on the data you have gathered from your buyer persona will work equally well as marketing, public relations or advertising.

Your strategy can incorporate a range of objectives. Regardless of how many are chosen, having a SMART objective (Table 4.4) is important in the development of your strategy.

Examples of SMART objectives could include the following:

- Increase unique visitors to our website by 5x from social networking sites (based on evidence from Google Analytics) over the next 5 months.
- Increase blog subscriptions signups by X per cent in 6 months by adding two new social media channels.
- Increase Facebook fans by X in 8 weeks.
- Increase Twitter mentions by 300 per cent in 6 months.
- Increase the number of interactions on Facebook page by five each week for the next 5 weeks.

Measuring objectives through key performance indicators (KPIs)

KPIs are the specific metrics that you will consider to determine whether your strategy is performing well and meeting your objectives. For example, you might look at a range of data points to determine whether a chosen tactic is working. KPIs are determined per tactic, with an overall eye on your objectives.

Targets are the specific values that are set for each KPI that are to be reached within a specific time period. They may include customer acquisition and retention targets, customer satisfaction targets, added value measures (the wow factor), level of customer engagement or quantifiable efficiency gains (WOW Blog, 2014).

If you meet or exceed a target, you are succeeding; if you don't reach it, you're falling behind on your objectives and you need to reconsider your approach (or revisit the values you have set for your target).

Companies have different perspectives on which KPIs matters the most. The important point is to align the KPIs with your business and campaign objectives and to actually measure them (Murray, 2019). Table 4.5 presents some examples of KPIs that you can use within your own commercial strategy.

KPIs focusing on converting to sales through free trials or webinars may be a suitable KPI in a B2B sector. For example, if a SAAS (software as a service) company sets a KPI based on converting sales after a free trial, the company can actually track results. For example, the KPI can focus on converting 50 per cent of SAAS users to sales after a 30-day demo (Mdirector, 2017). Linking

Table 4.5 KPI examples for businesses

Branding (stimulus and Zero Moment of Truth)	Conversion (First Moment of Truth)	Advocacy and loyalty KPIs (Second Moment of Truth)
• Visits/ page views • Website's organic traffic • Time on page • Pages visited per visit	• Conversion rates (from visitor to buyer) • Customer acquisition costs • Revenue per customer • Sales volume and value • Customer retention costs • Abandoned shopping carts • Profits per customer	• Repeat visits • Buzz indicators (web mentions) • Online product/service ratings quantity and quality • Net promoter score • New vs old visitors

Table 4.6 Examples of KPIs for the non-profit sector

Conversion: fundraising KPIs (First Moment of Truth)	Branding: marketing and communications non-profit KPIs (Zero Moment of Truth)
• Gifts secured • Donor and donation growth • Donor retention rate • Fundraising return on investment (ROI) • ROAS (return on advertising spend) • Donation conversions by channel: This KPI tells you how many donors took action when prompted by your organization and where they took the action. Look at donation conversions by channel (organic, social, email, referral, ad, etc.).	• Website page views • Repeat website visits • Email open and click-through rates • Numbers of related questions asked • Shares, likes, comments, amplification, applause – these apply to social media channels. Conversation rate refers to comments and replies to your content.

Source: Ibrisevic (2018)

KPIs with activity and evaluation is an effective way to keep a close eye on the activities that are delivering results and the ones that are not.

Table 4.6 illustrates some KPIs relevant to the non-profit sector.

4.4 Creating campaigns and reaching your objectives

Once you know your overall strategic direction and have clear objectives, you need to determine the specifics of your campaigns. Your strategy will be unique and, consequently, what you do to achieve your objectives must be done on a case-by-case basis. The eight **Cs** (Table 4.7) assist in shaping your campaigns and ensuring that they are built on the unique strengths, weaknesses, opportunities and threats of your organisation.

Campaigns to acquire and retain customers

In the Buyer Persona Spring, the key to acquiring and retaining customers is to maintain a conversation with them. This does not mean you are committing to a daily email or even weekly messaging, but rather a paced and sensible exchange that takes place over time and feels natural to your customers. This is where the content, channel and data building blocks of your digital marketing strategy must work together and develop iteratively (Tables 4.8 and 4.9).

Table 4.7 Guidelines for digital and social media strategy development (8 Cs model)

1 **Categorise.** Focus on the channels where you are most likely to find your buyer persona. This focus will produce the greatest chances of success.
2 **Comprehend** the rules of the channel by observing. Adhere to the policies and guidelines of the channel so that you conform to its expected norms. Your buyer persona will be more likely to do business with you if you know, like and respect their favourite channels.
3 **Converse** with, acknowledge and respond to other users of the channel. Always be a contributor and never a promoter. Display your knowledge of a product area, and show genuine concern towards the key issues of the channel to build trust for yourself and your brand.
4 **Collaborate** to build mutually beneficial relationships. Co-create and co-consume your products. Your buyer persona will personally connect with and trust a brand or product that they have invested their time in.
5 **Contribute** content to build your reputation and improve the community. Position yourself as a thought leader by showcasing your unique knowledge. Knowledge about the subject equates with a product that will most likely be of higher quality.
6 **Connect** with the influencers to help shape opinions about your product or service. Provide everyone with outstanding service. This combination of efforts will attract the attention of the influencers and give them ample reason to praise and promote you.
7 **Community** participation (and creation) can elicit valuable suggestions for improving products and innovative suggestions for new products or services. Encourage two-way conversations that lead to feedback and new product ideas from customers.
8 **Convert** your overall strategy into campaigns and tactics that will raise awareness, gain attention and create loyalty for your brand.

Source: Adapted from Barker et al., 2013

Customer acquisition and retention are important. As you collect more and more data about your customers you may consider a customer relationship management (CRM) system to help you navigate the volume of data that you have collected and to extract maximum intelligence from this data.

Branding campaigns

Digital marketing focuses heavily on developing conversations in order to build trust with your customers. Your brand is a powerful symbol for this trust and represents the unique qualities and values of your products and services.

Your brand building is part of the development of your content, channel and data building blocks (Table 4.10).

Table 4.8 Acquiring customers

Building block	Steps to customer acquisition
Data	1) Research the current market and assess the external situation. Use internal data that you may already have to direct this research.
Data	2) Create a buyer persona from your acquired knowledge so you know who you are looking for.
Data	3) Identify what products and services your buyer persona needs and desires.
Channels	4) Identify the channels where your buyer persona is regularly found.
Channels	5) Identify which channels you will utilise in your strategy. Which channels are appropriate and which are not?
Content	6) What value do your products and services bring to your buyer persona? Describe these benefits.
Content	7) Present content that engages your buyer persona, exudes the value of your organisation and is highly shareable.
Content	8) Create incentives for existing customers to become brand advocates, reviewers and influencers about your brand, products and services.
Channels/ content	9) Keep encouraging the conversation. Encourage likes, tweets and sharing of content.

Table 4.9 Retaining customers

Building block	Steps to retaining customers
Data	You've acquired a new customer. Engage them in conversation to learn about them.
Content	Give your new customer a personalised space for feedback and comments.
Data/content	Respond to comments and feedback. Celebrate positives and address the negatives. Attempt to exceed expectations.
Data	Collect additional data from your customers. Use additional methods including surveys. Incentivise completion if necessary.
Content	Develop loyalty programmes as part of your content production.
Data	When a customer leaves, try to capture their reasons for leaving. If possible, use this data to encourage them to return.

Source: Adapted from MailerMailer, 2011

Table 4.10 Actions to build your brand

Action	Activity	Content	Channels	Data
Increase brand awareness	For a new product or service, build awareness of its existence	Emphasis 'newness', highlight the values and benefits of your offering over the competitor	Inhabit the channels of your buyer persona. Choose to contrast their positioning or compete head-to-head with competitors	Identify the activities of competitors, the preferred channels and current value propositions
Improve brand perception	Positively influence the perception of yourself by aligning with leaders in the industry	Share positive testimonials, reviews and discussions	Use the channels of industry leaders and influencers	Curate the positive perceptions within the industry and what they look like
Position your brand	Even popular brands can create a more positive impression with their buyer persona	Differentiate your content from competitors. Be distinctive	Take your buyer persona on a journey to discover new, 'better' channels	Collect the responses to positioning. Are you bringing your buyer persona with you or turning them away?
Expand brand loyalty	A loyal buyer persona can market your brand indirectly by telling friends and family about you	Enable your buyer persona to share good content with others	Bridge your current channels to those used by the family and friends of your buyer persona	Where are the messages going? Are there new channels for you to inhabit?

Case Study 4.2   ao.com: setting an example with social media campaigns

Electrical appliances company ao.com (formerly known as Appliances Online) knows more than most about the power of social media (Price, 2014). A pure-play online retailer, it has created its brand from scratch since launching in 2000, relying extensively on platforms such as Facebook and Twitter to gain a share in the ultra-competitive white goods market.

'Fun and engaging content' is key to the brand's success online, says Andrew Kirkcaldy, marketing director at ao.com. 'We have to think a little out of the box because white goods aren't the sexiest of things to create content around', he admits.

Examples of recent content, which is all created in-house, includes filming a man who is in the Guinness World Records for balancing a washing machine on his head for the longest time and sponsorship of 'Tony the Fridge' (@tony_the_fridge), who runs marathons for cancer charities with a 42-kg fridge strapped to his back.

To get this content seen, ao.com has invested heavily in Facebook advertising to get the necessary reach. Consequently, ao.com now has nearly 1.6 million Facebook likes and is also active on Twitter, Pinterest and YouTube.

ao.com's YouTube channel regularly hosts live competitions to win white goods, as well as providing recipes and what it calls 'AO hacks' – tips such as how to keep your clothes fresh or how to put two plates in the microwave at the same time.

What ao.com has constantly found is that there is a direct correlation between its social media activity and the number of people coming to the website through search. Mobile traffic is particularly important to ao.com, with the brand's recognisable smiley face logo having to work across all devices.

Of course, with engagement online comes the potential risk of negative as well as positive feedback from customers. For ao.com's Kirkcaldy, the key is to respond quickly and honestly if someone has an enquiry or isn't satisfied.

'We have a customer service team of eight people who are on the sites managing the comments. They will usually reply to customers on social media within two minutes, ten minutes max', he says. Adds Kirkcaldy: 'If we've made a mistake, we admit it and tell the customer that we will sort it out as quickly as possible'.

Importantly, the same customer service agent will deal with the problem until it's resolved so the customer isn't passed around. Most of the time, ao.com will deal with the problem publicly, but it may be in private if the customer wishes to take the complaint offline. ao.com also regularly checks comments on Trustpilot, an independent online community where people leave reviews of retailers.

Finally, one important aspect of customer service for ao.com is the 'Facebook Feedback' booklet that all delivery drivers see and that contains positive as well as negative comments from previous deliveries. 'The drivers are the only people who meet our customers, so the impact they can have is massive. It makes them realise how important it is to make a good impression'.

Source: Price, 2014

4.5 Tactics

Many tools enable you to implement the specific tactics of a campaign once you have defined your digital marketing objectives and strategy. Each tactic brings specific benefits, for example, customer acquisition may best be driven by search advertising, while email is one of the most effective tools for selling more products to existing customers.

Table 4.11 expands on some of the most popular tactics available to you and their desired outcomes. Choosing which platform to invest your energy and resources in is important. Determine who your audience is and how they interact with your brand before establishing a presence. Remember that in order to make an impact you must post regularly and consistently.

Actions and control

In order to measure success, you need to define a clear and measurable call-to-action. A call-to-action is simply the action that you want your buyer persona to engage in at a specific point in the buyer journey. Many different calls-to-action exist (Table 4.12).

Getting to the sale (conversion) is the final step in a chain of actions. For example, one chain of actions leading to a sale may be as follows:

1 Click on a blog post link from Twitter or Facebook.
2 Sign up for an email newsletter at the end of a blog post.
3 Sign up for a webinar announced in a newsletter.
4 Have a representative call as a result of this signup.
5 Purchase.

Table 4.11 Marketing tactics, relevant campaigns and their desired outcomes

Tactics	Relevant campaign	Desired outcomes
Search engine optimisation (SEO) involves creating content that search engines index and serve when people enter a relevant search term.	Customer retention or acquisition	SEO has a key role to play in acquisition. It ensures that your offering will be well ranked in search results and allows you to reach new customers. Optimised websites are also by definition clear, relevant and well designed. These elements ensure a strong user experience, meaning that SEO also plays a role in retention.
Affiliate and partner marketing are lead generation systems where referrers are paid a 'finder's fee' for every referral.	Sales and return on investment (ROI)	Promotion of e-commerce websites. ROI is central to this tactic, as the commission that is paid is within the ROI parameters.
Search advertising (pay-per-click, PPC) means the advertiser pays only when someone clicks on their ad. The ads appear on search engine results pages.	Sales, customer retention and acquisition	PPC is keyword-based, which means an ad will appear on a results page in response to a search term. It allows an advertiser to reach people who are already in the buying cycle. It offers immediate search engine presence in contrast to SEO tactics, especially for new markets.
Online advertising include emails, ads on social networks and mobile devices, and display ads on websites.	Branding and acquisition	Online advertising raises brand awareness. This form of advertising can generally be targeted to physical locations, subject areas or past behaviours.
Video marketing	Branding, customer retention and value creation	An interactive and engaging format for capturing and retaining customer attention. A video can provide information, entertainment and inspiration – potentially all at the same time.
Email marketing	Customer retention and value creation	Build relationships with potential and existing customers by sharing valuable content and other messages. Targeted and segmented emailing means that a brand can direct messages to specific categories of customer to maximise results.

Source: Adapted from Stokes, 2013

Table 4.12 Examples of calls-to-action

Click Here	Do not use this kind of text. It is not a screen reader–friendly text. It is a classic web-based call-to-action mistake.
Download Now	Content that is delivered immediately satisfies immediate interest and encourages a conversation.
Buy Now	Your reader likes what they've seen so far. Now they can take the next step to buy.
Join Now	If you have gained sufficient reader interest, the next step is offered as a chance to belong, affiliate or associate more closely.

In each small incremental step of this chain of actions, the goal is to increase the level of interaction and engagement. Although the final desired action is probably to generate a sale, the best way to get there involves intermediate steps. The call-to-action is the important 'glue' that links each of these steps in a structured way.

4.6 Buyer Persona Spring as the core for the digital marketing strategy

The key decisions made to formulate the digital marketing strategy can be summarized in the Buyer Persona Spring table. Figure 4.9 provides a table of the touchpoints through the anticipated customer journey – stimulus, ZMOT, FMOT and SMOT. It also connects strategic business with the buyer persona through specific channels, content with their associated keywords, data and the summary of the buyer persona pain and trust touchpoints.

It is important to have an overview of strategic commitments that are shared in this table (Figure 4.9). The idea is to have a logically linked summary of key commitments that will be maintained for 3 to 5 years. The duration will depend on overall strategy timelines. The detail and length of this table should fit ideally one single A4 sheet and outline the overall direction for the marketing team. The table can be used for briefing external agencies and aligning any internal projects that will take place. As mentioned earlier in this chapter, annual review of this strategic commitment is recommended.

Figure 4.10 illustrates the application of the Buyer Persona Spring. To be able to create this, it is necessary to create a buyer persona (see, for example, Figure 3.1) and the customer journey map (Table 3.6). The Nigel Bloom digital marketing strategy would be different to the B2B buyer persona Lucy Bels (Figure 3.2).

The completion of this Buyer Persona Spring encourages constant sense checks against the buyer persona and their customer journey. For example, all preferred channels that a customer is likely to take need to be mapped out with

Digital Marketing Strategy (Buyer Persona Spring) for _____

Date: _____   **Completed by** _____

Strategic business objective for 3 years	Channels	Content	Strategic keyword terms	Data/KPIs	Buyer persona
	Stimulus •				
	ZMOT •				
	FMOT •				
	SMOT •				

Figure 4.9 Key decisions of the digital marketing strategy using Buyer Persona Spring table

content and related management and monitoring with related KPIs. It is an iterative process and by completing the Buyer Persona Spring it might be needed to revise the buyer persona and their customer journey so that there is a logical link. The key objective is to maximise the trust touchpoints and reduce/eliminate the pain touchpoints. The KPIs should also be helpful in capturing data for the strategic business objectives. There are going to be more KPIs, but there should be at least one or two that feed data into the business objectives. This helps a business on a continuous basis to see whether they are developing in the right direction. For example, the objective of sales is captured at the FMOT and the objective for keyword visibility is picked up at the stimulus stage.

Digital Marketing Strategy (Nigel Bloom) for _____ **London based florist**

Date: _____ 1st September 2021 _____ **Completed by** _____ **Ana and Aleksej**

Strategic business objective for 3 years	Channels	Content	Strategic keyword terms	Data/KPIs	Buyer persona
1. To double the sales online from £50k to £100k 2. Being on the first page of Google's search engine results page for the strategic keywords 3. Being the best and most reviewed florist in London	*Stimulus* • WeChat • YouTube • Instagram	• Valentine's Day romantic presents inspiration • Latest trends on Valentine's Day flowers • Quality of freshly cut flowers and care instructions	• Valentine's ideas • What to do for Valentine's Day • Gifts for Valentine's Day • Flowers for Valentine's Day	• Number of video views • Number of likes • Number of shares • Visibility for given keywords • Buzz indicators (web mentions)	**Pain points:** • Flowers that do not last a long time • Bouquets that do not look like the image on the website of the florist store • Delivery times that are not convenient **Trust points:** • Well-chosen freshly cut and conditioned flowers • A photo confirmation of the bouquet being bought • Flexible delivery, where time and location can be specified and changed as required
	ZMOT • Google My Business Reviews • Website	• Reviews of flowers and purchase process from past customers and responses from the business to acknowledge receipt	'same day flower delivery London' 'luxury flower delivery London' 'flower shop London'	• Visits/page views • Efficiency of website navigation • Website data is of high quality and relevance to the persona	
	FMOT • Website	• Product purchase details • Payment options and delivery process • Pictures of the product being bought	• Buy flowers online 'Store Name' • 'Store Name'	• Conversion rates (from visitor to buyer) • Abandoned shopping carts • Sales levels	
	SMOT • Google My Business Reviews • Instagram • Email	• Customer loyalty encouragement 5% discount on a second purchase within 3 months • Review request for Google My Business listing • Product care details	• Reviews of 'Store Name' • 'How to keep fresh flowers longer'	• Repeat visits • Number of positive reviews • Size of active customer database	

Figure 4.10 Digital marketing strategy for a florist in London targeting Nigel Bloom buyer persona

4.7 Summary

Strategy is the first step in positioning your brand. A strategic perspective lets you create a road map to reach your organisational goals.

In this chapter you have stepped through the development of strategy. Strategy is connected to the widest context of your organisation, including the sector in which you operate and the pressures that currently exist in the sector. However, strategy also connects this big view to the details of specific tactics you might employ to, for example, attract new customers.

In this chapter, we have emphasised the importance of planning campaigns that will bring your buyer persona into close connection with your organisation. Of particular importance is the need to constantly consider the three key building blocks of digital marketing: content, channels and data. Channels, content and data interact closely and are equally important to achieving the objectives of your digital marketing strategy.

4.8 References

Barker, M., Barker, D., Boermann, N. and Neher, K. (2013) *Social media marketing: A strategic approach*. Mason, OH: South-Western Cengage Learning, pp.26–35.

Corliss, R. (2012) *11 Savvy ways to use buyer personas to strengthen your marketing*. blog.hubspot.com/blog/tabid/6307/bid/33526/11-savvy-ways-to-use-buyer-personas-to-strengthen-your-marketing.aspx

Develop *customer acquisition and customer retention strategies*. blog.mailermailer.com/tips-resources/develop-customer-acquisition-customer-retention-strategies#

Ibrisevic, I. (2018) *20 KPIs for your nonprofit to track*. donorbox.org/nonprofit-blog/kpis-for-your-nonprofit/

MailerMailer (2011) *Develop customer acquisition and customer retention strategies*. blog.mailer-mailer.com/tips-resources/develop-customer-acquisition-customer-retention-strategies#

MDirector (2017) *Periodic table of B2B digital marketing metrics*. www.mdirector.com/en/digital-marketing/periodic-table-b2b-digital-marketing-metrics.html

Murray, M. (2019) *101+ key performance indicators and tips – Make the best KPI choices*. content-marketinginstitute.com/2019/06/key-performance-indicators-kpi/

Price, C. (2014) ao.com: Setting an example in social media strategy. *The Telegraph*. www.telegraph.co.uk/sponsored/technology/4g-mobile/news/11150963/social-media-strategy-example-white-goods-market.html

Stokes, R. (ed.) (2013) *E-marketing: The essential guide to marketing in a digital marketing world*. Cape Town: Quirk Education.

WOW Blog (2014) *Digital marketing strategy case study*. blog.wowconsulting.co.uk/blog/digital-marketing-strategy-case-study

Section III

Operational planning

5 Campaign planning and project management

Anna Tarabasz

5.0 Learning objectives

In this chapter you will learn how to:

- view a campaign from a strategic perspective;
- understand the stages of the campaign planning cycle;
- translate your strategic goals into SMART campaign objectives;
- estimate, budget and use evidence-based decision making processes to select and evaluate the performance of your digital marketing actions;
- communicate and document your project management processes using Gantt charts; and
- apply appropriate risk management techniques.

5.1 The importance of planning

Successful digital and social media marketing campaigns do not just happen. They are the result of good campaign project management actions, which are closely related to your digital and social media strategy implementation. The adage 'failing to plan is planning to fail' is true for many digital marketing campaigns. In the Global Project Management survey, findings show that planning is key; when proven project, program and portfolio management practices are implemented, projects are more successful (PMI, 2018). This chapter outlines how each digital marketing campaign is essentially a project and, therefore, good project management skills are needed to control digital marketing activities.

The 24/7 culture of online activities compounds the potential gravity of issues that an organisation can face by opening up digital channels of communications. Some of the major brands have digital customer service teams who communicate with customers around the clock. Other organisations make their online 'customer service times' public to reduce disappointment amongst their customers. This essential decision will impact all other activities in your digital presence. Nowadays, artificial intelligence (AI) and machine-based adaptive learning represent the next great frontier for marketers. Indeed, certain activities may be supported by chatbots and use of AI, but you know your customers best – are they ready for it or do they prefer limited timings and a human touch?

Staff burnout and high staff turnover rates are common in digital marketing agencies. Speed is a characteristic of the fast-paced digital industry and can have negative effects on organisational structures if not managed well. Organisations and their digital teams have expanded rapidly, and many are using the same management methods that worked in a small team environment – which do not work well in a larger team setting. Likewise, for a one-person organisation – owner manager – it is essential to be well organised, manage one's time and have good project management skills. Spending a whole day just on social media might not be an option for those in a busy organisation, but using tools to schedule and automate some of the engagement activity can be an option. For example, automatic subscription to mailing lists does not require any human intervention, but setting it up does take time and planning ahead helps in this respect.

On the positive side, the Buyer Persona Spring (see Chapter 0 for more detail) highlights how an organisation can engage around the clock, and this offers the possibility of ongoing interaction, especially if multiple aspects of this can be automated. Internal stakeholders have to be managed too. Considerations of how the marketing campaign impacts your people, finances, production and operations need to be made. In this way, having a common strategy used for aligning the processes and procedures of an organisation, in line with marketing activities, helps to focus and lead an organisation to success (Figure 5.1). Likewise, operational constraints have to be taken into account to make sure marketing does not over-generate demand for products and services, which could have a negative effect of not being able to satisfy demands.

If you plan to use digital channels for creating and curating content to engage your buyer persona, you will need to consider various factors such as products and services life cycles and seasonality. From this point of view, each campaign is essentially a project which has to be managed. Therefore, this chapter focuses on key project management practices related to stages of planning, acting, observing and reflecting.

This chapter stresses the importance of integrated activities across multiple digital channels within marketing campaigns, activities of which are prioritised by referring to your overall strategic business objectives. Collaborations with other departments and individuals across an organisation are essential; therefore,

Marketing	People	Finance	Production	Operation

Figure 5.1 The implication of marketing actions across an organisation

some of the projects can be managed outside of marketing team but have an impact on the deliverables of marketing activities. For example, customer service and postal delivery need to coordinate with marketing activities. Understanding digital marketing campaign project management and its key planning tools and stages offers insight into repeatable success patterns, which can be recreated and integrated into an organisation's culture. Whilst we focus on digital marketing campaigns, we recognise that digital marketing strategy implementation will also have an impact on other areas of organisation such as Human Resources – for example staff social media policy development and enforcement and recruitment of new in-house teams and external agencies.

5.2 Project management in the context of digital marketing campaigns

Project management of digital marketing campaigns is a combination of processes, tools and techniques used for intelligently organising resources in order to successfully meet the set digital marketing objectives.

Processes include communication protocols such as update meetings with relevant stakeholders, both internal and external. Tools include spreadsheets for tracking campaign activities and analytics packages for measuring success. Some of the tools are channel-specific, but others, like Sprout Social, Pardot, HubSpot and Net-Results, offer integrated channel management options. Techniques include the use of Gantt charts and identification of critical paths and risk management.

There is no single approach to project management that fits all organisations. For example, detailed project management methodologies such as PRINCE2 (**PR**ojects **IN** **C**ontrolled **E**nvironments) are popular in the UK, and the Das V-Modell is preferred for digital projects in Germany. But these two represent only the tip of an iceberg, as there are many more like PMI/PMBOK, Agile, Scrum, Kanban, Waterfall, Lean and Six Sigma. Digital marketing activities do rely, to a large extent, on the development of digital artefacts (e.g. e-commerce website application and mobile apps) and therefore, for large campaigns, these methodologies can offer more detailed guidance. Both of these two first-mentioned methodologies broadly fit into the four steps of planning, acting, observing and reflecting.

Importance of a proper canvas

At the beginning of your digital journey, you might ask yourself "where do I even start?". The answer might be simple – literally draw a sketch on canvas. The Business Model Canvas by Strategyzer can help you to define current and future value propositions which are informed by the newly identified building blocks of the Buyer Persona Spring. After analysing your current state and defining your planned future state through the Buyer Persona Spring (Chapter 2) you may now go even deeper through the Digital Engagement Canvas (Figure 5.2).

Digital engagement framework – using the Buyer Persona Spring for operational planning

Assets	Reach		Buyer Persona
What advantages do you have to be able to create value to this buyer persona? See your Business Model Canvas.	*How can you connect with your buyer persona for the first time?* e.g. advertising, public relations, social buzz. It is the stimulus stage of your ZMOT model.		*Who is the buyer persona?* e.g. highlight the pain points and trust points, objective.

Information	Technology	Processes
What channels, content and data do you need? Use notes from your Buyer Persona Spring.	**Technology** *What hardware and software will you need?* e.g. content management software for your website.	**Processes** *What operational activities are needed?* e.g. train staff, conduct monthly SEO audit, create content calendar.

Engage
How can you get the buyer persona to interact with you during the Zero, First and Second Moments of Truth? e.g. creating interactive product compassion options (ZMOT), customising the service/product during purchase (FMOT) and getting customer reviews and advocacy (SMOT).

Objectives	Co-created value	Trends
What are your objectives for this engagement? See your Buyer Persona Spring.	*What is the value created for this particular buyer persona?* See your Business Model Canvas.	**Trends** *What industry trends affect your organisation?* e.g. increased use of mobile users, video content use.

Figure 5.2 Digital Engagement Canvas

The Digital Engagement Canvas is a checklist and is used to identify new projects that support implementation of your digital marketing strategy. It uses a number of elements that are linked to the strategic thinking models such as the Business Model Canvas and the Buyer Persona Spring. To operationalise your strategy, a number of projects are needed. The links between these models are as follows:

1 Audience – it is your buyer persona as developed independently and integrated in the Buyer Persona Spring and the Business Model Canvas.
2 Objectives – defined by your Buyer Persona Spring.
3 Information – the content aspect of the Buyer Persona Spring.
4 Trends – as identified in your SWOT and PESTLE analyses.
5 Co-created value – identified in the Business Model Canvas as value proposition.
6 Technology – identified as part of the channels consideration for the Buyer Persona Spring as well as the data section. Now is the time to think about wider technological implications to support all your digital marketing activities and supporting services.
7 Process – the key activities as identified in the Business Model Canvas, but now you can be more specific in terms of how to enable your staff and organisation to deliver the key activities. These are considerations that go beyond digital marketing activities such as customer service and the product returns process.
8 Reach – using the ideas from the stimulus stage of the Buyer Persona Spring, you can identify what types of projects are needed to start buyer persona on their customer journey. For example, a need to commission a viral marketing campaign or a survey that can be used for new content creation (see more on content marketing in Chapter 9).
9 Engage – use the content from the Buyer Persona Spring as the SMOT as well as brand personality, which dictates the accepted tone of voice for engagement. Hot touchpoints and trust touchpoints of your buyer persona can help to identify these engagement ideas and generate project ideas.
10 Assets – using the insight from strengths that you identified in your SWOT analysis, consider what projects can help to maximise your strengths and reduce your weaknesses.

Objectives and key performance indicators (KPIs) leading to success

One of the key differences between managing a digital marketing campaign and a 'non-digital' marketing campaign is the availability of tools for the management, automation, capturing and reporting of data. Many of these tools have a free entry-level version (e.g. Mailchimp, Google Analytics and SEMrush). These tools allow the measurement and capturing of data even at the smallest interaction along the Buyer Persona Spring. Therefore, using data to set SMART objectives and track these through related KPIs and optimising resources intelligently is one of the most important skills of a digital marketing campaign manager.

Each channel, such as search engine optimisation (SEO) or social media platforms, offers its own set of KPIs, which can be measured and tracked automatically (subsequent chapters highlight the potential KPIs which can be tracked for each channel). Whilst this information is usually available for free, one of the first activities that a project manager, and the team if relevant, would have to agree on is which tools will be used for tracking this data. Sometimes it is useful to use more than one source of data for tracking your KPIs, since no one data set is 100 per cent reliable (see Chapter 12).

Creating and setting up KPIs for tracking SMART objectives helps to define and agree on what 'success' looks like (see Chapter 4 for an explanation of SMART objectives). To measure campaign impact, it is therefore useful for a campaign manager to be familiar with tools such as Google Analytics and Google Search Console for website traffic measurement (see Chapter 12 on web analytics). For example, tools such as Google URL Builder can be used for creating campaign-specific URLs for sharing with a specific campaign. Campaign impact can therefore be better tracked through Google Analytics. Capturing this data using one tool allows cross-campaign comparisons as well as measurement of factors, which might have not been the original intention. For example, noticing an increase in brand awareness through a higher volume of website visitors, for a campaign that was aimed at increasing sales and identifying user interface difficulties, is a secondary benefit of getting insight from your customer interaction. Live tracking of available metrics is equally exciting and empowering but at the same time may protect against major failure (see Box 5.2).

For campaigns that are repeated seasonally, use of consistent tools is also useful to ensure comparability of results. For example, a florist can compare the volume of website visitors and sales data in the run-up to Valentine's Day over previous years and predict accordingly. Understanding what the individual KPIs measure is also important. For example, for a social media KPI, simply using the number of followers or likes on your organisation's digital profile is not really helpful, especially where campaigns are outsourced and it is unclear how results are being achieved. Therefore, more qualitative measures could be used, such as the sentiment of comments and the number of meaningful interactions. For example, social media listening tools such as Sprout Social and Radian6 offer a qualitative analysis perspective on your data and provide KPI reporting for your social media. Many social media platforms such as Facebook and Twitter offer their own reach and engagement metrics beyond the likes of the page and the number of followers on your Twitter account. Even customer complaints and negative reviews have value for your organisation – those that pinpoint a weakness help you to refine and improve your offering, and customers who see the improvement are more likely to trust you in the future. At the end of the day, in a for-profit organisation, your objective is to generate income through delighted customers, and you need to remember that the difference between satisfied and delighted customers may bring down a business. This is because customers who are delighted are more likely to share their experience with others – those who just received an OK experience have nothing special to say on social media.

Having set strategic business and marketing objectives for the next 3 to 5 years, organisations cannot wait this long to see whether these have been met in order to determine whether the digital marketing activities were effective. Therefore, digital marketing strategy implementation involves breaking down the long-term objectives into distinctive transient campaigns (e.g. building brand awareness could be split into different viral marketing actions and sponsored articles, appearing every 2 months or scheduled to coincide with events relevant to your buyer persona). Not only are shorter campaigns easier to budget for, but they also reflect seasonality and the buying cycles of your buyer persona. Seasonality can be seen online using tools such as Google Trends or Google Ads Keyword Planner or, if you have an existing website, Google Analytics. Enabling e-commerce tracking from past purchase history can help here, so that you can export your data into external data analysis and manipulation tools such as spreadsheets to make more detailed and customised reports.

These campaigns or digital marketing projects are distinctive from other day-to-day operations (such as everyday maintenance of the website or new blog entries) in two main areas: first, they are time-bound and so they do not go on indefinitely and second, they are focused on releasing defined outcomes (e.g. brand awareness or conversions) and outputs (e.g. campaign-related collateral material such as web pages, video and images). For these particular reasons, the digital marketing campaigns, as well as digital presence seen from a broader, long-term perspective, offer three important points:

- an opportunity for sense checking – if the mix of channels and content is generating the desired outcomes;
- reflecting on this campaign performance compared to other campaigns by your brand, as well as your competitors; and
- points for refining the digital marketing strategy implementation tactics chosen to achieve long-term ambitions.

The success of a digital marketing campaign is usually defined in the 'non-digital world' through the judgement of interrelated aspects – the so-called triple constraint or the iron triangle, creating the project triangle (Figure 5.3). Each side of the project triangle cannot be changed without affecting at least one of the other sides. For example, through increasing the campaign scope (e.g. target audience), it is inevitable that other factors will be engaged – for example, more time would be required, and the budget will likely increase. A further refinement of three previously mentioned variables (scope, time and cost) is 'quality'. Quality is closely linked with scope and, in fact, some notations replace it altogether. Quality in digital campaigns encapsulates KPIs in the project. Defining quantitative and qualitative measures for quality assessment helps to define what 'success' looks like and the key priority areas for campaign activities.

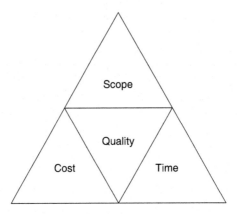

Figure 5.3 The project triangle

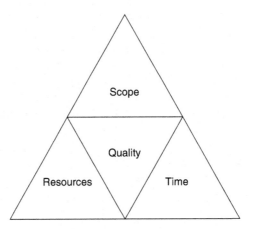

Figure 5.4 The digital project triangle

Therefore, the four variables that constrain the project of digital campaign assessment and planning criteria as represented in Figure 5.4 are as follows:

- **Scope** – specific objectives of each individual digital marketing channel.
- **Time** – start and end dates of the campaign.
- **Resources** – financial resources, in-house human resources, social capital.
- **Quality** – KPIs and data used for measuring the digital campaign impact (e.g. clicks, traffic, sales and shares).

These four aspects set out the constraints for each project and have to be clearly defined and agreed on amongst the relevant stakeholders at the outset of a digital marketing campaign. However, in a digital marketing campaign, cost does not apply in all scenarios. Some resources might have incurred costs in previous campaigns, but they would not have a direct cost for the current campaign. For example, an organisation might have a very strong brand advocate who creates content and leads an online community on their own because of self-interest and brand advocacy. The Internet culture is full of 'unboxing videos' – where individuals film themselves opening up a box containing a product and sharing the excitement with others by posting the content on video-sharing sites such as YouTube. If this benefits the brand, such campaigns may not really involve financial cost. This applies to a number of sectors that rely on volunteers and the community to help in developing a service or a product, and they use the resource of social capital. Social capital is essentially the likelihood of someone helping you because they know you and you have helped them in the past. Social capital cannot be quantified in conventional ways such as money, but if it is present, it offers a competitive advantage to an organisation (Heinze et al., 2013). Some basic indicators of social capital that a brand can have are the number of interactions it receives from its buyer persona representative when it asks them for feedback (read more on social capital in Chapter 8). For example, the 'My Starbucks Idea' website is dedicated to customers of Starbucks to share their ideas on how to make Starbucks better – the volume and the quality of the recommendations are an indicator of how much social capital Starbucks has.

The implementation cycles and importance of nine steps

Digital marketing strategy implementation does tend to go through a number of iterative cycles. By drawing conclusions from the lessons learned, you act on continuous improvement, constituting the basis for the development of the next iteration. This iterative nature is also characteristic of digital activities, since so many variables keep changing all the time – for example, when search engines release their ranking algorithm updates and refreshes, when social media platforms come and go, as well as the impacts of competitor activity on your campaigns.

The four phases of the action learning cycle (plan, act, observe and reflect) (Figure 5.5) will constitute the main themes in this chapter. Although their role will be described in the following sections, these stages can be defined as follows:

- **Plan** – refers to the setting of project triangle–related activities (resources, times, scope and quality).
- **Act** – indicates operational stages (message building, allocating and curating campaign content).
- **Observe** – involves results monitoring (KPIs), optimisation and risk management.
- **Reflect** – constitutes a basis for the next cycle of promotional activities.

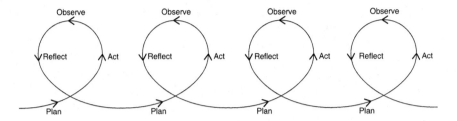

Figure 5.5 The digital marketing implementation cycle

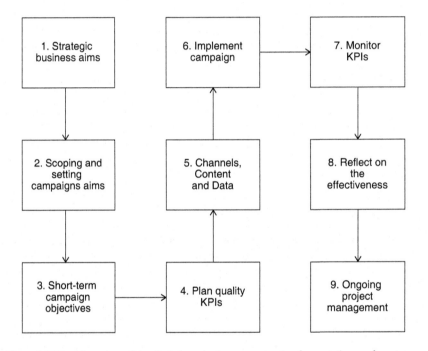

Figure 5.6 The nine steps of the digital marketing campaign implementation cycle

A more detailed example of a digital marketing campaign approach is illustrated in Figure 5.6.

Planning (cycle steps 1–5) – a digital marketing campaign starts with identifying your strategic aims. Such an approach requires you to define where you want to be in 3 to 5 years and predict what your organisation will achieve in this time horizon.

In the second step, based on the seasonality of your industry and key related events for your buyer persona, the scopes and aims should be set for individual campaigns. Previously mentioned florists preparing for Valentine's Day could have campaigns that are targeting the search term 'Valentine's Day flowers'.

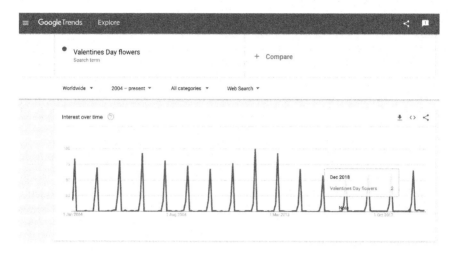

Figure 5.7 Interest over time data showing seasonality for "Valentine's Day flowers"

Source: Google Trends (www.google.com/trends)

Based on past performance, tools such as Google Trends offer insight into when your buyer persona will start their research journey. The search volume for flowers slightly increases in December, has a high increase in January and is at its highest in February (Figure 5.7). The data clearly points to the need for your organisational planning to focus on the 4 months from December to March for your Valentine's Day flowers campaign.

The third step of planning is translating a campaign into shorter-term specific, measurable, attainable, realistic and timely (SMART) campaign objectives. The setting of objectives is discussed in Chapter 4, and now the time periods are months and not years. This involves indicating the appropriate constraints from the project management triangle, such as deadlines and activities that are critical to the success of the project. Risk assessment is completed and the main risks are documented with management; mitigation of these is also identified. Whilst communication with all relevant stakeholders is important at each stage, before acting commences it is essential to get buy-in and agreement from all primary stakeholders. Face-to-face meetings are usually best for presenting and clarifying the plan for a campaign, but other forms such as written documents and virtual presentations are important. Organisations such as the Association of Project Management produce templates for project plans, which can guide you in thinking through an individual campaign cycle, time and resources for the individual 4 months.

After defining the quality KPIs to be achieved (fourth step), these can be grouped into monthly, quarterly and annual reports for measurement and reflection. For larger organisations, multiple projects on the same product could be grouped into programmes, and programmes of a particular brand can be grouped into portfolios. Programmes and portfolios show another level of abstraction when it comes to collecting and grouping KPIs. Whilst financial cycles can be broken down into tax timeframes, product and service trends need to take into account seasonality and competitor activity when setting these KPIs.

The **planning** phase is complete after documenting the communication channels and content (step 5), as well as creating a Gantt chart, which lists all the main activities. These can be adapted to your own needs.

Even though the **acting** phase (step 6) of the cycle consists of only one step, it is certainly no less important. The majority of project manager time is spent in preparing and briefing all parties at the planning stage. The acting stage is mainly driven by implementing activities specified within the Gantt chart and managing project-related risks. The planned activities are now being implemented. However, things don't always go to plan. The actual campaign implementation might need to be adjusted due to unforeseen circumstances. The already agreed-on list of project priorities offers a supporting guide for making minor adjustments.

The **observing** phase (step 7) focuses on monitoring your current activity and its progress in relation to the planned Gantt chart and the risk table. The tracking Gantt chart is produced to monitor the actual time and tasks undertaken to complete the project. The difference between the Gantt chart and the tracking Gantt chart is that the former is produced ahead of the project implementation and is based on estimation, whilst the latter is a documentation of actual time, resources and scope delivered. Any problems that occur throughout a campaign are also added to the tracking Gantt chart and risk management table and documented. The mistakes and errors of a campaign as well as all successes have to be documented so that future campaigns can use this insight to improve.

The last steps of the digital campaign implementation cycle are based on the **reflecting** stage (steps 8 and 9). This stage is used for reviewing the campaign results and effectiveness and the likelihood of achieving the annual and strategic aims. The tracking Gantt chart is compared to the estimated Gantt chart and risks are reviewed. Reflecting on past campaign management and reviewing against set objectives and KPIs helps to better estimate KPIs for future campaigns. Stakeholder correspondence and feedback are also taken into account when writing the campaign report. At this stage, your analysis should focus on determining which activities to continue and which to stop. The reflecting phase closes the cycle and, due to the approach of continuous improvement, constitutes the basis for the development of the next iteration.

5.3 Planning – starting a new project

The planning stage plays an important role in digital marketing campaign project management. Often, organisations focus on the short-term campaigns, not taking into account strategic priority areas. However, this kind of thinking does have its challenges, in particular when considering justifications of major investments in people or in tools such as a customer relationship management systems or an extensively customised e-commerce application. Such investments are needed to facilitate long-term organisational growth; hence, longer-term planning is needed to see a return on investment (ROI). For example, an email database needs to be used regularly and needs to be up to date in order to be useful for many years to come; spending a lot of energy on a one-off email campaign and finding that it did not work the first time because most of the addresses were out of date is not a reason to never use email marketing again.

On the other hand, *emergent strategy* allows for flexibility and gives freedom for individual short-term activities, which, with time, can translate into a repeatable pattern and become documented in a formal strategy document. The emergent strategy starts with **action** and is contrasted with *prescriptive strategy*, where the process starts with **planning**. Emergent strategy is more appropriate for dynamic industries and fast-changing activities such as digital marketing. The prescriptive strategy translates a long-term organisational vision into strategy and through tactics to programmes.

Defining aim and objectives

Based on an understanding of the strategic priorities, the short-term digital marketing campaign aim and objectives are set. These can be broadly grouped into two types – brand awareness and conversion-driven campaigns.

Brand awareness objectives

The aim of brand awareness is to generate positive publicity for the brand and its products or services. Some of the objectives could be focused on increasing brand mentions, engagement with the buyer persona, generating high-quality incoming links to the website or footfall to physical premises where relevant.

Digital content produced and optimised for this activity could be based on broad keyword search phrases (as discussed in more detail in Chapter 7). These campaigns assume no or limited awareness of brand, its product and services names.

Conversion-driven objectives

Conversion-driven aims can be focused on achieving any specific calls-to-action. For example, objectives could be to measure enrolments to an event, mailing list subscriptions, visits to physical premises, if relevant, and most importantly, the number of sales in volume and value. The type of content used for these tends to be more products- and services-specific.

Content should be produced and focused on more specific keyword search phrases that include both organic and paid search terms (discussed further in Chapter 7). This content would be focused on longer search terms bringing the buyer persona closer to the final decision making process.

Box 5.1 Florists

Two florists, A and B, plan their digital marketing campaigns. A aims to increase brand awareness and B aims to increase the number of bookings. Both florists are aware that January is the time of year when most buyer personas tend to research and arrange the details of their wedding flowers.

Basing their activity on the SMART objectives principle, both have to specify the precise and unique outcome (specific), that will refer to quantitative values (measurable), and be possible to attain (attainable), based on estimations from previous campaign experience where possible (realistic) and defined within a specific period of time (timely).

Because A aims to increase brand awareness, it defines its objective as:

> *'To develop and launch 3-month-long campaign for January 2021 comprising 1-minute-long YouTube video and four related blog posts and related social media networks amplification targeting subject of "wedding flowers ideas" and reaching 1,000 new company website visitors.'*

B aims to increase bookings and so defines its objective as:

> *'Double the number of wedding flowers related bookings in January 2021 compared to the year before by creating a 4-month-long campaign targeting "wedding florist in London UK", comprising a 1-minute-long You-Tube video, four blog posts, PPC and offering a bottle of champagne for every non-refundable booking deposit in January 2021.'*

The selection of channels for individual campaigns will depend on understanding the channel mix as proposed by 'the customer journey to online purchase' (see Chapter 3 for more details). All campaigns should prioritise the strategically committed channels of communication based on the understanding of the buyer persona to ensure that the right channels and messages are used.

Budget setting

In general, there are four main methods of planning the digital marketing budget (Table 5.1).

The percentage of sales and the affordability methods of budgeting emphasise that the marketing budget can be almost unlimited. This unlimited budget idea does not work for all industries; for example, a hotel with a fixed number of rooms cannot sell more rooms for the same period of time. But the concept

Table 5.1 Main methods of marketing budget planning

Budgeting method	Description	Advantages/disadvantages
Affordable method	Budget is estimated as the remainder of funds once all operational expenses have been deducted from overall revenues.	*Advantages*: spending will never exceed financial capabilities. Supports organic growth of an organisation. *Disadvantages*: usually results in under-spending on marketing, which leads to an uncertain annual promotion budget and ignores the effect of promotion on sales. Accessing external funds and investments for growth are not advocated.
Percentage-of-sales method	The budget is set at a certain percentage of current or forecasted sales per unit.	*Advantages*: very simple, emphasises the relationship between marketing spending, selling price and profit per unit. *Disadvantages*: leads to false impression of sales affecting marketing instead of resulting from them. No basis for choosing specific percentage ranges.
Objective-and-task method	The budget is set by defining specific objectives and determining the marketing tasks required to achieve these objectives. The budget is set to cover the costs of these tasks.	*Advantages*: forces managers to link the level of spending to expected results. Accessing of external funds where necessary to facilitate growth and transformational thinking is encouraged. *Disadvantages*: it is difficult to guarantee results without having past performance data. Large-scale investments that rely on borrowed capital create a risk for those organisations that expect activities to deliver sales to repay the borrowed capital.

Source: Adapted from Kotler et al., 2018

works well in digital content consumption, e.g. watching an online video or listening to a song.

Your budget will also depend on your digital channels mix selection. For example, while using social media networks such as Facebook and Twitter is free of charge, the human resources for monitoring and engaging in these networks takes time.

Ultimately, deciding what to spend should be based on what is sensible for the size of your organisation, your strategic ambitions and your available resources. As consumers increasingly use digital channels, your marketing channels need to follow them. Whether you establish a modest or robust budget, it is important to learn what will work for your organisation today and in the future (Association for Project Management, 2015). As your awareness of the Buyer

Persona Spring grows, you will also learn what works, so that you can set more realistic objectives for the next campaign.

5.4 Acting – executing your project

From a project management perspective, acting is an ongoing process and focuses on keeping the digital project triangle under control. This role is mainly focusing on leading activities such as stakeholder expectations management, team management, roles assignment, scheduling and workflow planning and amending Gantt charts. From a campaign operational perspective, acting involves researching and developing content and digital engagement tools, as well as implementing these in practice. In larger organisations, a project leader can be assigned, who oversees the activities of others. In smaller organisations it could be one person who is responsible for all activities – in this case, it is particularly important to allocate time to reflect on the campaign process (how things are done) and not just on campaign operation (what is being done). This chapter focuses on the project management perspective, and subsequent chapters will review channel-specific actions such as conducting SEO and implementing social media optimisation.

Campaign documentation

Documentation of all project-related information is placed in a single file – project documentation. This document is continuously updated as the project progresses so that it can be used for future project estimations and as a template. Dependent on the scale of your project, the project documentation could range from a single spreadsheet to a host of files that help to define the project based on the following five W and one H-questions: Why? What? Who? Where? When? How?

- Why is this project being done?
- What will be done as part of this project?
- Who will do what and how?
- Where will content be created and published?
- When will activities take place?
- How exactly all the above mentioned will be done?

Perceiving a digital campaign as a short-term project, the project documentation principally justifies and clearly defines your project as well as indicates its scope. If necessary, it also secures funds for the project from a previously established budget. Moreover, it assigns the roles and defines the responsibilities of project participants, and it can be referred to as a source of information for other team members.

For larger organisations, introducing a digital campaign project requires contributions from appropriate team members inside your organisation as well as external actors. Contributions could be knowledge of past similar projects, or implications of the current project on their activities. For this purpose, a project initiation meeting with them is a must – this outlines the project and makes clear the communication protocols and timeline of activities. Ongoing stakeholder management would be agreed and involves communicating with the wider organisation as necessary, e.g. as outlined in Figure 5.1.

The project documentation could have the following sections:

- Campaign name – name campaigns to make them distinct from one another.
- Aim and objectives – setting the direction and scope of the campaign.
- Business case – the reasons that rationalise the campaign activities as being worthy.
- Project team – outline of project sponsor, manager and other team members.
- Communications plan – how the project team will communicate, how frequent these communications will be and the contact details of these individuals.
- Quality plan – how quality will be assured and assessed during and at the end of the project.
- Deliverables – the expected tangible artefacts produced as a result of the project.
- Scope – detail of how objectives will be achieved, e.g. which channels, what content and what activities would be part of this campaign.
- Resources – what financial and non-financial resources are available to the project.
- KPIs – for tracking and assessing what a successful campaign looks like.
- Risk register – what activities can go wrong and how risks will be managed and mitigated.
- Work schedule – including the project Gantt chart and critical path analysis.

Project team

Team management techniques are a response to the 'What? Who? Where? When? and Why?' questions from the 5 Ws approach. While describing the initial roles in a project team (Mind Tools, 2016), you need to define the following:

- Project sponsor – the individual with ultimate authority and control over the project and its implementation.
- Project manager – the team leader, responsible for implementing the project, assigning roles and clearly defining responsibilities of other members. Person responsible for delivery of project on time, on budget, within scope and to the defined quality benchmarks.
- Team members – individuals with specific roles and responsibilities in a specific project.

Table 5.2 The responsibilities of project management

Do	Don't
• Keep a holistic overview of the project. • Take into account integration between tasks. • Delegate tasks to team members. • Schedule and communicate activities for yourself and others. • Manage and motivate the project team and act as a leader, and be prepared to be flexible. • Engage all relevant stakeholders and project team members with relevant information. • Control quality of project-related tasks and deliverables. • Manage project costs. • Assess and review risks related to the project. • Overcome obstacles arising in the course of the project – cooperation facilitating.	• Get involved in micro management – you can't control every single task of the project. • Get carried away with operations, forgetting the aim and objectives of the project. • Ignore poor-performing KPIs – if the project is not working, don't worry about stopping the whole project. • Leave questions from your team members unanswered. • Create authority based on negative team members' emotions (fear, bullying). • Rely on a single point of information – where possible, always consult multiple sources to make your decisions. • Rely on informal communications with all your stakeholders. • Prioritise the urgent over the important. • Assume you know it all.

By assigning roles to your remaining key members of your project team, you define their job descriptions. A team membership diagram showing the lines of authority and reporting for each project team member can help in complex projects.

The project manager is central to communications between team members and the project sponsor. It is often a difficult position, balancing operational reality with strategic priorities (Table 5.2).

Communication plan

Managing projects requires formal and informal communications amongst all the stakeholders, and agreeing on when these communications take place and their purpose is important. Regular communications, as illustrated in Figure 5.8, can be done at different frequencies with different team members – these could be to review and reflect on campaign progress and seek solutions to emerging problems. Problem-specific communications can also be set up to facilitate management by exception when intervention is required. Management by exception is based on the assumption that the team implementing the project can make deviations from the project plan as long as these are not significantly different. The project manager is only consulted when these go beyond certain agreed-on boundaries. Communication agreement is also needed on tools for documents sharing, contact details for video conferencing, and the phone numbers and email contact details of all relevant stakeholders.

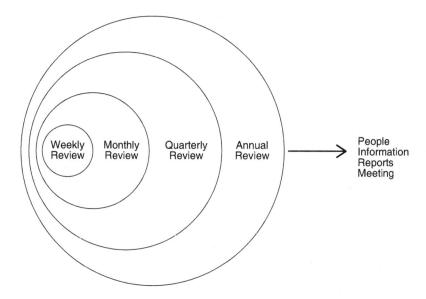

Figure 5.8 Communications plan

Work schedule

To complete a project successfully, you must control a large number of activities and ensure that they are completed on schedule. A delay of one activity or task may lead to negative consequences for the entire project, while prolonging another activity can have no impact on the overall project. For this reason, the idea of 'divide and conquer' works for projects, which is based upon the assumption that controlling smaller parts of the project helps to control the overall project.

Gantt charts are a common technique in project management and present a project in a visually accessible way. A basic Gantt chart lists project tasks, the individuals responsible for those tasks and when the tasks have to be undertaken (see Figure 5.9). In its simplest form, it uses bars on a horizontal timescale to show the start, duration and finish of activities.

Work schedule management is the process of developing, maintaining and communicating schedules for available resources. The Gantt chart must show all the work related to the delivery of the project according to the assigned time. An additional benefit that a detailed Gantt chart offers is the ability to log activity precedence. By calculating the duration of each activity and which activities rely on the completion of others, it is possible to estimate the project's longest time for completion. In project management, this longest sequence of activities is called the 'critical path'. On a Gantt chart, the critical path could be a line connecting the bar charts for the critical

Project task	Name and % responsible			Project Months					
	Aleksej	*Ana*	*Gordon*	1	2	3	4	5	6
Identify target market	50	30	20	X					
Client meetings	30	30	40	X	X	X	X	X	
. . . .									

Figure 5.9 An example of a basic project management Gantt chart

interdependent activities. Interdependent activities could be creating a web page before a pay-per-click (PPC) campaign is launched or driving traffic to that page. More sophisticated variations of Gantt charts can convey other project-related information such as cost per task, resource over-allocations and percentages of completed tasks.

Knowing the activities on the critical path allows you to allocate the best resources in your team and therefore increase the chances of your project being successful. Also, knowing the critical path activities offers you the ability to prioritise important tasks over those that appear to be urgent (e.g. responding to urgent emails instead of creating content for a video campaign). To create a Gantt chart and the critical path, answer the questions below:

- What are your time/cost constraints?
- What preceding activities need to be completed?
- How do individual activities depend on each other?
- Which activities can be done in parallel?
- What is the estimated duration of each activity?
- Who do you need for each activity?
- What is the skill level of each resource assigned to its task(s)?

To develop a Gantt chart, a number of tools are available, from simple spreadsheets and free online tools such as Trello, to specific tools including commercial tools such as Microsoft Project and free tools such as Gantt Project. Plans change and, therefore, there is a need to re-prioritise activities; in cases where the digital campaign is causing unintended negative consequences, it can be stopped and the project terminated.

5.5 Observing – optimising your efforts

During the acting phase of the campaign, a project might change the activities as the need arises. For example, a Google update algorithm is released which requires you to change your approach to your campaign. Factors impacting the digital project triangle, such as changes in budget, timeframes or illness of team members, result in the need for revision of activities. The knowledge gained from observations of a project has benefits for future campaigns and, therefore, documenting lessons learned is a key component in the optimisation of your future efforts.

Continual review of schedule and budget

During the project observation stage, the project manager has to make sure that the project is moving forward as per the Gantt chart schedule. As previously mentioned, online project management software tools are available to allow project managers to track project schedules, budgets, organisational resources and project-related material in real time. These tools also allow other members of the project team to view and update their contributions to the project, upload related information and inform others about the status of the project. Regardless of the complexity of such tools – whether you use a spreadsheet or an automated digital integrated project management service – you have to have a clear understanding of the costs incurred by the project. Whether working on an in-house digital project or for an external client, the lack of accurate financial information has a negative effect on the sustainability of the project and the overall organisation. To avoid such issues, while preparing a project, relevant finance monitoring systems have to be agreed and put in place, including the relevant software support.

'Re-prioritising' tasks

During the project management process, one has to anticipate risks associated with the project. For example, negative feedback from customers on social media may prompt a project management team to pause their marketing activities or bring in a customer services agent or reputation manager to manage feedback in real time. This exemplary form of unexpected outcome may force organisations to re-prioritise certain activities and introduce new activities into their project. Therefore, project managers must create flexible projects and be ready to re-prioritise their tasks due to unexpected risks from internal or external forces.

Maintaining a risk register

Risk management is a way of anticipating challenges and managing these to reduce their negative effect on a project's success. Risk management involves identifying risks, assessing their impact and probability, prioritising risks and then monitoring and mitigating these. The documentation of risk management is logged in a risk register, which in its simple form could be as illustrated in Figure 5.10.

Risk identification	Impact	Probability	Assessment	Management and mitigation
Not being able to gain number 1 position for a secondary keyword 'SK'	2	2	2 x 2 = 4	**Use a range of secondary keywords expectations**

Figure 5.10 Risk register

The first column states the name of the risk – risk identification. Then the **impact** of the risk is analysed and rated on a scale from 1 to 5 using the following interpretation:

1   Negligible
2   Marginal
3   Important
4   Serious
5   Catastrophic

The estimate of the risk occurring is noted in the **probability** column:

1   Impossible
2   Remote
3   Unlikely
4   Possible
5   Probable

The **assessment** column notes the assessment of individual rows for the risk and is a result of impact x probability. The scores for assessment can be colour-coded using this notation:

Red: assessment of 15 to 25
Amber: assessment of 9 to 14
Green: assessment of 0 to 8

The final column allows for documenting management and, where possible, mitigation tasks for this risk. The collection of all project-specific risks entered in the register allows the team to make a judgement on whether the overall project is still viable – for example, if all risks are on red and there is not much that can be done to mitigate these, the team need to consider whether the project should be terminated (Figure 5.10).

The project management team should identify possible hindrances and take steps to resolve them if they occur at any stage of the project.

Quality assessment

Quality assessment means that the project is able to meet the objectives of the project team and that it offers the desired quality and functionality. The main objective of quality assessment is to detect and rectify issues as quickly as possible. An early correction of errors tends to result in the reduction of surplus costs and offer overall schedule benefit. The major tools for quality assessment are testing and technical reviews. Technical reviews originate from the software development discipline and are becoming a crucial activity in digital marketing campaigns. They are based on expert peer review, where an expert examines artefacts or content and offers their feedback and overall assessment on the suitability of the artefact for the desired campaign. User experience testing is another commonly used technique for digital artefact quality assessment. User experience is based on involving representatives of the buyer persona and asking them to use the artefact. Their use of the artefact can be recorded, and users are interviewed about their experience of using the artefacts.

Monitoring results

There is no management without control functions. That is why the role of monitoring and tracking to obtain results is so important within the whole campaign cycle. This is, first, because it closes the whole cycle and thus allows the company to summarise the results obtained in relation to the previously established objectives. Second, and sometimes more importantly, this verification provides a basis to take further actions for future campaigns. Analysis of subsequent campaigns will allow expenditure optimisation and will provide invaluable knowledge for future decision making concerning the most successful digital marketing channels to choose, who should be the target of future campaign messages and which activities will yield the best results for your organisation. Knowing which channels do and do not work for your organisation can save you time and energy in the future. Of course, the digital environment is very fast paced, and new types and forms of digital communication tools are always emerging. Therefore, always scanning for new opportunities is good practice when planning and reviewing a project. Competitors and customers may change and evolve; hence, following their needs and interests is also important, as all knowledge gained from campaigns feeds into an understanding of the buyer persona.

Box 5.2   When high click-through rate (CTR) still means a campaign failure

When an electronic retail bank in Poland conducted a digital campaign, users were encouraged to click an advertising form and were transferred to a landing page relevant to the campaign. The campaign resulted in

3 per cent CTR, resulting in website traffic increases; however, the bank quickly found such traffic was not converting into sales and generated no income for the bank.

The bank's previously established banner campaign had given an inferior CTR outcome (around 1 per cent), but a higher rate of customers applied for the advertised online cash loans. So, what went wrong with the new campaign?

Between the two campaigns, neither the landing page nor the application form had been changed, and pricing conditions remained constant. It was all about the choice of a new advertising form. The new platform allowed a user to click anywhere on a web page, but only in specific places of the ad image. This resulted in confusion when users who clicked on a space were directed to a link not mentioned in the ad. The new advertising platform gave outstanding CTR results. However, since users were clicking and landing on a non-relevant web page, they were confused and did not proceed to apply for the loan. The loan application was a metric as well as the CTR. Despite the high brand awareness due to relatively high CTR of the new campaign platform, the overall campaign did not result in the desired sales.

The example of the Polish bank highlights the importance of measuring the effectiveness of the user experience through continuous observation. Instead of verifying the indicators and metrics, you should instead track your most important KPIs.

Reflection at the end of the project allows the project management team to assess its efforts and learn from its experiences. Reflection is not only about looking back; it is also a proactive step taken by the project manager to reassess their activities regarding the project. Project reflection, in part, allows the project management team the time to identify their strengths and weaknesses throughout the duration of the campaign and to learn from this for the sake of future projects. Key learning can be used to update the Buyer Persona Spring as well as information about the buyer persona itself. For example, by launching a campaign on social media channels and receiving positive feedback from your followers, your organisation receives a positive reinforcement that the strategy is working. This means that maintaining a similar direction for future campaigns is appropriate. On the other hand, as shown in the Polish bank example, with high CTR but low sales, not all high numbers inevitably show the full story of success. All campaigns require a full set of KPIs that will measure the actual success that you seek.

Preparing for premature closure of a project

Closing a project is a consideration that should be open to the manager and the team. In management by exception, the decision of project closure is certainly something that requires careful consideration of the advantages and disadvantages of doing so. Premature closure of a project can be disappointing for any project team, although the experience gathered during the project is always useful. However, you should consider it as a valuable lesson. For instance, closure may become the only way out if the budget for the project is no longer available.

Creating a post-project report (against initial goals and benchmarking)

Developing a post-project report is necessary, since it gives the project management team the opportunity to review the results of the project and determine its success. If the post-project report shows that the project was able to achieve the initial goals and meet the benchmarking required by the project team at the start of the project, this means it was a success. However, even if the original aim and objectives have not been achieved but secondary aim and objectives emerged as the project unfolded and these resulted in a beneficial outcome for the organisation, future projects can use the new aim and objectives as a starting point for new campaign considerations.

Undertaking a project debrief (with relevant stakeholders)

After completion of the project, the project manager should debrief stakeholders who were directly or indirectly involved with the project. The debriefing allows the project manager to understand the viewpoints of the stakeholders regarding the project and learn from others' experiences. The valuable feedback and constructive criticism received from the debriefing permit the project management team to learn from such experiences for future projects.

Making a concerted effort to praise achievements

Whilst the 'praise publicly and correct privately' rule has some critics, the general thinking is worth noting. It is the responsibility of the project manager to appreciate the project management team when they successfully complete the project. Praising colleagues for the successful completion of the project motivates them to do even better in future projects and makes them feel that they are valued as part of the team.

At the same time, the project manager has to lead the team when they are unable to achieve the desired goals of the project. The project manager must meet privately with the team members concerned and share constructive criticism so they do not repeat the same mistakes in the future.

5.6 Summary

After opening with an explanation of the main stages of the campaign planning cycle, we then explored the first stage of the planning cycle and considered the campaign setting objectives aligned with the overall digital marketing goals. You have learned how to set a planning budget and how the key message of the campaign needs to be thought through, keeping in mind the buyer persona and the digital media channels selected.

The key digital marketing campaign planning tools for documenting digital campaigns have been discussed. A project Gantt chart and a risk assessment table help you to keep on track of the project management triangle.

The four stages of planning, acting, observing and reflecting have been given attention from a digital marketing campaign perspective. Whilst project management time is spent mainly on the planning part of the campaign, there are tasks during acting, observing and reflecting that are essential for documenting the actual project and learning from these lessons for future campaigns.

5.7 References

Association for Project Management (2015) *What is project management?* www.apm.org.uk/WhatIsPM

Heinze, A., Ferneley, E. and Child, P. (2013) Ideal participants in online market research: Lessons from closed communities. *International Journal of Market Research*, 55(6), 769–789.

Kotler, P., Armstrong, G. and Opresnik, O. (2018) *Principles of marketing*. Harlow: Pearson Education.

Mind Tools (2016) *Project initiation documents. Getting your project off to a great start.* www.mindtools.com/pages/article/newPPM_85.htm

PMI (2018) *Success rates rise-transforming the high cost of low performance.* 9th Global Project Management Survey. www.pmi.org/-/media/pmi/documents/public/pdf/learning/thought-leadership/pulse/pulse-of-the-profession-2017.pdf

6 Developing an effective digital presence

Ana Cruz and Stelios Karatzas

6.0 Learning objectives

In this chapter you will learn how to:

- recognise what constitutes a digital brand presence;
- differentiate key concepts such as brand equity and social media branding;
- maintain digital presences to create content synergies;
- differentiate media types – owned, earned and paid;
- understand the role of user experience;
- develop information architecture that is based on your buyer persona;
- use key performance indicators (KPIs) to assess your digital presence.

6.1 Defining digital presence

Your digital presence is the sum total of all the online activities managed by your organisation (including websites, blogs and social media profiles) as well as the online activities carried out by your key stakeholders, such as employees and consumers. The interactions that are generated by this presence can make or break brands. Corporate brand managers no longer engineer brands. In a digitally connected world, brands are co-created.

You might see your digital presence as a means to an end but, if managed strategically, it can become an important asset in its own right for your organisation. Your presence is not only for sharing information but also to build credibility (Verisign, 2016), trust, engagement and brand loyalty. These positive responses can all be achieved by influencing attitudes and behaviour.

Influencing behaviour does not solely mean the completion of a purchase. For non-profit organisations, for example, the behaviours that are encouraged may be to support a cause financially, to sign a petition, to donate something or to recycle more and waste less. Of course, influencing and securing purchases remains a vital aspect for most businesses, so having clear calls-to-action (such as buy, like and share) within your digital presence is vital.

6.2 Brand building

Branding is a pivotal aspect of your strategy because it provides a focal point for your buyer persona. Your buyer persona can identify with your brand and will associate it with the value that you deliver. Your brand helps to clearly differentiate the products, services and experiences that you offer from those of your competitors. The work you have already undertaken that has been described in earlier chapters, for conducting external and internal examinations of the environment, the identification of a strategy and the process of defining and creating your buyer persona, supports the development of a robust market presence.

In the Buyer Persona Spring, your brand is an integral part of your organisation, although in small organisations this may currently be an underdeveloped aspect of your digital identity. If you are in this position, then brand building should be an integral aspect of your overall digital strategy and a key consideration for content, channels and data. A strong brand identity that is well communicated through key content on the right channels will appeal to your buyer persona and tighten the spring to your organisation (Figure 6.1).

Building your brand requires careful consideration of what your brand stands for now and what you want it to stand for in the future (in other words, the brand essence). How does your brand make your customers' lives better, safer, more exciting or more convenient? With popular commentary suggesting that attention spans are shrinking, why should your buyer persona pay attention to you, your product or your website? Why should your buyer persona use your application or read your blog? Consider the message conveyed immediately by brands such as Volvo (=safety), Apple (=simplicity) and Angry Birds (=entertainment). Each of these brand promises is clear, based on fundamental customer needs and consistently delivered by every aspect of the organisation. These messages are delivered by the entire organisation, not just through the products and services that they provide.

Each touchpoint between your organisation and your buyer persona is a moment of truth, where the promise of your brand needs to be consistently delivered. Apple's brand association with simplicity is translated into its product, packaging, web design, apps, interface and usability. Apple promises a life of beautiful simplicity where form follows function, where each interaction is intuitive and the 'I' at the centre (e.g. iPad, iPhone, iTunes) is all of us – individually. Your branding challenge is to develop a meaningful promise of value (the value proposition and unique selling point or USP) that is fully aligned to your organisation. Your organisation must then consistently live up to and deliver this promise of value. Your organisation can develop this alignment by responding to a series of straightforward questions (Figure 6.2).

- 'What do we say?' How do you communicate internally and externally? For example, social media policies for employees are just as important as integrated communications with your buyer persona.
- 'What do we do?' What are your products, services, experiences and interactions?

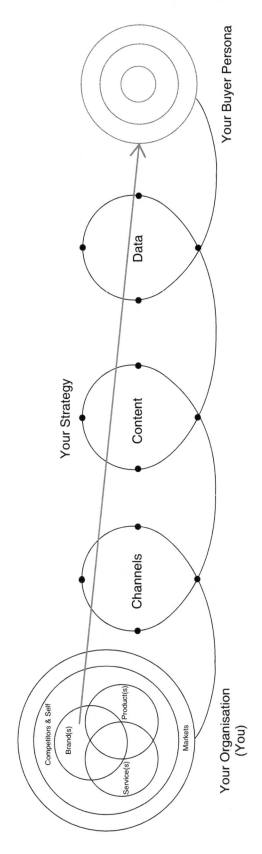

Figure 6.1 Brand building with the Buyer Persona Spring

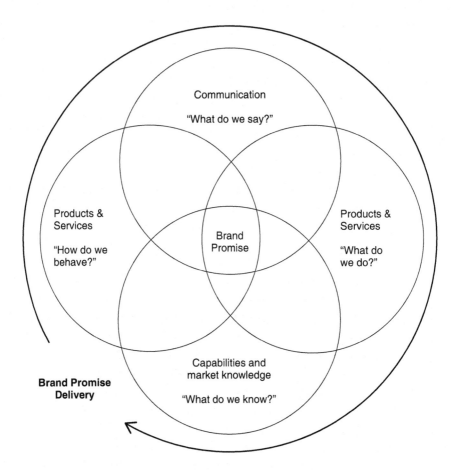

Figure 6.2 Embedding your brand's value within your organisation

Source: (adapted from Cruz, 2006)

- 'How do we behave?' What is your organisation's culture and behaviour? How do you facilitate engagement and conversation with your buyer persona?
- 'What do we know?' What capabilities and market and customer knowledge can be maximised through market research and social media listening? How much knowledge and understanding does your buyer persona have about your brand?

Brand alignment (or misalignment) can also be recognised in the Buyer Persona Spring (Figure 6.3). Brands that are misaligned will appear to be at odds with your products and services and will confuse or misdirect your buyer persona. For example, developing a brand that suggests luxury will be misplaced in a retail outlet full of discounted items. In contrast, a brand built on an image of convenience and value for money could be entirely appropriate, particularly if the image distinguishes you from competitors in a unique way.

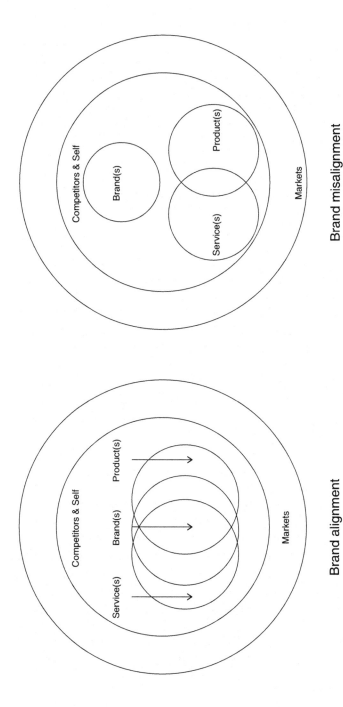

Figure 6.3 Brand alignment or misalignment in the Buyer Persona Spring

6.3 Brand equity

Brand equity is extra value customers perceive in a brand that ultimately builds long-term loyalty. It is considered an asset generated by the interactions and relationships between brands and their customers (Iglesias et al., 2019). Effective digital presence for your organisation requires a focus on building brand equity through brand knowledge, preference and loyalty. Organisations may own a trademark (the name, logo and symbols), but the brand and its equity ultimately lie in the head, heart and actions of your buyer persona, as is the case with the Newby Trust (Case Study 6.1).

Case Study 6.1   Newby Trust builds trust in their brand online

Even when organisations don't rely on online purchases, they still need to build their brand. The same principles of branding apply. The buyer persona must easily recognise what the brand is saying and doing, how it is behaving and what it knows.

For a small charity like the *Newby Trust*, the need to build brand equity is significant, as it acts as a trust for charitable organisations, and most of the public are probably unaware of how these types of organisations function. From its home page, the visitor is immediately drawn to what the organisation has to say (a trust that supports the common good). Scrolling down further we are directly shown what the Newby Trust does (makes grants to registered charities and small grants to philanthropic organisations).

The Newby Trust successfully communicates its brand behaviour through a concise and informative history section, and in describing how simple it has made the process of applying for grants. In this way, the brand has made an arduous, complicated and time-consuming procedure for receiving funding for charitable endeavours easier. The Newby Trust has successfully built its brand online and has enhanced its brand equity.

It has also taken steps to ensure that the basics of brand building are supported by other approaches, to ensure a positive experience for its buyer persona. For example, it repeatedly offers contact details and support for questions and more information. Additionally, the brand reveals its recently audited accounts to ensure transparency, a fundamental position for any trust organisation seeking to gain credibility and legitimacy. This action helps to further build the positive perception of the brand.

Source: www.newby-trust.org.uk

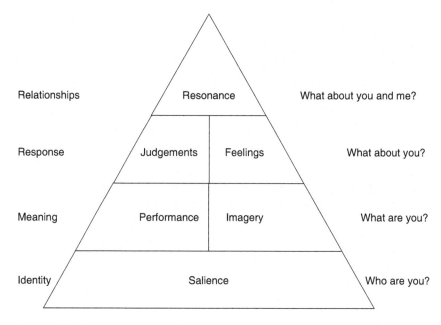

Figure 6.4 The brand equity pyramid

Source: (adapted from Kevin and Keller, 2019)

Brand equity is built as the buyer persona becomes aware of the brand and begins to value its offering, when they know what the brand stands for, when they respond to it and when they want an ongoing relationship with it.

The brand equity pyramid (Figure 6.4) illustrates these levels.

The variables that induce positive brand equity in retail include creating an emotional connection, an excellent online experience, responsive service environment, high levels of trust and high-speed fulfilment for orders. In a digital environment, brand equity means getting the hygiene factors right, including findability, speed of download, contemporary site design, intuitive navigation, robust order fulfilment and personalised support (Cavender and Kincade, 2014). The application of these key factors is discussed later in this chapter.

6.4 The rise of the social media–based brand

The rise of social media, plus advances in technology, mean that consumers are now capable of creating and publishing content themselves. This means that your brand is being co-created right now, whether you are part of that process or not. If we are aware of brand equity, this co-creation includes your organisation. Even if you are not currently creating your brand, your key stakeholders are. Your customers, employees, pressure groups and brand advocates are all working away at presenting your brand through user-generated content (UGC) such as videos, reviews and blogs. Without your participation there are no guarantees that this image of your brand will reflect you accurately or even positively. To build brand equity and achieve resonance with your buyer persona, your brand will need to facilitate relationships, interactions and conversations – to be a social brand that listens and engages. Your conversations should not just be dialogues but forums, with all your stakeholders able to talk to each other – for example, the ability to review products (on multiple channels), comment on blogs and use social media buttons to share, like and tweet (Case Study 6.2).

Case Study 6.2   Café Coffee Day stays relevant through engagement and staying 'social'

Coffee is one of the largest traded commodities in the world, with head-quarters in India. It is a ubiquitous daily tradition throughout regions and cultures globally. Attempting to compete in this market takes a special type of brand and strategy. Café Coffee Day began modestly in 1996 with one location and has remained, to this day, one of the top coffee brands in India, claiming to serve 1.8 billion cups of coffee annually.

Not only does Café Coffee Day have around 1,500 retail locations across India and beyond, but it also produces its own coffee from its own plantations, produces its own coffee machines and even manufactures its own furniture for its stores. Even though this vertically integrated strategy does offer cost-savings to the brand, they know that this is not enough to compete in today's social world.

Consumers in India are no exception to wanting to be able to engage with the brand and to be able to have their voice heard. Café Coffee Day knows there's no better place for this than social media. They have active accounts on all the key platforms (Facebook, Twitter, Instagram, YouTube and Pinterest) and stylize their content based on current demographic trends (i.e. beautiful pictures of coffee cups with laptops). Furthermore, they utilize each social media account strategically and post content according to each platform's unique environment.

For example, their Instagram account is full of social shares of their consumers delightfully consuming their products (crediting their consumer's social currency) or sharing empowering stories of women, while consuming their product for International Women's Day, while utilizing strategic hashtags like #WomensDay and #GirlPower. On their Twitter account, they have polls for consumers to vote on new flavours and product names, and on their Pinterest account they showcase visuals of their products and entertaining graphics like memes. They also cross-post content along their social media platforms in order to create consistency and fluency.

Café Coffee Day understands that coffee is a part of everyday life, so they are seeking inclusion into this realm. Since they know that their target consumers are socializing online daily, they must successfully communicate engaging content throughout social online platforms, including through their website, which allows users to easily find a location, find out about their newest products and find links to social media sites. Finally, they also keep users wanting to come back through promotions, rewards programs and, of course, great product.

Source: www.cafecoffeeday.com

Creating content that facilitates dialogue and sharing is one of the most important activities for delivering an engaging brand experience. The combination of your content, channels and data should enable this brand experience. There are many challenges to this work, and in contrast to traditional approaches to marketing, the digital environment is not necessarily brand-oriented and people want to connect with each other rather than a brand. Brands are not people – usually – but the metaphor of a brand personality is one way you can bring your brand to life. If the brand were a person, how would it behave? What are its values? How would it talk? What is its tone? These considerations will clarify the image that you want to project and will set the tone for all your conversations and interactions with your buyer persona.

Building your brand requires you to create and offer content through channels that will get you invited into the conversation and that get others talking about the brand. Listening – and gathering the data that results from this listening – is a fundamental principle for effective conversation (see Chapter 8 on social media for more details about listening online). Your strategy must include data that closes the loop and listens to your buyer persona in a way that enables you to respond intelligently and personally.

6.5 Social media presence

In order to build your brand, a social media presence is essential. Please see an in-depth discussion of the social media presence in Chapter 8. Almost all social media, including Facebook, Twitter, YouTube and LinkedIn, allow customisation features for brands as well as individuals. The composition of your social media presence will be shaped by the brand you are creating and will be a key consideration for your channels.

A key starting point for a successful social media presence starts with your name (for example, twitter.com/EU_Commission). In order for your name to rank well in search engines, your social profile name should appear in the most familiar way that users would search for your organisation.

Most social media channels also allow you to have a profile picture. Larger businesses will use their brand logo and consistent naming of the brand. This approach applies to all organisations. Sometimes your brand name will not be available. If the brand name is already taken, use words like 'official' or the brand's location after the name (for example, UniversalBG for a company based in Bulgaria). Another option is to use your specialism to gain a naming advantage. For example, you could use specialist sector positioning such as ' sports financing'.

Some social media channels allow a background picture. This can be used for pictures of new products or services and can be updated regularly. As with usernames, profile pictures should stay consistent through all of your channels to deliver a consistent message and brand personality.

6.6 Developing a network of profiles

It is very important that each of your social media channels as well as your primary website are well interlinked. This consistency makes it clear to your buyer persona that your brand wants to engage. Consistency also enables better data collection to track which channels produce results – whether this is sales, engagements or actions. On the channels that allow a biography, there is an opportunity to share your brand philosophy, brand personality and USP. Keep it short. All your channels should also be linked from your organisation's website, making them consistently visible as well as through email signatures, business cards and forum signatures.

There are different types of social media buttons for web pages – most importantly, 'Follow' and 'Share'. The 'Follow' button links a social media profile and allows a visitor to follow your brand through multiple channels. The 'Share' buttons allow the user to share content across social media channels and can also incorporate a counter that allows some basic activity data to be gathered. A higher number of shares for a particular piece of content is also a proxy measure for the trust that is being placed in your brand by your buyer persona. Measures of trust are particularly important for e-commerce web pages. Writing a review can be an onerous task, but a like or a share is a quick way for a visitor to endorse one of your products or services. However, there is a risk in publicly displaying sharing counts, as low numbers all too clearly reflect low popularity.

Organisations use social media channels to connect with their buyer persona. One of the most effective channels for doing this is a blog. Developing a blog and then amplifying the content of the posts through other channels contributes to the longevity of your content (Figure 6.5). The nature of social networks is such that they are constantly changing, so it is a risk to invest a lot of energy into a social media network that might become less popular in 2 years.

Figure 6.5 The centrality of a blog in your brand development

If you have a blog, your customers can access your content without signing up to a particular network, and the content will always be available through a search engine, offering a safer longer-term social media presence. Also, all social network profiles can be used to amplify blog content that is based on the main website – driving traffic and engagement to the main digital profile of your brand. Social media is discussed in greater depth in Chapter 8.

6.7 Owned, earned and paid content

One of the most crucial ways for a brand to stand out is through engaging content which makes users want to comment on and share it and which sparks conversations. There are three different channels where content can be placed: these are described as owned, earned and paid (Figure 6.6).

Owned channels and content include corporate, product and brand web-sites, blogs, campaign sites, social media profiles and mobile applications. This category also includes bricks-and-mortar stores and offices which connect your buyer persona with your digital activities.

In contrast to your owned content and channels, both paid and earned con-tent are external endorsements of your brand which can be earned through genuine positive word-of-mouth or paid advertising. Paid-for content has

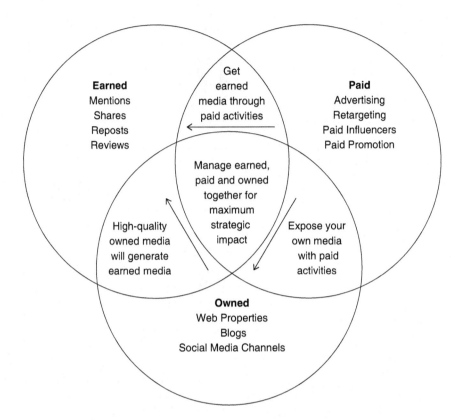

Figure 6.6 Owned, paid and earned content and channels

Source: adapted from www.titangrowth.com/what-is-earned-owned-paid-media-the-difference-explained/

lower levels of credibility when compared to earned content, but it can still be a powerful tool. For example, online and offline advertising and retargeting (where an ad follows a website visitor who left your website without a purchase) can be effective ways to generate brand awareness and drive traffic to your website (one of your owned channels).

Organisations also pay influencers to share or endorse content. Paid endorsements, both online and offline, must be clearly labelled as advertising to comply with good practice guidelines for advertising and codes of ethics. Paid endorsement and paid content introduce specific ethical considerations when it is unclear whether the endorsement is genuine positive word-of-mouth – earned content – or just a paid-for promotion. Failure to disclose a paid endorsement is misleading and can have serious consequences, as illustrated by the Fyre Festival example in Box 6.1. The role of influencers and the need to be transparent when collaborating with them is further discussed in Chapter 8 as part of influencer engagement.

Box 6.1   Fyre Festival

Promoted on Instagram by social media influencers and models Kendall Jenner, Bella Hadid and Emily Ratajkowski, the festival was promoted as the ultimate luxury music festival. Due to take place on a private island previously owned by Pablo Escobar, the festival promised to be a unique immersive experience. The endorsers did not disclose that they had been paid to promote it; however, their endorsement was effective. The tickets were sold out in 48 hours. Instead of a luxury experience and gourmet food, festival goers experienced serious problems related to security, food, accommodation and medical services. The founder was found guilty of fraud and the case is the focus of two documentaries released by Hulu and Netflix in 2019.

Source: www.bbc.com/news/newsbeat-46904445

Earned mentions in the form of reviews (UGC) have become the third most trustworthy source of information at a global level (Nielsen, 2013, 2015). Thus, product reviews have become an important aspect of earned media due to their potential impact on sales. For example, Ho-Dac et al. (2013) researched the impact of online customer reviews on the sales of the new Blu-ray players and the already mature DVD players. The study's findings indicate that positive or negative online customer reviews increase or decrease the sales volume of the different models belonging to weaker brands, but they have no impact on the sales of strong brands. However, a high number of sales leads to more positive reviews, which in turn can help increase brand equity.

Due to the importance of reviews in the customer journey's ZMOT consideration stage (see Chapter 3), organizations need to be responsive to good reviews as well as proactive on how negative reviews are handled. This is further illustrated in the research discussed in Box 6.2.

Box 6.2   Most optimal way to deal with negative reviews

Brunner et al. (2019) researched the most optimal way to deal with a negative customer review. They explored the effects of different response scenarios in which a brand and/or satisfied customer responded to a negative review aiming to rebuild the consumer's trust and purchase intention. When a weak response was provided by the brand and compared to a customer response, consumers perceived the customer review as more trustworthy than the one provided by the brand. However, when compared to a strong brand response, there was a significantly higher product purchase intention when compared to the negative customer response.

In a strong brand's response, it was considered as credible as a single customer response to a bad review. This suggests that the consumer's prior brand knowledge plays an important role during the online purchase decision. The study identified that a combination of a detailed brand response and a response from a customer has a significantly higher effect than a single response from a consumer in isolation. In the case of a weak brand response, customers perceived higher risk and uncertainty in buying. Therefore, in order to reduce concerns a bad customer review should be responded to in detail by a brand to reduce the impact of the negative opinion.

Generally, consumers understand that there might be times when not all goes to plan and are happy to give a second chance to a brand that listens to consumer reviews and responds in detail to show how they addressed the issue raised if necessary.

Genuine positive customer reviews are a powerful endorsement for brands; however, with fake reviews being on the rise trust becomes key. Therefore, it is important that your buyer persona is reassured by being able to check the veracity of reviews. Companies like Amazon are now implementing a Verified Purchase Label that accompanies real reviews (Cohen, 2019). This confirms to the buyer persona that the customer in fact bought the product. Trust is at the heart of robust brands. Thus, it is key that you reassure your buyer persona of the veracity of the information that you present in your digital presence including veracity of the reviews from previous customers (for more on trust touchpoints see Chapter 3).

6.8 Building a successful user experience

Your owned channels are the ones that you have the most control over. You can respond most rapidly to external changes through your owned channels, and your owned content is the most malleable to your brand's proposition and positioning. Of all your potential paid channels and content, your website is probably the most central to your entire digital marketing effort and strategy. How easy or difficult it is to use and navigate your website is known as the user experience. A successful user experience translates into positive experiences that can lead to contentment, positive behavioural intentions and even emotional connections with your brand.

Your aim in creating a positive user experience is not merely to satisfy your buyer persona with reliability, convenience and functionality; it is to 'wow' your buyer persona into wanting to return again and again to your website and to share their experiences throughout their network. User experience is a crucial step in converting a user into one of your brand advocates.

Your goal is to improve customer satisfaction and loyalty through the utility, ease of use and pleasure provided by the use of your owned channels. Mahlke and Thüring (2007) describe three user experience factors that assist in evaluating a website experience and to positively influence future user decisions and behaviours. The findings are relevant to date.

- *Perceived instrumental qualities*: what users notice as being easily usable and useful (e.g. controllability, effectiveness, learnability). This should include access for every user, regardless of any disability, and should follow W3C (w3.org) guidelines such as always having alternative text for images or providing transcripts for podcasts and videos.
- *Emotional reactions*: how enjoyable the interaction is and how the content transforms the user's hedonic state of being (subjective feelings).
- *Perceived non-instrumental qualities*: what the user believes to be appealing and attractive (visual aesthetics).

User experience is inherently focused on the user and on where value will be generated through the user's experience of the channel.

6.9 The principles of user experience design

The fundamental objective of user experience design is centred on the end user. The user experience should meet a user's expectations regarding ease of use, while offering a simple process for accomplishing a goal that is obvious to the user. It is important to recognise that search engine robots are amongst the primary audience for any website and require easy-to-access information in order to index the website so that it will rank well on search engines and other users can find it more readily (this point is discussed in further detail in Chapter 7).

Slow-loading content on a site is a fundamental *faux pas* of usability. Users are no longer willing to wait for content to appear. Another common mistake is a busy layout that distracts users from clear calls-to-action and inhibits readability. Similarly, when there are no search options or feedback mechanisms, users can get stuck while trying to find what they want and be unable to proceed to a completed action. A clearly visible search option that leads to a truly functional internal search function is an essential feature that allows users to freely look for what they want while also introducing a data-collection opportunity that helps you to identify what users are looking for; the website search data can be captured through a system such as Google Analytics and reviewed in regular reports (see the analytics discussion in Chapter 12).

Usability is about being able to make fundamental use of your website, whether it is being accessed from a mobile device like a phone or tablet, or from a variety of web browsers like Mozilla Firefox and Google Chrome. Anything that prevents efficient task completion, takes someone off course, causes confusion, creates an error, allows the misinterpretation of content or leaves the user unable to understand the navigation are all important considerations when user experience is the focus of your attention.

6.10 Usability guide and testing

According to the US government's online guide to usability (usability.org), there are five steps in creating a usability guide: planning, analysing, designing, testing and refining. These steps are incorporated into the overall user experience design processes, with a specific focus on how easy the website is to use at all times. The easier it is to use, the more a user's attention is directed to all other aspects of the user experience.

Besides simply using a guide and testing, there must also be a process for understanding and identifying usability issues through user testing and observing actual users. Hedegaard and Simonsen (2013) found that usability designs that include emphasis on dimensions of hedonic affect and emotion, pleasure and enjoyment and fun score much better in usability testing. Albert and Tullis (2013) have identified, through in-person studies, that there may be verbal expressions of confusion, indecision or dissatisfaction, and nonverbal facial expressions and eye movements. After issues of this type have been identified, they can be categorised further with severity ratings, for example, from low (annoying but does not result in task failure) to medium (issues that contribute to but don't directly result in task failure) to high (issues directly related to task failure). Issues can then be placed in priority or non-priority categories. Severity issues can also be analysed and reported by frequency per participant or group. It is also constructive to illustrate and collect positive outcomes and possibly focus on them for further development.

The Web Content Accessibility Guidelines (WCAG) developed by the main international standards organization for the Internet provide a set of recommendations for making web content more accessible (WCAG, 2019). The focus is primarily for people with disabilities and for all user agents, including mobile phones. WCAG 2.1 became recommended by the World Wide Web Consortium (W3C) in 2018. It consists of 12 guidelines (untestable) organized under four principles: websites must be perceivable, operable, understandable, and robust (see Table 6.1). Each guideline has testable success criteria. The W3C's Techniques for WCAG 2.0 is a list of techniques that help authors meet the guidelines and success criteria. The guidelines and success criteria do not change, but the techniques are periodically updated (WCAG 2.0, 2018).

Schmutz et al. (2018) investigated possible effects of WCAG 2.0 recommendations on nondisabled users as a function of age and the type of device. The research employed website accessibility (high accessibility vs very low accessibility), age (younger adults vs older adults) and type of device (laptop vs tablet). The results showed that higher accessibility increased task completion rate, task completion time and satisfaction ratings of nondisabled users. While user age

Table 6.1 Four principles to make web content more accessible according to WCAG 2.1 and W3C

Perceivable	Operable	Understandable	Robust
Provide text alternatives for any non-text content so that it can be changed into other forms people need, such as large print, braille, speech, symbols or simpler language. Provide alternatives for time-based media. Create content that can be presented in different ways (for example simpler layout) without losing information or structure. Make it easier for users to see and hear content including separating foreground from background.	Make all functionality available from a keyboard. Provide users enough time to read and use content. Do not design content in a way that is known to cause seizures. Provide ways to help users navigate, find content and determine where they are.	Make text content readable and understandable. Make web pages appear and operate in predictable ways. Help users avoid and correct mistakes.	Maximize compatibility with current and future user agents, including assistive technologies.

did not have any effects, users showed faster task completion time under high accessibility when using a tablet rather than a laptop. Younger users liked the websites more when presented on the tablet rather than the laptop, while older users liked the websites more when using the laptop rather than the tablet. Besides this preference, the results confirmed the benefits of accessible websites for nondisabled users. The findings suggest that the beneficial effects may now be generalised to a wide age range and across different devices, thus providing further encouragement for practitioners to apply WCAG 2.0 to make web content more accessible.

6.11 Responsive design

Mobile devices such as tablets, ebook readers and smartphones are growing in popularity. Your digital presence needs to be capable of operating on these platforms too. Building a mobile site demands a responsive design – a web design created for an optimal viewing experience on multiple screen sizes, with easy-to-read content and large navigation buttons that better support small screens and touch-based scrolling navigation. Mobile devices deliver your content on the go, alongside other screens and amongst a crowd to people who want to access information quickly and easily. Done carefully, your brand and content can be delivered into the heart of a group of like-minded people, alongside that of competitors and at key points in a discussion.

Building a responsive design is a similar task to that of building a great user experience. Simplicity is the key, offering fewer options, using plain language, keeping formatting simple and sticking to conventions. Because mobile devices have smaller screens, content must be organised to include the most pertinent information at the top of a page. Mobile devices rely on touch input, so your functionality should be straightforward. Mobile devices generally also have slower connections, so your web pages should reduce any data transfer to a minimum and keep content and actions on the same page to save data costs for the user.

There are some specific challenges to responsive design, including the complexity of development and the need to reduce a website to a bare minimum so that it can adapt to all devices and browsers and overcome the inconsistencies of website functions on different devices (especially considering the speed at which new devices are being developed).

Case Study 6.3   Wix.com offers an easy-to-use platform to create, host and optimize websites for small businesses

Internet users are browsing the web at around 2x the rate on mobile devices than on traditional desktop ones. This means brands that do not optimize their web presence will be left in the dark.

Small businesses no longer have to fear large budget allocations for website development and optimization. Now there are sophisticated tools that allow small businesses to create, host and optimize their website with little hassle. The Israeli web-development company Wix.com offers exactly this. Whether a small business wants to increase brand awareness and drive traffic to their brick-and-mortar store or they want to develop their very own online store, Wix.com has them covered.

Since many small businesses are weary of committing to long-term contracts or of paying upfront for products or services, Wix.com allows users to build their very own website free of charge. This way, small businesses can discover for themselves how easy it is to create their own websites using Wix.com's templates. Once they are ready to use their

Figure 6.7 Wix.com logo

Figure 6.8 Wix.com responsive design

own URL and remove Wix.com's branding from their website, they are then charged for the service.

In order to remain aligned with consumer preferences, Wix.com offers a mobile site creator and optimiser in parallel with the desktop developer, so small businesses can ensure that their websites are responsive. The completeness of the editing tools means that users do not need to undertake any additional technical editing to deliver a strong user experience. Users can preview their website at any time for both desktops and mobile devices to confirm that both are fully optimised before publishing.

Furthermore, all proprietary and third-party plugins and apps offered on Wix.com's website builder are responsive. If a small business requires event registration, for example, then they can effortlessly install the Simpl-e-Schedule app. Once the app is installed on the website, the app will automatically be optimized for mobile devices as well.

Finally, Wix.com offers a comprehensive support section so users can search through many frequently asked questions to solve their issues or learn more about their products and services. They also showcase previous customers to enhance trust and inspire users to create their own responsive website.

6.12 Website infrastructure

With your owned content and channels defined – based on your strategy and the clear definition of your buyer persona – and your website look and feel and page layouts determined, your next step is web development. The development process will take you from the design phase to an interactive website that will connect you with your buyer persona.

The first step in your development process is choosing and registering your domain name. It is easy to see whether your preferred domain name is available – simply type the name into a search engine or web browser and scan the results. Finding a suitable domain name may sound easy, but there are many factors to consider. You might want your domain to be your brand name, if available. However, you may also want to add or subtract from your brand name to make the domain name as catchy and memorable as possible. However, be cautious of being caught up with naming trends, for example, Flickr or those offered by the Web 2.0 domain name generator (www.dotomator.com/web20.html).

Depending on where your target audience is, you may choose to use a local domain (such as. gr for Greece or. bg for Bulgaria) if you are primarily serving local markets. But you can also just as readily register a familiar 'global' domain, such as. com,. net or. org, or one of the new global top-level domains (gTLDs) such as. makeup or. watches (newgtlds.icann.org/en/program-status/delegated-strings). Another consideration is whether to have multiple domain names to avoid competitors or others registering similar names, while still being able to link those domain names to the main site. Trademarking and intellectual property rights apply online in the same way as they do offline, so there are limits to your choices both legally and ethically. Finally, including keywords in the domain name can help with search engine optimisation (SEO) to make smaller organisations more visible to communicate the purpose of their site.

Another question you will need to answer is whether the website should be static or be based on a content management system (CMS). Static websites have historically been perceived as the cheaper and more secure option (Garner, 2014), since they are hosted without the aid of a database. However, with the maturity of open-source CMSs such as WordPress, there are really no technical, design or marketing reasons to use a static website.

Most hosting companies freely offer pre-installed open-source CMSs (such as WordPress for information sites or Magento for e-commerce sites), which simplify website development for smaller organisations. These systems are easy to use and customise, with many free themes and plugins that make website management easy for those with limited technical knowledge. There are many guides, online courses and help sites for these popular systems, which provide a relatively low-cost form of technical support. There are a number of plugins that allow a CMS to be integrated with other systems such as a customer relationship management (CRM) system or a simple mailing list management system (such as Mailchimp).

6.13 Information architecture

The best websites are shaped with a strong understanding of their buyer persona's interests, needs and expectations. The content, visual design, organisation and navigation should all work in harmony to enable users to find key information easily and readily complete critical tasks. This arranging and grouping of information can also benefit the website's visibility for search engine spiders to create better SEO results (see Chapter 7 for more details). The term 'information architecture' refers to the organisation and structuring of a website. Better information architecture creates a more coherent, intuitive and satisfying experience for your buyer persona.

With a well-defined buyer persona, a clear understanding of your organisation and a definite digital strategy, you should be able to identify the keyword phrases or keyword terms that are of highest relevance to your organisation and your buyer persona. This understanding should produce high specificity (combinations of two or more words), have high search volume (determined by search engine data from Google's Trends or Keyword Planner tools) and should ideally have low levels of competition (indicated by the keyword difficulty tools). These terms should be identified and categorised into themes. The themes will help you determine the pages your website needs, in addition to the more 'standard' content of 'Home', 'About Us' and 'Contact Us' pages.

Having identified the main themes, you will then need to outline the content structure based on these themes. A hierarchy of subcategories should incorporate all of the keywords that you are targeting. The highest levels of your website hierarchy should include the most important but general information, while lower levels of the hierarchy should have less importance overall, with more specific information. Some keyword terms might not fit into the hierarchical structure, but these can still be utilised through blog posts and as part of the overall ecosystem of content that answers all the needs of your buyer persona.

This hierarchical site structuring should then intuitively lead to the creation of a site map (the visual representation of the logical structure of the content). The site map can be translated into a web page that will help to outline the navigational structure for your website in a manner similar to the way a table of contents helps to organise a book.

Good navigation should include menus and submenus similar to the contents page of a textbook. Your buyer persona will be familiar with this system. From a design point of view, it is important that your buyer persona is not presented with more than seven options – simplicity is important for user experience. Your keywords now act as content labels which users will click on, so the words should be meaningful and representative of what users can expect to find on the resultant page. With this increasingly extensive architecture now defined, wireframes can be created as a guide to integrating all of the indispensable page elements in an organised and purposeful manner and to help you brief and collaborate with designers and developers.

6.14 The AIDA model for creating content

Once your information architecture is well defined, you need to set out the content that will align with the keywords that you have identified and will convey the essential aspects of your brand's message. One formal model for designing content is known as AIDA. This model presents four key stages in converting prospects into customers (Table 6.2).

Brand awareness is increasingly generated through search engine results pages (SERPs). As a result, the more search engine–friendly your website and all your channels are, the easier it is for your brand to build awareness.

As the stages of the buyer journey progress, it can become increasingly difficult to engage the buyer persona. At the interest stage, relevance and usefulness are key. Your engagement must answer why your buyer persona came to the site and what they want to know. This is why a clear USP is of paramount importance for successful marketing. Make your content easily accessible. Use images and video, and write well-formatted text that is designed for online readability and scalability. Use familiar structural elements such as headings and bullet points. Write in short sentences and use short paragraphs.

Develop a desire in the buyer persona by creating an exciting and relevant user experience. It is also about displaying the content necessary to make a purchase decision, either through video, images or text. Other ways of evoking desire include associating your products and services with social causes, celebrity endorsement and online promotions (free trials, discounts, gifts, competitions and one-time offers). Once desire has been crafted, there should be a clear and logical call-to-action that can be found through directional cues that lead the eye towards it.

During the final action phase, the attention of the user has already been gained, but an obvious call-to-action should be visible, such as a large clickable button saying 'Buy Now', 'Donate Now', 'Sign Me Up' or 'Free Trial'.

Table 6.2 The AIDA model for content creation

Attention (or Awareness)	Create attention and awareness for your brand, your website and other channels and your products and services. You can measure the success of this stage through the number of visitors, number of impressions, number of pages visited and average duration of a website visit.
Interest	Spark interest in your products and services through engaging content that is created by you for the brand and also by its advocates. Success for this stage can be measured through the number of engagement interactions such as comments and re-shares, as well as how many new conversations are generated that are related to your brand's activity.
Desire	Generate desire to buy your products and services through positive third-party reviews and special offer campaigns. Measures of success include the total number of new mailing list subscribers, new followers on your owned and external channels, and repeat visitors to your website.
Action	Move your buyer persona to complete the desired activity on the website or through social media channels, which has the ultimate business objective of, for example, making a purchase or causing a change in behaviour. Success at this stage looks like the number of sales, the total value of new sales and number of 'earned' positive UGC reviews and comments.

These buttons usually have contrasting colours and clearly defined parameters with bold borders for emphasis. Some best practice advice for calls-to-action involves keeping the number of calls-to-action to a minimum and using active language. Any statement that includes words such as buy, call, register, subscribe or donate will use active language. Since a website user can potentially enter your website from any web page, having a call-to-action on every web page is a good way to measure the attractiveness and success of each page. Calls-to-action could be as simple as asking the user to follow you on a social media network or as complex as a full e-commerce interaction.

6.15 Content and website design

Visual content has become imperative for web designers. In a visual culture, 'seeing is believing' is more than a cliché. Humanity is generally drawn to visual information (pictures or videos) more efficiently than text, and this particularly applies to international audiences where written text may be inhibiting their understanding of your content. You can use this knowledge to create a website that wows your buyer persona (Case Study 6.4).

Case Study 6.4 Mikiya Kobayashi makes their breathtaking design obvious from the first click

Some brands have not forgotten that what should truly make you stand out from the crowd is the actual product or service that you are offering. Therefore, if you are a brand that truly believes in your offering, then it should be evident in every form of communication with your prospective customer. Japan's Mikiya Kobayashi has made this central to their online content.

From the moment you land on their home page, you are already immersed in the work of the design firm. The captivating images with breathtaking design fade into one another creating an effect where you can't wait to see more. Maintaining a minimal navigation architecture allows the brand to be in control of how the user interacts with their brand, so when all the home page asks you to do is scroll, you 'scroll'.

Figure 6.9 Mikiya Kobayashi logo

Henceforth, you are further captivated by more displays of past work in a mesmerizing portfolio exhibition. As you scroll over each image, you find out more about each project and are impressed by the recognizable brands that were collaborated with. This adds further credibility to the already remarkable designs, since you realize that industry leaders also share this same intrigue in their designs.

On offer for the website's navigation is a 'hamburger' menu bar, as to not infringe on the aesthetics of the rest of the website experience. Mikiya Kobayashi understands the design world well. Its main purpose is not to sell new designs, but it is to intrigue prospective clients of the quality of their design that could be imagined for future projects. This is why no real specifics (prices, availability etc.) are listed online, so the prospective customers will be incentivized to contact the brand directly through its stimulating imagery.

Finally, you can find more about the brand by clicking their profile. You will find the founder's profound story and his accomplishments, including being an adjunct professor and the myriad of awards that he has received. This simple, yet effective way of showcasing the brand's profile through the founder's story and timeline allows the customer to see the brand as more tangible and trustworthy.

Thusly, Mikiya Kobayashi is using their content and design to truly create a unique customer experience.

Source: www.mikiyakobayashi.com

Even though visuals by themselves are good for grabbing attention, pictures and video bring greater value when they are combined with text. The important points in the (concise) text should always be highlighted using bold and italics in combination with headings and subheadings to create visual hierarchies. If more information is required, bulleted or numbered lists and easy step-by-step outlines can be used.

Sparking the senses and enticing curiosity are key. But this must be supported by practical content that is valuable to the user, is conveyed in a professional manner and does not contain typos or grammatical errors. And, just as the principles apply for user experience, language must be easily understood by most readers (unless it is targeted to only a very specific buyer persona). If facts are stated, they should be backed up or referenced to ensure credibility and encourage trust in your brand. All of this content should be presented in a personal tone that adds a human touch to your brand.

6.16 Summary

An effective digital brand presence is the sum of all your digital activities. These include not only content and channels managed by your organisation (websites, blogs and social media channels) but also activities carried out by your key stakeholders when they are engaging with your brand. A robust presence provides a platform to communicate, engage and co-create value for your organisation and your buyer persona. Aligning what the brand and the organisation say and do, how they behave and what they know is vital in order to deliver a unique brand promise and experience.

A robust digital presence begins with an understanding of your own organisation, your buyer persona and the user experience you are setting out to provide. The open ecosystem of social media introduces the prosumer (a person who both consumes and produces media) and UGC. It is vital to listen and to (co-)create value, content and experiences that people would like to share and talk about. This interaction and engagement can be maximised with the use of paid and earned channels to drive traffic to your owned channels and content.

Your website can be optimised by creating an excellent user experience which enables an augmented experience for the user. Your user experience should pay special attention to usability and should incorporate processes of constant testing of the channel and its content to ensure that it is appealing to your buyer persona. Throughout the processes of building this design, your buyer persona is at its heart, from the creation of content all the way through to the testing stage and thereafter.

Highly usable websites not only increase traffic from consumers but also optimise the potential to rank higher on SERPs, bring higher social media channel engagement and, ultimately, increase positive brand awareness. The focus on usability must also extend to ease of use for accessing your website from mobile devices. Having a keyword-driven website information architecture is another vital component to satisfy your buyer persona's needs.

6.17 References

Albert, W. and Tullis, T. (2013) *Measuring the user experience: Collecting, analyzing, and presenting usability metrics.* Waltham, MA: Morgan Kaufmann.

Brunner, C. B., Ullrich, S. and De Oliveira, M. J. (2019) The most optimal way to deal with negative consumer review: Can positive brand and customer responses rebuild product purchase intentions? *Internet Research*, 29(1), 104–122.

Cavender, R. and Kincade, D. H. (2014) Management of a luxury brand: Dimensions and sub-variables from a case study of LVMH. *Journal of Fashion Marketing and Management*, 18(2), 231–248.

Cohen, J. (2019) *How to spot a fake review on Amazon.* www.pcmag.com/feature/369119/how-to-spot-a-fake-review-on-amazon

Cruz, Ana (2006) *Industrial brand strategy: Mapping a learning journey.* Unpublished PhD, dissertation, University of Manchester.

Garner, D. (2014) *A Content Management System (CMS) or static website: Which is right for you?* www.dmgbluegill.com/blog/content-management-system-cms-or-static-website-which-right-you

Hedegaard, S. and Simonsen, J. G. (2013) Extracting usability and user experience information from online user reviews. In *Proceedings of the SIGCHI conference on human factors in computing systems,* pp. 2089–2098. ACM.

Ho-Dac, N., Carson, S. and Moore, W. (2013) The effects of positive and negative online customer reviews: Do brand strength and category maturity matter? *Journal of Marketing,* 77(6), 37–53.

Iglesias, O., Markovic, S. and Rialp, J. (2019) How does sensory brand experience influence brand equity? Considering the roles of customer satisfaction, customer affective commitment, and employee empathy. *Journal of Business Research,* 96, 343–354.

Kevin, L. and Keller, S. (2019) *Strategic brand management: Building, measuring, and managing brand equity.* Harlow: Pearson.

Mahlke, S. and Thüring, M. (2007) Studying antecedents of emotional experiences in interactive contexts. In *Proceedings of the SIGCHI conference on human factors in computing systems,* pp. 915–918. ACM.

Nielsen (2013) *Under the influence: Consumer trust in advertising.* www.nielsen.com/us/en/insights/news/2013/under-the-influence-consumer-trust-in-advertising.html

Nielsen (2015) *Global trust in advertising report.* www.nielsen.com/wp-content/uploads/sites/3/2019/04/global-trust-in-advertising-report-sept-2015-1.pdf

Schmutz, S., Sonderegger, A. and Sauer, J. (2018) Effects of accessible website design on non-disabled users: Age and device as moderating factors. *Ergonomics,* 61(5), 697–709.

Verisign (2016) *Five reasons every small business needs a website.* blogs.verisign.com/blog/entry/five_reasons_every_small_business

WCAG (2019) *Web content accessibility guidelines (WCAG) overview.* www.w3.org/WAI/standards-guidelines/wcag/

WCAG 2.0 (2018) *Web Content Accessibility Guidelines.* www.w3.org/TR/WCAG20/

7 Search engine optimisation

Strategy implementation

Aleksej Heinze

7.0 Learning objectives

In this chapter you will learn how to:

- create a search engine optimisation (SEO) strategy and implement it;
- research and develop a strategic keyword plan for your buyer persona, including identification of channels to amplify the content;
- understand technical SEO and be able to diagnose potential issues; and
- implement the four pillars of SEO.

7.1 The importance of search engines

Search engines are popular because they bring a form of order to the Web. Information and resources are immediately available in ways that would be impossible without them. The increasing number of Internet-connected search devices such as personal assistants and smartphones make search for video and image content one of the major trends. Voice search, in particular, allows people to ask long and near-conversation-like search queries which a search engine tries to match to relevant search results.

To harness the power of search engines, your organisation needs to generate high-quality digital content that is relevant to your buyer persona. When this quality content is used with search engine marketing techniques, you can maximise your brand's visibility within search engine results pages (SERPs) and increase the chances of interaction with your desired buyer personas.

It is generally acknowledged that the vast majority of search engine users do not go beyond the first SERP. This means that if a web presence – a web page, social media profile, app or post – is not found in the top half of the first page of the SERP, your chances of attracting users to your brand's web presence are significantly reduced. SEO is the process of increasing the presence of an online profile in the SERPs for relevant keyword terms.

Knowing your buyer persona is an essential first step before substantial resources, in terms of your time or money, are allocated to a specific channel. SEO plays a pivotal role in digital marketing. The CMO Survey regularly identifies the role of SEO as a top investment priority and practitioners (Moorman, 2019). This is because where someone goes through the ZMOT of the customer journey they are likely to use a search engine and they are just a step away from the FMOT – ready to make a purchase.

For the Buyer Persona Spring, SEO is an essential part of your strategy. SEO most readily and clearly draws together content, channels and data. The importance of SEO within each of these building blocks is equally significant. Leading practice in SEO defines many of the parameters for determining the quality of your content, provides a linkage amongst all of your preferred channels and gives you the most accessible forms of data for your organisation to make informed decisions.

This chapter will offer insight into the key techniques and tactics that will help to get your organisation's website ranked in organic SERPs.

7.2 The business models of search engines

When you are working with search engines, you are communicating with automated computer databases. These databases are constantly collecting, storing, evaluating, sorting, ranking and sharing information. A basis for a search engine's business model is focused upon a fast and positive user experience – ensuring that relevant, high-quality content is returned quickly for any given search query. A successful search engine marketing (SEM) strategy is based on how well you know each specific search engine's standards and requirements. There is no single search engine that is dominant in every country in the world. Although Google is a major player in the majority of North America and Europe, Baidu dominates the Chinese market and Yandex is the leader in Russia. Understanding the search preferences of your buyer persona is the first step in developing your SEM strategy.

SEM traditionally includes a mix of pay-per-click (PPC) and organic (nonpaid) search campaigns. PPC is paid advertising, which has an immediate effect on the results at the top of a SERP; in contrast, organic search is a longer-term activity that is achieved through creation and optimisation of content. However, while there are many tactical differences between PPC and organic search, there are also direct strategic synergies that you should plan to recognise. For example, a well-optimised organic SEO web page is likely to have a positive effect on the quality score of a paid campaign if you are targeting similar search terms.

Working with a search engine algorithm

One of the key challenges with SEO is that brands wishing to rank well in SERPs are entirely at the mercy of each search engine's algorithm for identifying high-quality content for a particular keyword term. The initial formula of PageRank (Page et al., 1999), which essentially took the number and importance of incoming web links to a web page to rank its importance, has been substantially revised and the results of this are no longer publicly available.

Adding to this complexity, all search engines regularly update and refresh how high-quality content is both defined and recognised. Google alone implements around 500 changes to its internal search algorithm each year. Most of these changes are minor, with trivial impact, but a handful of these updates each year can require a change on most websites. Google has made this situation ever more complex and dynamic, with over 10 per cent of their updates now based on artificial intelligence and machine learning involving no human intervention.

Algorithms are secretive and highly complex mathematical formulas that provide the search engines with instructions on how to rank the importance and relevance of a page. Continual amendments are made to the algorithm, which are rolled out with the aim of improving the quality of both search results and the web pages that are discovered behind the results (further recommended reading are three specific Google algorithm updates – 'Hummingbird', which specifies how search queries are handled, 'Penguin', which relates to incoming links to a website, and 'Panda', relating to the quality of content). A number of updates do not require anything to be fixed by website users such as, for example, the Broad Core update of June 2019 (Search Engine Journal, 2019).

Organisations that ignore changes to Google's and other search engines' algorithms risk losing highly ranked positions on their targeted SERPs. In some cases, the search engine will apply penalties to pages that contravene what is currently regarded as leading practice. These penalties can be applied manually or automatically and will depend upon the severity of the violation to a search engine's algorithm. By understanding and adhering to current leading practice, your brand gives itself the best possible chance of achieving high rankings naturally for specific keyword phrases.

Sometimes organisations are not operating on an even playing field for SEO when it comes to how large brands fare compared to smaller organisations. For example, a search engine can easily remove a small organisation from its listings if they contravene any of its guidelines, and there is little that the small organisation can do except to rectify their 'error'. However, and in contrast, if a large multinational is found to be spamming, they are likely to receive a much lesser punishment. This reflects an economic reality in that the search engine needs the large organisations for the scale of their advertising revenues and the expectation that search engine users will find these brands through the search engine. This was evident in the case of BMW in 2006 (Malaga, 2008). The brand's website was found to be violating quality guidelines (by creating doorway pages). It was publicly removed from Google SERPs but then speedily reinstated once the problem was fixed. A number of other short-lived Google penalty examples have been imposed on brands such as JCPenney, Interflora, Rap Genius, Halifax, Thumbtack and Expedia. Controversy has rumbled on over time around search engines giving preferential treatment to large brands, but these brands equally had to respond by fixing their digital presence in order to regain strong SERP performance.

The ethics of SEO

Some SEO techniques have been described as an active attempt to manipulate or 'game' the search engine ranking algorithms. This approach is also commonly referred to as 'black hat SEO'. These are techniques that generally have only short-term impact and risk having a website penalised. This is when your organisation needs to take a clear ethical stance in defining your SEO strategy. The argument that is often used by black hat SEOs to justify their approach is that they are not breaking any laws. They say it is only search engines that set the rules regarding leading practice and, as they are solely commercial entities, they have no legal basis for their position.

This book solely advocates pursuing ethical 'white hat SEO' techniques. These are the techniques that adhere to the rules and boundaries of practice set out by search engines. These working practices are often found under webmaster guidelines and can be searched for with the phrase 'webmaster guidelines' in combination with the name of the search engine you are working with. The links should lead you to specific breakdowns of current recommended practice. For example, Google's resources are generally found at www.google.com/webmasters/. Once you are familiar with the additional advice from third-party resources such as Moz, Search Engine Watch and Search Engine Land you can develop your competitive advantage in SEO.

Ultimately, SEO is a balance between satisfying search engine quality guidelines and the expectations of audiences who use search engines. The challenge is to achieve this balance without removing the 'human' element from your brand. Whenever you are in doubt about your SEO decision, the user should be given priority. In Google's 'What we believe' section – 'Ten things we know to be true' – the emphasis is 'focus on the user and all else will follow' (www.google.com/about/philosophy.html).

7.3 How search engines work

In this section the focus is upon Google. The rationale is straightforward – it is currently the most dominant player in the world, with 80 per cent of the global search market share, and the second largest is Baidu with only 11 per cent (Netmarketshare, 2019). Where Google leads, other search engines usually follow. Although this is not to say that understanding how Google works will provide all the answers for other search engines.

In essence, a search engine's spider or a 'bot' finds web page links and then automatically makes a copy of the online content behind each link, analysing and assigning meaning to what has been found. The meaning that is assigned is based on the algorithmic variables, including the body text, the keywords used and their positions, links, synonyms and word proximity, semantic entities, as well as other variables. There are different types of Googlebots for web content: news, images, video, mobile content, AdSense and AdsBot (Search Console Help, 2019). Each bot gathers relevant variables, such as the links out of a page (these are noted for future crawling by the bot) and the content checksum

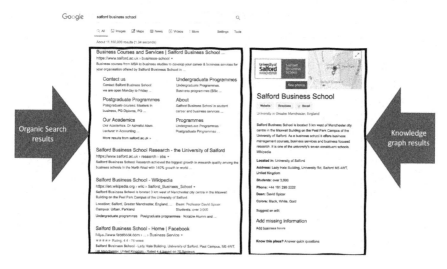

Figure 7.1 Screenshot of Google SERP for search term 'Salford Business School', including the knowledge graph on the right-hand side of the page

for the page, which is compared by the indexer (changes are compared at that point with previously stored pages). The frequency of change is also recorded and estimated to schedule future visits. Sorting also occurs at this point, like the creation of a large book index.

After a user types in their query, they are presented with a list of content that Google believes will satisfy the original intent of the query – these are the SERPs. Typically, the content that is returned in SERPs includes a mix of paid and organic results. Each result includes a link with a short title and a description, as well as optional add-ons such as thumbnail images, videos, site links and knowledge graph data. The knowledge graph is a short summary answer box, found underneath the search box (Figure 7.1), providing a direct and relevant summary response to the user's query without the need for further clicks through to the source page. For example, if you search in Google 'How old is Larry Page?', the knowledge graph gives you a direct answer. The knowledge graph uses a number of reference points, including structured data on source web pages, and can contain images, text descriptions, maps, social media profile links and other related content.

Structured data is an important method for providing additional information to help search engines understand web content and is discussed later in this chapter.

7.4 Creating an SEO strategy to engage your buyer persona

In order to reach your buyer persona, you need to systematically set out to plan and optimise your website and social media content. Your strategy should adopt the action learning cycle that is emphasised throughout this book in order to monitor, assess and respond to the success (or otherwise) of your campaigns and tactics.

A typical SEO strategy is based on five key steps:

1   Understand your buyer persona's keywords.
2   High-quality content development.
3   On-page optimisation.
4   Off-page optimisation.
5   Technical optimisation.

1   Understand your buyer persona's keyword research – this involves iden-
     tifying the main keywords that are essential to your brand, are likely to
     be search terms used by your buyer persona and echo the content that is
     or could be on your website. As your SEO strategy is a long-term com-
     mitment, these terms should be generic enough to be valuable to your
     organisation for years instead of focusing upon individual products or
     short-lived slang. Three key questions will assist the definition of your
     keywords:

     1   For each term, at what point is your buyer persona in their buyer journey?
     2   Why is your buyer persona asking this question at this point?
     3   What content is your buyer persona expecting as a result of their query?

     Generic intentions can be identified through the specific keywords being
     used in terms of their stage in the buyer journey and the scale and type of
     content that your buyer persona is expecting as a response (Table 7.1).
2   High quality content development – this involves developing or editing
     your content to reflect your keyword research for a specific service, prod-
     uct or brand. See Chapter 9 for more detail on the actual process of content
     development. Content starts with strategically identified and committed to
     subject areas that are driven by keyword research. All buyer persona infor-
     mation needs and touchpoints should be addressed by either your digital
     profiles or those of your partners to make sure that their ZMOT and the
     rest of the journey to purchase is satisfactory.
3   On-page optimisation – this includes using the words from your research
     as the basis for developing your website navigation and to shape the hier-
     archy of your web pages – your website architecture. Thinking about the
     logical sequence of website navigation for your buyer persona will assist the
     development of a relevant website architecture. This architecture should
     also reflect the logic of the changing intention of your buyer persona as
     they progress through their buyer journey.
4   Off-page optimisation – this includes the development of your content and
     channel that will generate relevant links back to your main 'owned' website.
     These actions include encouraging (and checking) incoming links generated
     from social media (e.g. using Google Analytics) and from other sites where peo-
     ple are talking about your brand, services and products (e.g. Talkwalker Alerts).

Table 7.1 What a keyword reveals about your buyer persona's intention

Type of intention	Intention	Example	Rationale	Content	Assumption (things your buyer persona knows)
Information	Exploratory investigation signalled by plural terms and phrases	'Digital cameras', 'Cameras'	The early research stage in the buyer journey	Your buyer persona is interested in detailed reviews, decision making guides and comparisons content to inform their decisions	At this stage your buyer persona does not know what they need to know
Navigation	Your buyer persona is seeking a particular website or content	'Panasonic', 'Sony', 'Canon'	Focused seeking behaviour partway through the buyer journey	Offer rich content product information on your website and social media channels	At this stage your buyer persona tends to know where they want to go
Transaction	Buyer persona wants to actively do something such as buy or download	'Panasonic Lumix DMC–LX100 12.8 MP Compact Digital'	Your buyer persona is looking for the best price for this particular type of camera	Persuade with your price and perhaps current delivery or bundling offers	The camera description itself

This work can be done through the amplification available at your owned social media channels. You also want to reach potential industry authorities, industry commentators and bloggers. These earned channels will then ideally engage with and link to your content if they find it relevant and valuable.

The monitoring of competitors is important in SEO, as all SERPs change regularly. In some market sectors these updates occur many times each day; in other sectors the changes may be much less frequent. Being aware of competitor activity and their relative ranking improvements or demotions for specific keywords allows you to anticipate their subsequent actions. A range of freely available tools makes monitoring of your competitors relatively straightforward. Google Alerts and Talkwalker Alerts can keep track of content changes – and public mentions of your competitors. More detailed SEO analysis is offered by tools such as SEMrush and SimilarWeb, which provide insight into your competitors' action and their visibility on SERPs, traffic overview and the keywords they use. Analysis of the backlink profiles often unveils their off-site SEO strategy by revealing patterns of outreach and site types – see tools such as Link Explorer. Likewise, understanding the content types that they are developing – their content 'hubs', for example – may well provide an opportunity to gain advantage by moving more rapidly. The Skyscraper SEO technique is based on the principle of identifying what content works for your competitors and developing similar content but better, therefore building an even greater presence and engagement with your buyer persona.

The quality of external links coming to your website is regarded as a key factor in off-page optimisation. Opportunities to build up your backlink profile and emulate that of your competitors should be explored at every opportunity.

Personalisation and geo-location are also increasingly coming into play in relation to your page ranking in SERPs. For example, when a person is logged into a Google product, their browser history will influence what is shown to them in the organic SERPs.

All of this insight aids your data use and will support your expanding knowledge of your own organisation as a digital business.

7.5 Strategic keyword research

Keyword research is pivotal for SEO. Keyword research helps you to focus your energies on generating content that is important to your buyer persona, in their own language, in ways that improve engagement.

Your tactical search engine keyword research informs the wider 'strategic' keywords that apply to your organisation as a whole. For example, a strategic keyword phrase for a florist in Chorley, UK, could be 'florist in Chorley', whereas a tactical phrase could be specific to a product or service that is offered for a short period of time, for example, 'Mother's Day roses'. While the specific flower in the phrase might change, the phrase continues to relate to the industry.

Search engines continuously calculate the relevance of the content produced by your organisation in relation to the phrases that users put into search engines. Because search engines base their business model on selling advertising space (see PPC in Chapter 10), they offer potential advertisers information about the keywords that users have entered into their search engines in the past. This information is used to predict the potential volume of individuals interested in that content. Keyword volume and trends data for search engines are accessible through built-in ad management platforms such as Google Ads.

The keyword research process

The overall process of generating keywords is influenced by a number of factors:

- Your marketing objectives.
- How many buyer personas are being targeted and optimised.
- Budgetary constraints.
- National or regional cultures.
- Language, including regional dialect differences.
- The search engine(s) being targeted.

Keyword research needs to be recognised as a combination of art and science; nonetheless, it can be addressed through a methodical three-stage process.

Stage 1 – keyword brainstorming

Start with an initial brainstorming session, usually in a meeting with your team and, if possible, representatives of your buyer persona. Keywords are inspired by customer needs, as well as your products and services. Additional insight can be gained from focus groups, surveys and social media analysis. Thesaurus lists and other similar sources will help you to find synonyms for words that you have already selected. For example, for someone interested in having their house rewired, they might search for 'house rewiring', 'property rewiring' or 'rewire my home'. Using a semantic keyword search that relies on the meaning of a word or an ontological approach is a good start. For example, list all terms related to a domain or an entity (site topic) – you can also use a range of other 'related' and 'extending' (stemming) terms to enhance topical relevance. For example, it is likely that 'house rewiring', 'property rewiring' and 'rewire my home' may also be semantically found when searching for 'home electricians' or 'house renovations'.

Stage 2 – keyword refinement

To increase the search volume of keywords in your 'target list' there are a number of online tools available that will suggest additional keywords for you.

These tools typically offer relevant data, such as the number of searches conducted each month in specific locations, as well as the term's popularity and competition (others targeting the same term), to help you make an informed decision.

For example, tools that require website access are:

Google Search Console	https://search.google.com/search-console
Google Analytics	https://analytics.google.com/analytics/

Keyword tools that do not require existing website access are:

AnswerThePublic	https://answerthepublic.com/
Baidu Index	https://index.baidu.com
Google Keyword Planner	https://ads.google.com/home/tools/keyword-planner/
Google Trends	https://trends.google.com/
SpyFu	www.spyfu.com/
SEMrush	www.semrush.com
Moz keyword explorer	https://moz.com/explorer
Keyword Tool IO	http://keywordtool.io/

Stage 3 – keyword prioritisation and selection

Now that you have a long list of potential keywords, you need to prioritise the value of your terms with consideration of your buyer persona's preferences, as well as the objectives of your activity. There are four aspects of keyword selection. They are, in order of priority (Figure 7.2):

1   Relevance
2   Specificity
3   Popularity
4   Competition

Selecting keywords benefits from systematic analysis applied to each of these priorities.

1   **Relevance to the business objectives and your buyer persona.** Use your judgement and understanding of the buyer persona's pain and trust points to define an initial set of keywords. You can use a ranking system, where you rank terms from 0 to 3, where '0' is irrelevant and '3' is highly relevant. Higher relevance is better.
2   **Specificity of the term.** In general, the longer the keyword phrase, the more specific it will be. If you are scoring your terms, give higher scores

Figure 7.2 Selecting keywords in order of action priority

Figure 7.3 Short tail vs long tail keywords

to longer phrases. For example, using the 0 to 3 system assign scores ranging from '0' for one-word-long keywords up to '3' for the longest-phrase keywords you have in your list.

There is a continuous trade-off between 'short tail' and 'long tail' terms (Figure 7.3), and this highlights the importance of understanding the user intent behind different types of keywords. In the case of a user completing a search using a single search term with high search volume, e.g. 'Salford', users are unlikely to know what they are looking for and may be at an early exploratory phase of their research. Users arriving at your website through these 'short tail' queries are more likely to quickly 'bounce off' if they do not find the exact information they need and will return to a search engine. Research has shown (Person, 2015) that individuals who are using long search phrases or 'long tail' keywords are more likely to convert into customers, as they are more likely to know exactly what they want from their search. Single-word terms generally indicate that the users are at the start of their buyer journey. The buyer journey is reflected in summary

Figure 7.4 Google Ads Keyword Planner tool search result for January 2019

through the evolution of the keywords being used, for example, from 'cameras' to 'second-hand cameras' to 'second-hand digital SLR cameras'. Therefore, the more specific the search term that enables a user to reach your website, the higher the likelihood that you will convert a visitor into a customer.

3   **Popularity of the term.** The average monthly search volume is a good indicator, but it can be significantly affected by seasonality. As a result, your research should consider the annual average search volume in order to even out the seasonality of a term.

For example, 'Valentine's Day flowers' in the UK has a high search volume in January (1–10K – see Figure 7.4) and February (10–100K – see Figure 7.5), but not much volume in other months. This means that the averages are a good comparator with other terms where seasonality is not as significant – for example, 'birthday flowers', which attracts an average monthly search volume of about 20,000 searches. It can take months to achieve good organic rankings for a competitive term. If a term is relevant and has high seasonal peaks, the highest seasonal peak should be chosen when considering it as a term with others. Therefore, in the case of Valentine's Day flowers, it is a good strategic term to develop some good content marketing activity which is release in advance – say in December or January to build up the visibility and the popularity of the relevant web pages.

If you are scoring your keywords using the 0 to 3 system, allocate '0' to those terms that have no search volume up to '3' for those terms with the highest search volume.

4   **Competition for the term.** Data regarding competition for individual searches is drawn from paid search results. As a result, it is a less useful

Figure 7.5 Google Ads Keyword Planner tool search result for February 2019

indicator of competition for organic SEO; nevertheless, it provides an indication of the competition. In particular, Google Ads provides a good indication of competition by assigning a value between 0 and 1. Other tools, including Moz and SEMrush, offer similar indications of competition through their keyword difficulty tools.

Your interpretation of these third-party competition scores enables you to apply your own scores. With this priority, the highest competition attracts the lowest score for the keyword phrase – '0'. The less difficult a keyword phrase, the higher your chances to rank for it – assign these terms '3'.

Having scored all keyword terms based on the four priority criteria, you now add your scores together and use the total of each term as the determinant for a keyword's inclusion. Terms with higher scores will indicate which terms should be chosen primarily for individual pages, while the lower-scored keywords can still be used but as secondary supporting terms.

Using keyword mapping to inform your information architecture

Once all your relevant keywords have been identified and graded, they are grouped into themes. These themes will inform and shape your website's information architecture. Themes are important for capturing the more sophisticated semantic value of the grouped keywords – in other words, themes offer clarity regarding the content that you are optimising. The themes are part of the logic expected by search engine users as well as the search engines themselves (Amerland, 2013). At this stage, you will grade your terms as being of primary or secondary importance for individual web pages. You should aim to have one primary and two or three secondary keywords for each page. Because of the

Figure 7.6 The hero, hub, help framework

semantic understanding of content generated by a search engine there is no need to include every single variation of your keyword on your website as long as the main themes are clear. Each of your pages should focus on a different primary keyword, otherwise your pages will be competing against each other in SERPs.

The content structure you employ on your web pages should systematically support your themes and keywords. For example, YouTube suggests the use of the 'hero, hub, help' framework. This approach ensures that the site is well struc-tured to accommodate your 'theme'.

- Hero content introduces your brand to your buyer persona as the solution to their problem.
- Hub content will address your buyer persona's needs before they are aware of your brand.
- Help content supports your buyer persona once they have bought your goods and services (Figure 7.6).

Hero content – aims at increasing brand awareness and attracting large audi-ences to your content. The result of this content is brand awareness and poten-tial for future navigational search results.

Hub content – is based on the main product and services and offers regular fresh perspectives of interest to your buyer persona. This content would tend to satisfy informational search queries.

Help content – is a must-have for your organisation, and it helps your buyer persona to resolve the transactional and navigational search questions they might have in relation to your brand, products or services.

Keyword-informed website information architecture

When designing and mapping keywords onto pages, one term could be primary on one web page and secondary on another; hence, a keyword map (which is usually laid out in a tabular format) that outlines your website information architecture should be developed. This map includes each web page and online profile against its relevant keyword terms.

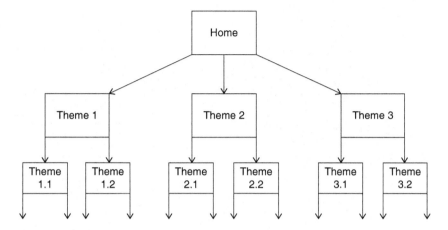

Figure 7.7 Thematically organised website structure

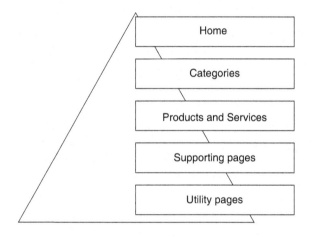

Figure 7.8 Traditional website architecture

Once all the pages have been identified, it is important that they are organised in a logical structure, which reveals semantically related themes and sub-themes. Figure 7.7 outlines a website's organisation by themes.

Traditional website structures (Figure 7.8) prioritised products and services at the second level and then used individual categories to break them into smaller product groupings. Supporting pages such as guides and instructions were then positioned at the next level down. At the bottom level of the structure were the terms and conditions and other information that is not often required.

To show the location of individual pages within its hierarchy, the use of breadcrumbs is advisable (Figure 7.9). Breadcrumbs are good ways to help

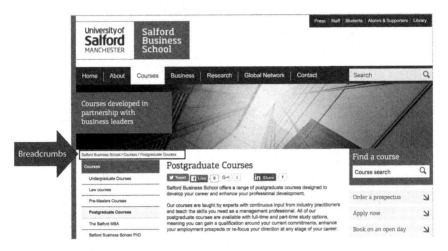

Figure 7.9 Navigational breadcrumbs

both the user and the search engine to understand where the page is located in relation to the structure of the overall information architecture and how to navigate towards and away from it.

7.6 Implementing your SEO strategy

Identifying the most relevant keyword terms allows you to develop a map for a website and strategic themes for your content, as well as enabling you to refine the focus for individual web pages and blog posts. But, the implementation of the actual optimisation process comprises four steps in what can be described as the four pillars of SEO.

The four pillars of SEO

The impact of SEO is at its greatest when your strategy brings together all four pillars of SEO. In fact, neglecting any one of the pillars of SEO can leave your website vulnerable to algorithm changes and could even have a negative impact on your long-term SEO performance. If the four SEO pillars are better optimised than your competition, your website has a higher chance of ranking above competitors in organic SERPs.

1 High-quality content

High-quality content was always important for web pages, but this is even more so since Google penalises websites with low-quality content in their ranking in SERPs. The key attributes of high-quality content have been outlined by Google's Amit Singhal (Singhal, 2011):

- The content must be relevant to your buyer persona.
- The content is unique – it is not duplicated across the rest of the site or copied from somewhere else.
- It is media-rich (including images and video), with carefully considered links to other relevant pages within your site.
- It includes a clear call-to-action (e.g. email signup, download, subscribe, call a number, comment or share).
- Do not 'over-optimise' to the point of incomprehensibility, and avoid the blatant use of unnatural keyword stuffing.
- Write to engage the user, not just to the benefit of search engines.

Having content that is relevant to the buyer persona and assists them on their buyer journey is arguably the most important factor when it comes to search engine ranking. This is simply because search engines want their users to be satisfied with the SERP they see as a consequence of their queries. For content to be appealing to the buyer persona, it has to be targeted to a specific keyword phrase, as well as being relevant, original, detailed and in accessible formats. Once an individual is engaged with your content – when they arrive via organic search to a web page, video or image – the traditional model of attention, interest, desire and action (AIDA) applies. This model is explored in more detail in Chapter 6 in relation to content marketing.

2 On-page optimisation

The second pillar of SEO is on-page optimisation. Once your keyword research is conducted and relevant content topics have been identified to formulate the overall website architecture, a detailed page structure can be developed. This structure is implemented by integrating the keywords in HTML (hypertext markup language) tags on your web pages. These tags are mainly based in the header part of the web page and include title and description tags as well as tags in the body section of a web page including headings, paragraphs, links and images. Your keywords should appear within page names (URLs), page titles, page descriptions and your top- and second-level headings (also known as H1 and H2 tags). Figure 7.10 compares the code view of a page and the effect of the title tag on what is displayed in a web browser window. In this case, the keyword targeted is 'Salford Business School'.

One of the main reasons the meta tags for title and description as well as web page URLs are specified at this level is that this information is often used by search engines to describe the page on SERPs.

However, this information is sometimes ignored, as illustrated in Figure 7.11 where Google changes the URL from

www.salford.ac.uk/business-school
to
the University of Salford > Business School

Figure 7.10 Title tag code and its visual impact

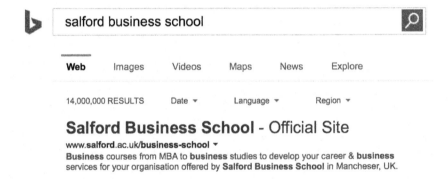

Figure 7.11 Google SERP with tags, titles and URL replacement

Bing, in contrast (Figure 7.12), uses the URL in combination with page description tag and the page title tag. When Google is unable to fit in the full description and title, it abbreviates the information with an ellipsis (. . .). This is similar to Bing's SERP, which is able to fit in the complete description although it also needs to abbreviate the title.

The example of Figure 7.12 and the abbreviated description reveal why titles, descriptions and URLs should not exceed the recommended maximum lengths. Search engines often change the maximum length, but it is also influenced by variables such as the device and screen size, i.e. whether the search is done on a mobile phone, tablet or desktop computer, and the operating system used. The space used in SERPs is calculated in pixels – which means that including a lot of wide characters such as 'm' and 'w' as well as highlighting the keyword by the search engines could push the results off the page. All of these limitations reinforce the need to keep your titles and

Figure 7.12 Bing SERP for 'Salford Business School' search termIn addition, your information architecture should avoid duplication of keywords in your description or
title, as this will confuse visitors and potentially be penalised by search engines.
A number of content management systems (CMSs) offer different formats for
your URL structure. Some contain numbers – effectively counting the content
on your site – while others are formatted in text. The textually formatted URL
is preferred, since it makes use of natural language and helps the site visitor and
the search engine to understand what your content is about.

Table 7.2 Description and title tag length recommendations

HTML tag	*Approximate length*
Meta title tag	60 characters
Meta description tag	160 characters

descriptions tags below the maximum length (see Table 7.2). But, be conscious of the fact that even these recommended variables change. You can
keep up to date with the latest on-page recommendations through SEO tools
such as https://moz.com.

In some earlier advice and texts about on-page optimisation, the keywords
meta tag is recommended. However, this tag now has no influence on SERPs,
and visual examination of this tag can be used by your competitors on the
terms that you have used to optimise your web page. As a result, it is not advisable to use this as part of your on-page optimisation.

TEXT OPTIMISATION

Text refers to the main visible content of your website. It is a cliché that 'content is king' for organic SEO, but it still remains true for search engines as
well as readers. Users are people who scan content. It is important to break up
pages with headings, images and bullet points. The use of bold text and quotes
can also draw attention to the key messages, guiding both readers and search
engines.

For search engines, one of the simplest routes to evaluating content is the quality and the semantic relevance of the text. Long-form content – for example, an article which explores an issue in detail – tends to be preferred by search engines to content that is shallow and has fewer than 600 words. A number of studies have indicated that web pages with over 2,000 words tend to rank better compared to those that have fewer than 500 (Lincoln, 2015). However, it is wholly dependent upon the type of content – for example, blog posts are better if they are longer, whereas product descriptions may not need to be as long. However, including user-generated content (UGC) in the form of, for example, reviews on product pages increases the depth of the text and value to the reader as well as the semantic keyword value. This is where the craft of being able to structure content in an accessible way – using headings, bullet points, images and video – is important to benefit those who want to take a quick look and get the key facts, as well as those who want a more detailed explanation that ultimately increases their trust in your brand.

The key message about good-quality content is that it should not be about selling to people – it should focus on helping your buyer persona to advance their buyer journey towards a purchase decision. A good example of how in-depth descriptive content is structured for e-commerce sales is found in an Amazon product description page. The page contains the main information in bullet points and relatively short descriptions – information that is available through every other online retailer. However, Amazon also includes user-generated reviews – information that is unique and often goes into considerable detail. This approach provides Amazon with almost limitless and free in-depth content, which is also appreciated by potential purchasers. The key lesson from Amazon is that content does not always need to be written by the organisation. If your web page allows for comments in combination with your original article, a lively discussion adds value for the reader and is a good strategy for SEO content development.

LOCAL SEO

If your organisation has a physical premises, you can also benefit from location-based optimisation. With the increasingly common use of mobile phones as a substitute for other devices, location-based information is becoming equally important. Effectively your website must be mobile-friendly. A reflection of the importance of mobile is Google's release of a mobile-friendly test tool which can guide your appropriate development (search.google.com/test/mobile-friendly).

As a local organisation, you need to claim your free Google My Business listing and populate it with your own content, which is ideally based upon keyword research around your products and services. The Google My Business listing also allows you to invite your customers to review your organisation.

With a physical location, you should also ensure that your name, address and phone number (NAP) are consistently presented on your website – a common approach is to include this in the website template which then appears in either the footer or the header of all your web pages. NAP information can also be presented using schema.org markup, which is described in the technical section later in this chapter.

IMAGES OPTIMISATION

Images should also be an aspect of your SEO strategy. Images play a major role in the description of product and services where individuals want to 'see the product or service in use'. Not only are images offering useful content to your buyer persona, they also offer additional content for image-specific search engines (Figure 7.13). As with text-based SERP, a brand should protect its image results by publishing its own images that present positive reflections of your brand. When selecting images for a web page, they should be relevant to the page and if they are abstract, they should offer some connection rather than simply being used for decoration.

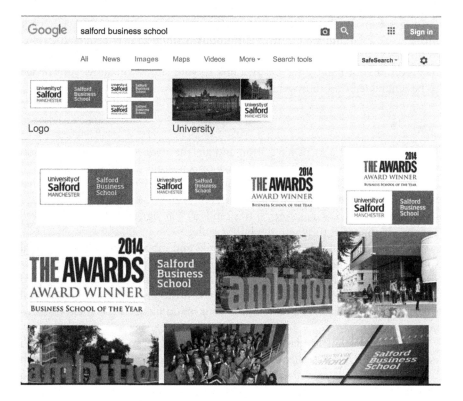

Figure 7.13 Salford Business School image search results

Image optimisation offers three places for the primary keyword to be integrated:

1   The file name. Most images taken with a digital camera tend to be a number by default, e.g. dmc123.jpg. To improve image optimisation, files can be easily renamed to include the primary keyword, e.g. oak-tree.jpg. In this case, oak tree is clearly visible to the search engine and also the user.
2   The alternative text for the image – or the 'alt' tag attribute. This tag is important for visually impaired users (including search engine bots) – this alternative text attribute offers a text description of the image, and if images are disabled, the alternative text is displayed instead.
3   Caption or description of the image – this information is usually easy to edit in CMSs such as WordPress. This text appears next to the image and allows the search engine to associate the meaning of the image with the accompanying text.

The process of integrating images on a web page will depend to some extent on your CMS. It is always good to have a minimum set of requirements for the images that you use, which should include descriptive file names that contain relevant keywords and setting the alternative text.

Images can also be a great source of 'virality' for content. Allowing your image to be used under a Creative Commons attribution licence (creativecommons.org/licenses/) increases the likelihood of sharing and re-use, with the inclusion of your name and, ideally, a link to your site if you allow your image to be embedded on other websites.

LINKS

Links are a crucial part of navigation and are the main source of information for Google, as they determine which page on a website is important and which is not. The text used for navigation should ideally mirror the keywords that have been identified for a particular page. For example, a page about 'oak trees' should be linked to as '<u>oak trees</u>' – this sends a clear signal to the reader as well as a search engine as to where the link is going.

There is a difference between internal links and inbound links from external sources. Internal links can be (almost) conversational and as keyword-rich as you want, external links not so much. Try to avoid using exact-match keyword links, as this can look spammy, especially when the links come from external pages to your website – if in doubt, use your brand name as the anchor text to your site.

Each external link is classed as an endorsement of your page by a search engine's bot. Therefore, when linking to external pages which you do not wish to endorse, use rel='nofollow' so that the search engine is instructed not to count this link as an endorsement of the page.

Links in images are also followed by search engine bots, and the 'alt' attribute is interpreted as the anchor text. However, search engines are not always consistent in following links that are in images. If you must link to a page through an image, always provide an alternative navigation path using a text link.

Positioning a page's primary keyword links higher in the page content and inside dense text paragraphs is also likely to achieve better results than simple lists of links or site links positioned at the bottom of every web page.

3   Off-page optimisation

Links to a web page and the text used in this link – anchor text – are an important off-page optimization factor. The influence of anchor text and higher SERP ranking was identified by the SEO industry and, as a consequence, a number of organisations have over-optimised their websites using spammy link-building techniques. The Penguin update (initially announced in 2012), as well as other Google algorithm updates, have targeted poor link-building practices and now penalise websites with over-optimised anchor text linking to the site. High-profile examples of the application of these penalties include JCPenney and Interflora.

This straightforward example highlights the need for a balanced SEO strategy and sound links ecosystem that connect to your most significant pages. Your off-page optimisation relies upon tactics that build up incoming links to your web pages.

A number of tools allow for competitor benchmarking of incoming links (e.g. www.semrush.com, www.opensiteexplorer.org or www.similarweb.com).

These tools compare the number of inward links a website has in comparison to your competitors and suggests the approximate competitive advantage. The assumption made regarding this comparison is that if one website receives more quality external links than its competitors, it is then more likely to be better ranked in SERPs.

If you are targeting local visitors, it is helpful to get local directories to list the NAP information in the same format that it is listed on your own other profiles. The links that you build from local relevant websites will also have an overall positive impact on your SERP visibility.

Universal search results that include the specialist search results from News, Image Search, Videos and Local/Maps are also included on a number of SERPs. Previous studies confirm that seeing a thumbnail or a map on a SERP attracts attention. Your brand can increase its visibility by targeting each of these options.

Different rules apply to these different specialist search engines. For example, for video optimisation on YouTube, the title and description are important in the same way that a web page would be optimised, but in this case the tags and keyword should be used extensively. The official YouTube Creator Playbook and www.tubebuddy.com offer further guidance on creating engaging and optimised video content. From an SEO perspective, all your 'owned' channels should link to your brand's home web page. Individual elements of video and audio content should also have links to the relevant web pages on your site.

4 *Technical optimisation*

Technical SEO is the methodical optimisation of on-page technical elements to improve the findability and crawlability of your content by search engines. Having a technically sound site can also improve the overall customer journey by improving elements such as site speed. Since 2019 Google has prioritised the indexing of the mobile version of a website. This means that all new websites are evaluated on their accessibility and speed on mobile devices (Mueller, 2019). Chapter 11, on mobile marketing, explores the mobile SEO considerations but in short, digital presences that allow web pages to be viewed and interacted with by a user on a mobile device are better placed to rank well on SERPS compared to those that offer poor mobile user experience.

On-page and off-page optimisation factors all rely on computers being able to read and understand your content. Technical optimisation brings the additional benefit that it can improve the impact of your other optimisations. There are many technical elements that can be optimised and each brings benefits.

XML SITEMAP

Giving a search engine the location of all your web pages requires indexing. The need for indexing a website has resulted in a common sitemap standard. The sitemap.xml standard provides a concise format that allows a website owner to list a page link, when it was modified, how important it is from 0 (not important) to 1 (very important) and how often it is updated.

The information for a site index is gathered automatically by most CMSs. The URLs included in a sitemap.xml are added to Googlebot's crawler queue and then indexed and made findable by Google.

The Google Search Console (www.google.com/webmasters/tools/) allows website owners to alert Google about a site when a sitemap link is submitted. Once submitted and crawled, any resulting errors will assist you in resolving SEO difficulties. Your sitemap.xml must continue to be accurate in order to have a positive impact on your SEO strategy.

Larger websites maintain index sitemaps to enable the distributed management and administration of different sitemaps. This approach helps search engines, as well as website managers, to manage their energies in maintaining the accuracy of individual sitemaps.

ROBOTS.TXT

Google has the benefit of being linked and reading your sitemap directly, but other search engines require more information. A long-standing common standard is used to allow all website owners to communicate with the many

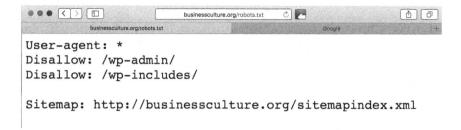

```
User-agent: *
Disallow: /wp-admin/
Disallow: /wp-includes/

Sitemap: http://businessculture.org/sitemapindex.xml
```

Figure 7.14 Robots.txt example from the www.businessculture.org website

different search engine bots that might visit the site. As part of the standard, the file is consistently called robots.txt.

Robots.txt is examined by a visiting search engine's bot. The consistent format and structure of this file mean that it must be located in the root (top level) of your website – in other words, as part of the standard, robots.txt will always be found at www.your-domain-name.com/robots.txt. The businessculture.org website, for example, has its robots.txt file located at http://businessculture.org/robots.txt (Figure 7.14).

Robots.txt files are openly accessible and visible to any user, as well as web robots. This means that you can look at the robots.txt file of any of your competitors. In the robots.txt file you can specify which search engine bots you want to communicate with and tell them which pages and folders of your website they should not be visiting, as well as the location of your sitemap. Examples of web pages that are often disallowed include any password-protected sections of your website as well as sections that might be used for website development or experimentation. You can keep up to date with the latest guidelines offered by each of the search engines you are optimising for by searching, for example, for 'sitemaps supported by Google'. You will be able to use the latest standards for the inclusion of sitemaps for video, images and mobile.

Directing a search engine bot not to crawl a web page using the robots.txt file is not as effective as using a password-protected page. If a web page has been visited by a search engine bot and that bot did not access your robots.txt first, it may be ignoring the robots.txt standard. Use the 'robots.txt tester' in the Google Search Console to check your robots.txt file against what is expected by Google (and, by implication, most other search engines).

STRUCTURED DATA

If your website offers, or will be offering, a common type of information concerning, for example, events, reviews, places or persons, there are recognisable methods of sharing this information and making it available to others through a search engine. A range of advanced markup structures – called schemas – have

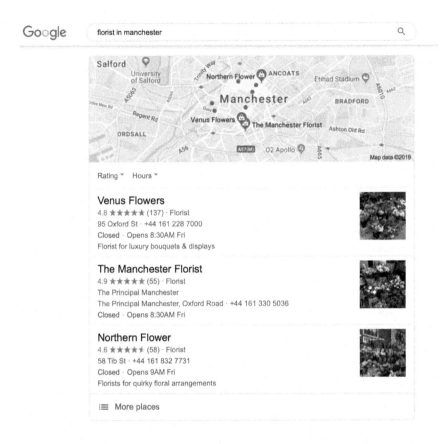

Figure 7.15 'Florist in Manchester' SERP, with star ratings and NAP information

been defined for common types of information that assist in making your website stand out from competitors in the SERPs.

There are a number of schema types, but the most popular are publicly available and documented at schema.org. These schemas offer a range of options to make your website content as accessible as possible to a search engine as well as including additional data in SERPs to differentiate your organisation from your competitors, for example, star ratings and NAP information that is particularly important for local SEO (Figure 7.15).

MOVING PAGES

Inevitably over time your website structure will change and individual web pages will change their URL. This may be the result of a new CMS or a redesign. The 301 redirect method allows website owners to define the old and new names of a web page and ensures that all of the accumulated page history and positive ranking is moved too. With 301 redirect, you map all the old URL addresses with the matching new addresses.

If you just remove a web page from its current URL it will produce 404 'Page Not Found' errors. Inevitably any change in information architecture will produce some of these errors. Instead of greeting users and search engine bots with the blank web page that is generated by your website hosting provider or CMS, you can create a custom 404 'Page Not Found' page.

Your custom 404 page can direct visitors back to your home page. This will cover the situation to some extent. Adding a link from your custom 404 page to the human readable version of your sitemap is another alternative that might assist the visitor in finding the right page.

A number of automatic server response codes can assist you in diagnosing reasons for a page not being correctly indexed. A record of the codes that your users received can be retrieved from your web server's logs. Your goal is to maximise the number of 200 responses and reduce the number of failures your visitors are experiencing.

503 – The web server is not available since it is being worked on at the moment
404 – Page Not Found
407 – Proxy Authentication Required
410 – Page is gone and Google should remove it from its index
412 – Precondition Failed
301 – URL has been permanently redirected to another URL
302 – URL has been temporarily redirected to another URL
200 – OK

More codes are defined at www.w3.org/Protocols/rfc2616/rfc2616-sec10. html. As you become more conscious of the impact of technical optimisation you will also benefit from learning the meaning of individual HTML tags (the markup language that builds web pages).

7.7 Benchmarking SEO activities

There are a number of key performance indicators (KPIs) that enable you to evaluate your strategy against the four pillars of SEO (Table 7.3).

Some of these current tools are worth closer investigation, as they will positively support your SEO benchmarking efforts.

Found SEO tool – www.found.co.uk/seo-tool/ – is a free technical SEO audit tool that offers a prioritised 'traffic light' system of the required changes to your site. A more comprehensive, but paid-for, technical SEO auditing tool is DeepCrawl (www.deepcrawl.com). DeepCrawl will crawl a site before it has launched and will recognise thin content, redirects and many other technical aspects.

Table 7.3 KPIs for SEO

SEO pillar	Examples of KPIs	Example tools
Content	Number of comments Time spent on page Completion of call-to-action Traffic generated Keyword visibility in SERPs	Google Analytics Google Search Console Tool/ Webmaster Tools SEMrush Moz
On-page	Reduction of errors such as duplicate titles, descriptions and headings	Screaming Frog Yoast's WordPress SEO plugin
Off-page	Number and quality of links to a page Number of shares to a page	Link Explorer – Moz

Technical	Reduction of technical errors such as w3c
	  validator approval and website speed
	  approval
		Found SEO Tools
		DeepCrawl
		Google Search Console

Search Console – e.g. https://search.google.com/search-console/about – Most search engines have their own form of 'Webmaster Tools' which allow a website owner to link their website directly to the database of a search engine. It offers a technical view of your website, as it is indexed by a search engine. Any technical indexing issues will be highlighted as well as noting the number of times a web page has been shown in search results and in what position.

Google Analytics – www.google.co.uk/analytics/ – This free analytical platform shows who the audience of your website is, how they arrived at your site and how they engaged with your web pages.

Screaming Frog – www.screamingfrog.co.uk/seo-spider/ – This tool requires download and installation on your computer. It crawls your website as a search engine bot would do and lets you know which pages are internally linked and which are 'indexable' by search engines.

SEMrush – www.semrush.com – This is a full suite of tools for online marketing covering SEO and PPC as well as social media presence and online video advertising.

Moz – https://moz.com – This is a set of tools for SEO analysis. It audits for on-page, off-page and technical issues. The tool is supported by a vibrant community of SEO professionals you can connect with and collaboratively troubleshoot problems.

7.8 Summary

You should now be aware of the fundamental concepts concerning organic SEO. Key SEO concepts include the creative aspects of offering relevant content, crafting and refining your keyword selection for each web page, as well as more technical concepts such as the use of primary keywords in the header of the page, indexing your site and considering what happens when something goes wrong for your visitor.

SEO is continuously changing and requires constant monitoring and evaluation. The strategic commitment and expectation of results vary by industry, but these can take from a minimum of 3 months up to several years, dependent on the resources and the scale of the task at hand. To succeed with your own SEO you need to stay connected to the SEO community and keep up to date with the latest industry trends and tools to ensure that when your buyer persona uses a search engine, it is your organisation that they find.

7.9 References

Amerland, D. (2013) *Google semantic search: Search Engine Optimization (SEO) techniques that get your company more traffic, increase brand impact, and amplify your online presence.* Indianapolis, IN: Que Publishing.

Lincoln, J. E. (2015) *The SEO and user science behind long-form content.* searchengineland.com/seo-user-science-behind-long-form-content-230721

Malaga, R. A. (2008) Worst practices in search engine optimization. *Communications of the ACM*, 51(12), 147–150.

Moorman, S. (2019) *The CMO survey, highlights and insights report,* August 2019. cmosurvey.org/results/august-2019/

Mueller, J. (2019) *Mobile-first indexing by default for new domains.* webmasters.googleblog.com/2019/05/mobile-first-indexing-by-default-for.html

Netmarketshare (2019) *Desktop, mobile and tablet search engine market share.* netmarketshare.com

Page, L., Brin, Motwani, R. and Winograd, T. (1999) *The pagerank citation ranking: Bringing order to the web, technical report.* Stanford InfoLab. http://ilpubs.stanford.edu:8090/422.

Person, S. (2015) *Off with Your head terms: Leveraging long-tail opportunity with content.* moz.com/blog/long-tail-content

Search Console Help (2019) *Google crawlers: See which robots google uses to crawl the web.* support.google.com/webmasters/answer/1061943?hl=en

Search Engine Journal (2019) *History of Google algorithm updates.* www.searchenginejournal.com/google-algorithm-history/

Singhal, A. (2011) *More guidance on building high-quality sites.* googlewebmastercentral.blogspot.co.uk/2011/05/more-guidance-on-building-high-quality.html

8   Social media

Alex Fenton, Mostafa Mohamad and Ashley Jones

8.0 Learning outcomes

In this chapter you will learn how to:

- understand the dynamics of social media-based communities and their composition and behaviours;
- conduct a social media audit including competitor analysis;
- recognise the importance of a blog as a centre of digital presence development;
- use amplification strategies to develop brand presence;
- explore the concept of social capital and its relationship to brand engagement activities; and
- develop tactics for measuring the quality and quantity of social media-based engagements.

8.1 The importance of social media

Social media has fundamentally changed the way we communicate. Organisations are recognising this trend and increasingly telling their story through social channels to connect with audiences.

Social media channels connect people and enable them to communicate amongst themselves and with your organisation. In distinction, the term 'social media platform' emphasises technological infrastructure, such as a website and/ or the applications which facilitate interaction.

The Conversation Prism developed by Brian Solis and JESS3 (see conversationprism.com) highlights the range of social media channels that are currently available. These platforms offer a range of options for engagement with your buyer persona, but you do not need to use all of them. You can filter out the irrelevant and marginal channels by understanding the diversity of options and identifying those that best connect with your buyer persona. Once you have identified the channels preferred by your buyer persona, you can evaluate whether there is an opportunity for opening another avenue of conversation. The decision to engage on a channel is an aspect of your Buyer Persona Spring (see the introductory chapter), and with this decision you are shaping your overall digital marketing strategic direction.

The Conversation Prism emphasises the strategic use of social media beyond marketing functions to include sales, customer service and operations. In this chapter, for the purpose of simplification, we will differentiate between social networks that are primarily for business-to-business (B2B) or business-to-consumer (B2C) interactions. In reality, most platforms can equally play a role in both B2B and B2C settings.

8.2 Social media strategies

Social media interaction broadly falls into four main functions – marketing, sales, operations and customer service (Figure 8.1).

When you open a social media channel of communication, you should be conscious of the different applications and techniques expected for each function and the results through key performance indicators (KPIs) for measuring their success (Table 8.1).

| Marketing | Sales | Operations | Customer Service |

Figure 8.1 Main functions for social media use

Table 8.1 Main strategies for social media use in organisations

Marketing

Application	Techniques	KPIs
Use conversation to understand your buyer persona's needs	Survey your buyer persona about their interests	Improved buyer persona understanding, their pain points and trust points
Gather feedback about your brands, products and services	Use competitions to encourage co-creation	Up-to-date contacts
Offer high-quality content about your offering	Amplify and encourage positive feedback	Positive brand mentions
Encourage positive reviews and learn from negative experiences	Identify and support charitable causes that are important to your buyer persona	Engagement numbers
Social capital acquired

(*Continued*)

Table 8.1 (Continued)

Sales

Application	Techniques	KPIs
Identify influencers and engage them in mutually beneficial ways Involve your influencers in interactions and co-creation as part of your extended 'sales' team	Brand ambassador programmes for endorsing your products and services, including exclusive information, offers and benefits Affiliate marketing agreements giving direct recognition for individual sales	Sales numbers Number of brand ambassadors Number of affiliates Social capital acquired

Customer service

Application	Techniques	KPIs
Customers log their support questions online so that they can be resolved publicly Enable customers to help one another and solve problems related to your products and services on your platforms	Develop support-focused forums on your website or owned social media channels which give the option to moderate Create support-dedicated accounts on networks such as Twitter Reward community participation and support with intrinsic motivators	Number of support issues resolved online Volume of publicly available and indexed support topics Number of participants in online support interactions Decreased volumes of support phone calls, emails and other private interactions Social capital acquired

Operations

Application	Techniques	KPIs
Internally focused interactions that act as knowledge management tools Help each other find better ways of doing their job Platforms for sharing internal communications	Use private social networks for internal interactions that support your organisation Enable public interactions to show a human side of your organisation	Percentage of organisation participating in maintaining organisational knowledge Volume and accuracy of internally available documents preserving organisational knowledge Decreased volume of email and attachments

Case Study 8.1 Public Desire

A number of organisations offer good examples of the four functions being enabled through social media interaction. In marketing and sales, Public Desire (Figure 8.2) was initially built its brand using social media channels in 2014. The buyer persona base (16- to 25-year-old females) spent large amounts of time on Instagram and were interested in fashion, music and food. Public Desire then created relevant content including images, mixing products and inspiration to appeal to their customers' interests and drive extremely high rates of engagement. The social following grew from a zero base to 100,000 followers in less than 6 months. This interaction is translated into new visitors to the Public Desire website and ultimately e-commerce sales.

The reasons for engaging with a brand such as Public Desire on social media can be grouped broadly into intrinsic and extrinsic motivation factors. Extrinsic motivation refers to rewards that originate externally to an individual – social media–related examples of this include competition prizes, money, praise and acknowledgements. Intrinsic rewards originate inside an individual – social media–related examples include mastery of a subject, love, curiosity, belonging, learning and autonomy.

While a brand can develop its social media presence using competitions, the motivators being applied should be a balance between extrinsic and intrinsic. Extrinsic competition rewards, in particular those that have material benefit, should not be used too frequently, as there is a tendency to attract people who have only a superficial connection to a brand (Heinze et al., 2013).

To develop a sustainable online community such as Public Desire, the key emphasis should be placed on the intrinsic motivating factors such as pride in belonging to a brand, curiosity and learning. Public Desire crowdsourced an understanding of what their customers like by offering them the opportunity to share their preferences of shoes. These stated preferences are then translated into products, which the same customers can purchase. The motivation for the followers here is both intrinsic – being able to buy and wear a pair of shoes that they like – as well as extrinsic – being acknowledged by the organisation for the shoes that are designed around their own preference. A key mechanism for fostering intrinsic motivation in your brand is to offer high-quality information that resonates with your audience (Poor Rezaei and Heinze, 2014). The importance of high-quality content for social media connects with

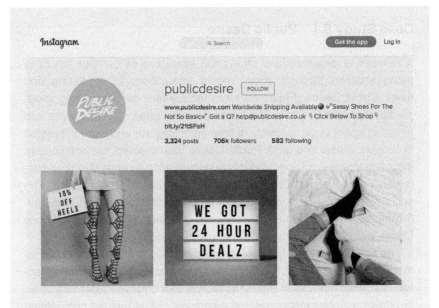

Figure 8.2 Instagram account for Public Desire

the SEO (Chapter 7) and content marketing (Chapter 9) chapters. In the case of Public Desire, this high-quality content is represented by reporting the latest news in shoe fashion.

Source: www.publicdesire.com

8.3 Social capital and social media

In Table 8.1, one of the KPIs that is used for measuring success in social media engagement is social capital. There are different types of capital. Physical capital refers to objects such as machines, buildings and computers. Human capital refers to labour, creativity and the knowledge of people. Social media, in contrast, is primarily concerned with brand building, with a heavy focus on communities and content. This is the basis of social capital and, if done well, results in drivers of engagement such as followers, views and likes, which can lead to revenue, as demonstrated in the case of Public Desire.

Social capital is the value of the relationships built through your social networks, the connections between people and the levels of trust that exist for your brands. As discussed in Chapter 5, social capital is one of the reasons that digital campaign planning does not always have direct costs associated with it, since social capital is difficult to quantify in financial terms. Social capital in the form of social connections and embedded trust is crucial to the functioning of social media. Social capital is therefore the lifeblood of social media channels, and understanding how this form of capital works is critical to the effective use of social media in digital marketing. It is notable that social capital can be built up with the buyer persona through appropriate social media content and interactions to build relationships with the brand.

There are three different types of social capital (Cofré-Bravo et al., 2019): bonding, bridging and linking. With a social media focus, these three types of social capital can be defined as:

- Bonding social capital includes the closest social connections. These connections are found between you and family members, friends, work colleagues, your employees (if you have any) and perhaps similar types of people from similar backgrounds, locations or those with shared interests. Loyal and happy customers who are also your brand advocates could also be considered part of this group and are the core informants in shaping your buyer persona.
- Bridging social capital includes connections with people from across different groups. These may be acquaintances, friends of friends or secondary connections. An occasional associate, client or customer of your organisation would be part of this category.
- Linking social capital is the broadest and weakest of connections. This type of social capital reaches out to people across the globe. Many of these people will be unfamiliar to your buyer persona and are less likely to benefit directly from your products and services. However, the aim of engaging with these connections is to find those who would be familiar to your buyer persona and an opportunity for your organisation to create stronger bonds with them. This type of social capital also provides the pool from which recommendations and referrals can develop.

Each of these types of social capital plays a different role in campaigns. If you are prospecting for your buyer persona, it is wise to reach out as far as possible between groups and use the power of networks to increase your social brand value. Having thousands or millions of people talking about your brand globally can help your brand awareness KPIs; however, it may not help you to reach your conversion KPIs if you do not successfully connect with your buyer persona.

You should not ignore the value of linking social capital. There is potential power in weak ties amongst a larger volume of people (Evans et al., 2019). In social media terms, linking social capital provides you with those followers who do not engage, or who may be your buyer persona but are not yet aware of your presence. An overall goal for your marketing strategy is to use the combination of content, channels and data to make those with the weakest social capital connections become more strongly connected with you and your organisation.

8.4 Online communities

Building on the concept of social capital, there are other ways to consider online communities. The 1 per cent rule of Internet culture divides online users into three categories: 1 per cent creators, 9 per cent contributors and 90 per cent lurkers (Figure 8.3).

Observation of this distribution comes from naturally occurring online communities.

- **Creators** – these are approximately 1 per cent of an online community. This 1 per cent consists of the people that visit social media regularly and actively create content (Fueller et al., 2011). They have strong ties with the community and are often creators and key influencers within the network. Identifying the creators for your brand and building your social capital with them will refine and focus your buyer persona while also influencing your online community. The creators are referred to as influencers and these are discussed in more detail later on in this chapter. Essentially, knowing and identifying influencers allows organisations to develop connections and work in partnership with creators to influence the contributors and lurkers.
- **Contributors** – approximately 9 per cent of the community regularly post to social media. This group are not as influential as creators, but they have a good understanding of the digital landscape in relation to your brand. Not all brands will have creators, but you should always be able to

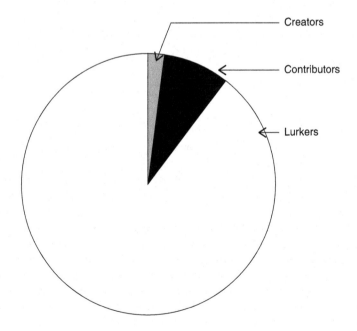

Figure 8.3 The 1 per cent rule of Internet culture

find contributors. For example, search for the name of your brand, products and services on a social network and see whether anyone has mentioned you. These individuals might be interested in writing a post for your blog, which they can then amplify through their own networks.

- **Lurkers** – the majority of your community, the 90 per cent, will consume your content, but almost never post or contribute to social media (Ferneley et al., 2009). These are the more weakly connected silent listeners and readers. Lurkers are the vast majority of your audience, so it is important to keep them engaged in a way that keeps them comfortable. For example, lurkers can be engaged through low-level interactions such as subscribing to your social media feed, blog feed or mailing list. Monitoring the behaviour of lurkers through analysis of visits lets you learn more about your wider audience. A regular mistake in thinking about social media is to assume that low social media engagement means that nobody is listening. However, this assumption means you might be forgetting about the 90 per cent.

8.5 Cultures

Culture is the way we do things and it is important to recognise that it differs. You are trying to reach people around the world who are enmeshed in different cultures. The global reach of social media is a key reason for organisations rethinking their marketing strategy (Ansari et al., 2019). Consider each culture that you are targeting separately. You need to develop knowledge and experience of what type of content is best delivered through which channels, in the right language and tone at the right time, in order to produce positive engagement. Your own research into each culture that you want to connect with will be important to understand individual nuances and preferences. Even if you are simply trying to reach people in your own language and time zone, it is still important to consider more regional cultures. Equally, the required content and needs of new and weakly connected followers will be different to core fans and creators.

Culture does not always neatly align with national boundaries or equate to a common spoken language. Within a single country, different groups behave differently depending on location, heritage, education, age and experience. Identifying the culture of your buyer persona will shape what social media platforms you will use and how you can best engage with them. Social media analytics data can tell you something about the country, city, devices and interests of your buyer persona (Lee, 2018). Social media analytics will also tell you which social networks are driving traffic to your website – the overall goal of your social media efforts. Becoming knowledgeable about the culture, habits, likes and dislikes of your buyer persona is essential (a cultural awareness of your buyer persona is part of the development process discussed in Chapter 3). This can be done through a combination of digital tools that measure and record – explored later in this chapter – as well as communicate with your buyer persona.

8.6 Sustainability of your social media platform

Social media platforms come and go, and there are major geographic differences when it comes to managing and developing social media activities. This presents a challenge for your organisation. For example, Facebook can be a good network for B2C communications in Europe and North America; however, it is currently blocked in mainland China (see full list maintained on Wikipedia for blocked sites in China and other countries). An alternative and more robust approach is to adopt the tactic of creating a website, blog or both where you control the hosting, data and content. This channel can be used as the main hub for engagement with your online community. The website and blog should therefore be at the centre of your channel implementation (Figure 8.4).

A website and blog are your key owned channels for creating synergies with other social media channels and should also be the central hub for your content. This enables amplification across your owned channels and provides content that your buyer persona can share across a wider network of channels.

8.7 Blogging platforms

A blog provides a good way to combine text, images, video and other media into high-quality engaging content. There are many different blogging platforms – some are free, some can be set up on your own website and some are existing websites where you create an account. Usually, an organisation sets up a blog as an extension to their website (e.g. as www.yourwebsite.com/blog). This sub-folder structure also offers SEO value as well as boosting the social media visibility of your organisation. An alternative sub-domain structure (e.g.

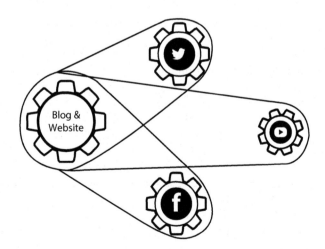

Figure 8.4 A blog and a website are pivotal channels in your social media strategy

www.blog.yourweb site.com) is also an option, but this is considered by search engines as a separate website, which means that you may gain fewer SEO benefits for your core website.

There are many different blogging platforms and software. The key to selecting the right platform depends upon your strategic goals and the KPIs you have defined. Some of the most common options for blogging are the following:

WordPress

WordPress is an open source blogging platform. This means that the software code is free and is developed by many thousands of people around the world. Because of its low cost, powerful features and wealth of themes and plugins, including the look and feel of the interface, it is used on a vast number of websites as both a blogging platform and CMS.

There are two options for WordPress:

*   WordPress.com is the 'hosted' version of WordPress, where you can set up a new blog or website very quickly. The basic functionality is free, with some 'paid for' additional features such as your own domain or further choice of themes and functionality. This option is more suitable for individual bloggers. Blogs on WordPress.com tend to rank well in search engine results pages (SERPs), but there are limited options for more advanced SEO configurations (such as the techniques described in Chapter 7).
*   WordPress.org supports the fully featured WordPress system. Essentially, WordPress can be set up on a web server and this will give you complete access to the look, feel and functionality of the website. Many organisations use this option as a CMS for their own website as well as using it as a blog. Many commercial web-hosting companies offer WordPress installation as part of their web package for a reasonably low cost. This is the option used by individuals and organisations to set up websites that require more customisation and functionality. With this version of WordPress, SEO plugins such as Yoast are available, and these allow much more control over the search engine friendliness of your pages as well as giving you better data collection and analytics integration.

Blogger

Blogger.com is a Google-owned platform specifically set up for blogging. Like WordPress.com, it is a freely hosted service, but has an entirely different look and feel. Blogs can also be set up from a custom domain owned by the user (such as www.yourwebsite.com) using DNS to direct a domain to Google's server but are often accessed via a sub-domain such as yourwebsite.blogger.com. Although the service is secure, Google has not updated Blogger for some time. There is some risk in using Blogger, as the lack of updates has led to some public speculation that Google may eventually close down or move Blogger to another service.

8.8 B2C platforms

Facebook

Since its inception in 2004, Facebook has grown to become the largest social network, with 2.4 billion active users visiting the social network on a daily basis in 2019. Launched originally at Harvard University, it was then initially made accessible to other US universities. Facebook has now become the *de facto* platform for individuals to connect with friends and family outside of China and some of the other countries where it is blocked. As a result of this focus, Facebook has also become an attractive channel for marketing. Organisations can create groups or fan pages as well as having the option to buy Facebook advertising to reach customers. Facebook is a mechanism for reaching new customers and engaging existing customers with new content. The platform enables easy setup of competitions as well as engaging in real-time interactions. Facebook popularity has levelled out and in some cases seen a decline in part due to negative press regarding the security and accuracy of the channel and scandals relating to this. The Facebook Cambridge Analytica scandal in 2018 is a high-profile example where Facebook user data was used inappropriately, causing an international outcry which led to some people quitting Facebook (González et al., 2019). Despite these scandals, Facebook's dominance in the market continues to grow, as it owns several of the other key messaging and social platforms including Instagram, WhatsApp and Facebook Messenger.

Facebook Messenger Chatbot is particularly one of the artificial intelligence innovations which is used by many organisations to offer automated website chat functionality (Batish, 2018). Due to its ease of use and high penetration rate amongst potential users, the Facebook-powered chatbot is one of the most popular options for organisations to try out chatbots.

Twitter

Twitter has risen to become a popular channel since it was launched in 2006. It is the best-known example of a micro-blogging platform that allowed users to communicate in a maximum of initially 140, and then in 2017 280, characters, and these are referred to as 'tweets'. Twitter was the driving force behind the hashtag (#) concept, which allows its users to identify a certain topic or conversation with a tagged keyword. It influenced other social networks to utilise the same idea, and now a hashtag is a common feature on most social networks. In 2019, Twitter boasted more than 330 million monthly active users, which is marking a decline from the top active monthly users of 336 million, which were reported in 2018. This is just another reminder that the Twitter ecosystem has struggled to capture a large share of the social network market. Unlike Facebook, Twitters' active user engagements have seen several declines since 2015.

Twitter profiles are usually public by default, but in relatively rare cases they are set to private. Trending topics are a feature of Twitter real-time capabilities, which allow users to see the currently most talked about topics. Communities thrive on Twitter because it is easy to use, it is easy to share tweets and it works in real time. Twitter content, as a result, is highly responsive to current affairs and breaking stories, which, in turn, makes tweets more attractive to share. For example, TV shows and programs rely on the Twitter hashtag idea to keep the engagement with their audiences. This is the idea of the second screen, where someone watching a TV programme is actively discussing it with other Twitter users on their mobile device or so-called second screen. One of the major talking points of the last few years with Twitter has been the high-profile figures who use the platform, most notably, Donald Trump, as never before has a US president been so accessible to so many people, and his activity is the topic of huge divisive conversation. In addition, Tesla CEO Elon Musk is famed for using the platform, and his tweets have been known to reduce the share price of the company due to their controversial nature (Best and Caylor, 2019).

Instagram

First released for public use in 2010, Instagram is a photo- and video-sharing app and is amongst the newest of the major social media channels. The platform has enjoyed rapid growth and engagement from users, and there are now 1 billion monthly active users on the platform (as of early 2019). The content that is shared is solely image- + video-based. This focus has helped to drive Instagram's success as a result of the increasing image quality available through mobile phones. This image-based focus has enabled individuals, organisations and brands to explore their creativity and to tell visual stories. Brands have especially lauded the platform for its ability to build a visual brand and gain a highly engaged audience. Acquired by Facebook in 2012, the platform introduced advertising in 2015. In recent years, the platform developed the stories feature to huge success, which is now predicted to be the main way we use social media. There are already one billion monthly active users of stories on Instagram.

One of the key features that Instagram offers is Instagram shopping via posts. This allows a user to see an item and, if they are interested, go directly to the shopping page of the organisation's website. Instagram shopping is not currently available in all markets. The four categories that were available in 2019 are eCommerce, Travel, Property and Auto – car sales.

8.9 B2B platforms

LinkedIn

Founded in 2002, LinkedIn is a B2B-focused social network, allowing users to post their professional work history, education and other professional achievements. LinkedIn is aimed at people who want to expand their professional networks as well as develop their career opportunities. The addition of company pages, and closed and open groups, allows conversations around business-related topics. LinkedIn is primarily used in the English-speaking world, but is translated into over 20 languages including Arabic, simplified Chinese and Russian. Known primarily as a B2B social network, the network is used to connect, promote brands and engage with new customers, colleagues and subject-specific interest groups.

LinkedIn has gained huge success in recent years as it developed from a networking platform into a content platform. As people realised they could become influential on the platform, this led to it being used more similarly in behaviour to Facebook, Instagram and Twitter and, more recently since the rise of video, YouTube for B2B.

Xing and Viadeo are two of the European competitors to LinkedIn and offer similar functionality to link professionals together. The key difference between the platforms is language. Viadeo was founded in France in 2004 and has a total of about 5.6 million individuals in France (as of 2019) and over 720k recruiters and over 7 million of business reviews in 2019. Xing, founded in 2003, is popular amongst German-speaking users in countries such as Germany, Austria and Switzerland and has over 16 million users (August 2019) in this core market.

YouTube / Vimeo

YouTube and Vimeo are video-streaming services. Both are free to use but place certain limits on the videos that can be uploaded in terms of content and length. The usage figures for these platforms, for YouTube in particular, are staggering, with people constantly choosing what they watch from billions of available professional or amateur video clips. Web video continues to be watched and created by a wide audience, with popular content including clips from favourite shows, 'how to' tutorial videos and even interactive or 3D content (which is often tagged as 'SBS', meaning side-by-side). Creating video content that your target audience will engage with and want to share should be a key aspect of your content. Videos hosted on these channels can then be embedded into your own web pages or blog posts and shared on social media platforms.

Google+

Started in 2011, Google+ ('Google plus') was Google's fourth social network project. The channel was significantly promoted by Google. Despite some impressive initial figures and close integration with search engine results, Google+ was ultimately shut down in April 2019.

In an earlier edition of this book in 2016, Google+ was considered a potentially useful platform with a growing user base. The closure of Google+ provides a stark reminder and key lesson regarding social media: if you build an audience on a social platform, you never truly own the audience, content or data. This is a risk to consider when trying to build a long-standing brand and underlines the importance of not having total reliance on one particular social media channel. Social media therefore should be used primarily to drive traffic where possible to a platform you own, such as a website, as noted earlier in the chapter. For example a blog, over which your organisation has full control, is a less risky social media commitment.

WeChat

Released in China in 2011, Tencent's WeChat system has evolved from a simple chat app to a multi-functional tool with more than 1.1 billion active monthly users (early 2019). WeChat has the widest range of uses of any social network at this point in time. It can fit into the B2C as well as into the B2B category and because of its particular use for business, it is integrated here in the B2B section. Although the majority of accounts are based in China, there is also a growing and significant percentage of users from outside China. WeChat enables videos and photos to be shared and altered, as well as calls, video conferencing calls and collaborative games. The release of an application programming interface (API) has also enabled an ecosystem of new apps to rapidly develop that range from support mechanisms to flight bookings.

The rise of WeChat is unprecedented and is filtering into the West now, with many brands beginning to understand how they can use these channels to reach the highly valuable Chinese market. Unlike Facebook and Twitter, the main business model is the value-added services that WeChat offers. It is therefore not relying on social media advertising to operate as a business. The value-added services are particularly developing due to the high adoption rate of the WeChat Pay – an opportunity to transfer money through this social network. Being at the core of many payment transactions for a wide range of applications that use WeChat as a core, this social network offers a backbone to digital marketing not seeing in the western apps.

For example, a customer can visit a restaurant, scan a QR code with their WeChat app and the restaurant menu will be loaded. Based on this menu, they can order their dishes and then pay for the meal – all using the WeChat app. It is no longer a social network but a social interaction platform that connects businesses and people in multiple ways.

8.10 Social media optimisation

The main reason for measuring KPIs in social media is to enable you to look beyond headline figures, such as the number of followers on Twitter or the number of likes on Facebook, and drill down to your success in engaging with your buyer persona and achieving your strategic aims. In social media terms, you are aiming for engagement with creators and to convert lurkers into contributors. Unless you are using networks with payment transactions that can be measured the value of social media interaction has to be aligned with your communication objectives. To achieve these aims, you need to understand your buyer persona's social media interests and actions.

Understanding your buyer persona using social media data and tools

Your buyer persona uses various channels, which creates large volumes of data. You can also inhabit these environments and use this data to better understand your buyer persona. Techniques such as social network analysis (SNA) and netnography can be used to gain additional insights from market research and better understand social media–based communities.

Netnography

Netnography is defined as a text-based output/result of digital/online environment/field work (Kozinets, 2018). Netnography is derived from the word ethnography (the study of people) but is specifically adapted to study online communities. Netnography has been described as quicker and cheaper than traditional ethnography and is more natural and unobtrusive than offline focus groups or interviews. The technique has been used for both academic and commercial market research. Listening to what people say interactively online is the central focal point of netnography. The careful analysis of conversations online and participation is therefore a vital tool to round out your knowledge and improve the description and understanding of your buyer personas on an ongoing basis. Simple analysis of conversations can be undertaken by constructing a wordle or word map from the text being analysed. In this way, keywords and phrases can be identified in individual interactions as well as across entire communities. More sophisticated tools (e.g. Radian 6) can also create a concordance of terms that provide further context for the keywords that have been used. Netnography can also be blended with other data such as interviews and SNA to create richer understanding of social media communities (Fenton and Procter, 2019).

Social network analysis

The concept of analysing offline social networks with SNA has been part of research for many decades (Groeger and Buttle, 2014) and has been used to identify the structure of networks. These networks can assist in identifying the focus and types of social capital within a network and, ultimately, can map the influence on buyer behaviours. These tools for SNA date back to around 2000 with the release of 'network.S.tools'. SNA has been used to, for example:

- understand e-word of mouth marketing;
- identify key influential people within networks;
- discover how people connect with each other over time;
- explore weak ties between people (Granovetter, 1973);
- identify key influencers, who are candidates for further qualitative analysis through netnography or interview (Griffiths and McLean, 2015); and
- understand social media capital and the 'structure' and 'form' of social relations (Jarman et al., 2015).

NodeXL, Gephi and Followerwonk

There are various tools that can be used for SNA, a form of analysis that can be computationally intensive. These tools can be used to produce data and visualisations of networks in order to understand the role of an individual in relation to their interactions with an online community (Jarman et al., 2015). NodeXL is a popular and low-cost tool for conducting SNA by gathering data from Twitter or other channels into an Excel spreadsheet.

Gephi is not as functional for gathering social media data, but the visualisation tools can be more powerful and clearer than NodeXL. It is also possible to import data from NodeXL to Gephi to take advantage of the strengths of each pro-gramme and produce clearer visualisations of social networks and personal inter-relationships. Both NodeXL and Gephi require installation on your computer.

Another tool used to gather social media data is Followerwonk. This online tool has the capability to visualise Twitter networks geographically and compare different user accounts. This comparison is not possible using NodeXL or Gephi. Followerwonk is used to understand where in the world potential fans are based and identify connections and new contacts based on the contacts of your competitors. It is possible to further look at the content of tweets from particu-lar regions using Followerwonk.

In Figure 8.5, a network map of Salford City Football Club @salfordCityFC Twitter followers using NodeXL reveals the number of links and connections that the club account has with one of its owners and key influencers, Gary Neville @GNev2. The figure also shows the links that exist between the club's other Twitter followers who are also connected to the club's official account.

Hashtags (#)

The word 'hashtag' entered the dictionary in 2014. Hashtags are an important part of your social media activities, as they offer a shared designation for all the interactions that happen in relation to a single topic. They take the format of a hash (#) character, followed by a word or words with no separating spaces. A multi-word example is this book's own hashtag '#passion4digital'. Hashtags became popular on Twitter, as they allowed users to separate and order their conversations and made it clear which topic they were communicating about. This trend for segmenting topics and conversations has since been picked up by other social media channels including Facebook, which now allows users to tag their content to make it more discoverable. Whilst the hashtag is still an important part of social channels, its relevance is fading over time.

There are no costs associated with hashtags and setting one up is as simple as adding a # to the front of a word, words (with no spaces) or a number. Hashtags work best when they are short and readable. Considering the num-ber of Twitter users and volume of daily tweets, it is important to check that nobody else is using your preferred hashtag. For example, #thenewmobile-phonecampaign does not make a good hashtag, as it is too long and the words blend into one another, sometimes forming unfortunate new words. Be creative

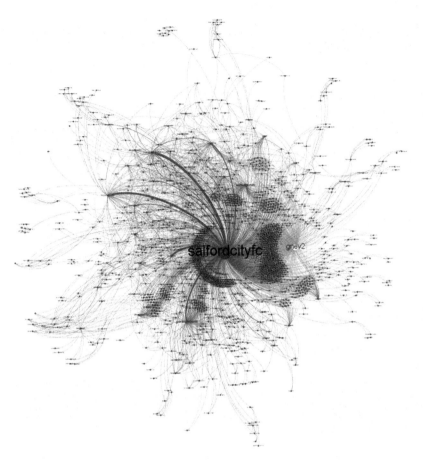

Figure 8.5 A network map of Salford City Football Club Twitter followers using NodeXL

and combine and shorten words into something that is original and distinctive for your organisation and its messages.

When setting up a specific hashtag, make sure you publicise it well and use it in all your communications to encourage its wider use by your buyer persona. You should not try to 'own' your hashtag and keep it constrained, but rather view it as a part of your brand collateral that you want to spread widely. For example, our book uses the hashtag #passion4digital – join in and share your thoughts with others about digital marketing.

Case Study 8.2 Always: #LikeAGirl

Always' buyer personas are female consumers looking for feminine products. In this case, Always has identified a challenge faced by its buyer

All   Videos   Images   News   Shopping   More ▼   Search tools

About 418,000 results (0.62 seconds)

The #LikeAGirl Campaign - youtube.com
(Ad) www.youtube.com/Always_LikeAGirl ▼
Check Out The Brand New Always #LikeAGirl Video Online Today!
Girl emojis · Confidence during puberty

#likeagirl on Twitter
https://twitter.com/hashtag/likeagirl

Always (@Always)
24 secs ago - View on Twitter

76% of girls think female emojis shouldn't only be portrayed
doing feminine activities. Watch & share! #LikeAGirl
cards.twitter.com/cards/7...

Amanda DeVito (@AmandaDeVito)
19 mins ago - View on Twitter

Recent trend towards transformational leadership and its
emphasis on empowerment and collaboration – #likeagirl.

Our Epic Battle #LikeAGirl | Always
always.com/en-us/about-us/our-epic-battle-**like-a-girl** ▼
Join Always in our epic battle to stop the drop in confidence girls experience at puberty. ... Let's
champion all girls to be Unstoppable #LikeAGirl. ... See how we changed the meaning of "like
a girl" from an insult to the ultimate compliment it really is!

Always #LikeAGirl - YouTube

https://www.youtube.com/watch?v=XjJQBjWYDTs
26 Jun 2014 - Uploaded by Always
Join Always in our epic battle to keep girls' confidence high
during puberty and beyond. ... "When the words ...

Case Study: Always #LikeAGirl | D&AD
www.dandad.org/en/case-study-always-**likeagirl**/ ▼
#LikeAGirl. Always needed a way to appeal to a next generation of consumers in the face of
growing competition from rivals that were gaining traction with ...

Images for #likeagirl   Report images

Figure 8.6 Always #LikeAGirl Google SERP

persona – that is, being 'like a girl' has diminutive connotations and is
sometimes even seen as an insult. In response, Always created an emotionally charged campaign that challenges the prevailing stereotype of
girls as being inferior when it comes to engaging in sporty activities. The
campaign is structured around a video that shows an audition for a video

shoot where unsuspecting actors are asked to behave 'like a girl'. Both female and male actors are asked to simulate running, throwing and fighting. In the first half of the shoot the individuals are asked to perform the activity and are then asked why they portrayed girls in an inferior way. The actors, once they had a chance to reconsider their actions – which could be interpreted as an insult to girls – are asked to re-shoot the scene again. The campaign used YouTube as the primary channel and allowed interaction in the comments. Since it engaged the target audience on an emotional level (see the discussion of what makes content viral in Chapter 9), it reached lurkers as well as creators who were sharing and engaging with that video.

The video generated comments on YouTube and on a number of other social networks where the same hashtag, #LikeAGirl, was used. The hashtag is short and memorable, with every word starting with a capital letter (sometimes called CamelCase) – this makes it easy to read and write. A Google SERP for the term #LikeAGirl (Figure 8.6) is now consumed with Always-related content and the results from Twitter and YouTube all appear at the top.

The SERP is showing images as well as the video thumbnail – the use of images is an important social media optimisation tactic.

A picture is worth a thousand words

Visual material, in particular good-quality images, is crucial for blogging and social media. Studies have consistently demonstrated that blog posts or social media posts that feature good-quality and relevant images resonate with the audience. As a consequence, these posts are more likely to motivate the audience to engage with and share content (Mawhinney, 2016). As technology improves, the quality of media we can access improves, and therefore the information on the Internet is becoming more visual.

Images can be obtained from a variety of sources. It is important that images are original, high-quality and relevant. You should check that you have the rights to use an image for your intended specific purpose – this means that you should not use images found elsewhere on the Internet without purchasing, acquiring the image owner's permission or having the rights to use them for the intended purpose. There are several places where you can obtain images:

- Stock libraries – free or paid for. There are many libraries that offer relevant images for purchase or download. Do check the usage rights and fine print for what you are permitted to do with the images even if you have paid a rights fee.

- Take your own photos – using your own camera or working with a photographer, either professional or amateur, produces original material that is customised to your brand.
- Creative Commons was started as a way for people to relax the copyright of the materials that they create. You can search for Creative Commons images on sites like Google or Flickr. Check the usage rights carefully, as there are different types of Creative Commons licences, and make sure the original author is always credited.

Working with images is easier with a good image editing package (Photoshop or GIMP) and a basic working knowledge of image editing. Even learning just how to resize, crop, brighten and fix images in order to improve the quality of your imagery will positively boost your brand.

8.11 Finding key influencers

Influencers can be differentiated into many types – nano, micro, macro and mega. Each of these can be of benefit for different purposes. These can be differentiated by their range of followers and or subscribers on their social network. It is important to only count the audience reach on channels that are relevant to our buyer persona and not all the channels where the influencer is.

- **Nano** – (up to 1,000 followers or subscribers). These tend to have a high level of engagement and are very active. They tend to have a high trust level with their audience and can be very influential for complex engagements.
- **Micro** – (audience of 1,001 to 10,000). Developed a subject expertise in a particular domain. These are usually enthusiasts for a particular topic and have a longer-term popularity and trust with their audience. They tend to have a good tone of voice and a style for communication which resonates with their followers.
- **Macro** – (audience of 10,001 to 100,000). These tend to have a more professionalised approach to their social media management. These can have agents and might be very interested in paid engagements and promotions. The drawback is that it might be more difficult for them to show real affinity with your brand since they might already work with multiple brands in your area.
- **Mega** – 100,000+ followers. These tend to be celebrities who have the followers because of who they are and not what they do on social media. Also, this category can be occupied by social media stars and social media personalities who engage on social media as a way of making a living. The exposure may be very high, but the engagement with your brand and their audience might be low. Beware that your website and digital services are able to withstand the demand of potential traffic that these mega influencers can generate.

By using tools such as a CRM (customer relationship management) system, SNA and netnography, you can better define and engage with your buyer personas. This allows data to be used to define who the audience is, and you can then identify appropriate social networks, key influencers and audiences who fit your brand. You can identify potential influencers using search engines (such a search engine) and SNA, as well as employing straightforward observation. These methods will also identify the locations where the interests you are targeting are being discussed and presented.

For example, if you are researching lifestyle or beauty and fashion, you will need to locate the digital presences of large fashion publishers who make use of guest and celebrity writers. These writers will often have their own blogs, Instagram account or YouTube content. These are the channels and specific locations where you also want to have visibility and reach out to these audiences and, ultimately, your buyer persona.

Once you have located communities that fit with your own brand's content, you can begin to identify the influencers in each of these communities. Learn the expected behaviours and culture of each community as a lurker before scaling up your activities as a contributor and then a creator. Once you have established your credentials in the community, reach out to the influencers in ways that fit the expected behaviours and culture of the specific community.

Contacting key influencers and building your own social capital with them is a key step in becoming part of a community. If you are approaching influencers with a reach that numbers in the hundreds of thousands or millions, you are going to have to stand out against a lot of noise. These are busy people who are used to – and largely immune to – a lot of contact requests and communications. Do something that makes you stand out to them in a way that catches their attention – for positive reasons – and starts the conversation off on a good note. A personalised, friendly message delivered through a social media platform such as LinkedIn, person to person, is better than a generic message that fills up an influencer's email inbox or Twitter timeline. Consider offering something helpful to them or promote a cause that they will be likely to support.

In recent years, influencer advertising has come under scrutiny from advertising standards bodies, and many high-profile influencers have been punished for incorrectly labelling paid advertisements, so it's crucial that any work you do with influencers meets advertising standards. Another issue with influencer advertising is that influencers are able to easily manipulate their followings and engagement in an attempt to entice brands into working with them. With few tools available for brands to check whether an influencer's following and engagement are genuine, this leads to wasted marketing budget and low ROI. It is important to undertake due diligence in influencer evaluation and study the reality of the engagement levels over a longer period of time.

Becoming a key influencer

An influencer is someone who has authority and wide respect for their knowledge, experience or abilities around a topic. An influencer is a driving force in their subject area and will be a thought-leader in some way. If your aim is to become a key influencer, you need to consider a number of separate issues.

Content – Content is central to a digital marketing strategy and the Buyer Persona Spring. There are clear synergies between good content and engagement. This synergy is a combination of creating and curating content that will thrive within your community and is the first step in becoming a key influencer. Give the buyer persona what they want (see the SEO and content marketing chapters) and, more importantly, can engage with.

Growth – Being able to grow your account on your platform of choice will boost your efforts to becoming a key influencer. The steps to boosting your efforts are platform-dependent, but generally involve you developing content and connecting with others who are positioning themselves as – or already are – key influencers. The basic element in growing your presence on any social platform is to follow those whom you consider to be your audience and to engage with them in relevant conversation. You want to be at the forefront of any emerging trend conversation. Your knowledge and the opportunities to exhibit your knowledge are invaluable opportunities to grow your audience and followers to a size that will have you regarded as an influencer.

Building an engaged community

Building a community on a social network can reap significant benefits, if it is done correctly. In recent years, both UNILAD and The LAD Bible have revealed how social media has enabled a new trend in publishing. These communities have effectively killed off the printed 'lads' mag' and have grown their markets (and their value) to levels that the print magazine could never have imagined. These social media publishers provide content that their audiences want to see, effectively collecting and curating content gathered from across the Internet around a particular topic and placing it in coherent streams on channels where audience interaction is a key element of the experience (Facebook). The LAD Bible now focuses heavily on delivering video content to Facebook – a result of a change in algorithm that positively encourages this form of content. As a result, The LAD Bible has reaped the rewards resulting from this change. What once started as a hobby, focusing on providing content, has become a community with millions of followers that can now be monetised for advertising purposes. Building a community online, in the right way, can be a game-changer. Building a community does not involve having to create a new platform, but rather is about building an affiliation with your buyer persona in the right place in ways that fit into their lifestyle preferences and patterns, including, most importantly, their channel preferences.

Building a community utilises the same key principles for becoming an influencer. You need to focus on content and growth. Knowing where to find your buyer persona and working with creators in that space will make your community grow. Building an engaged community involves constantly giving out a high-quality stream of content. UNILAD and The LAD Bible both spent 3 years building their model of giving before they were in a position to safely ask for something back from their audience. Community building requires a genuine passion for what the community says it is about, a degree of dogged perseverance and the constant building of trust. If you provide the audience with what it wants, you will reap the benefits – but it will take the commitment of time.

Creating a niche

Creating a niche enables you to build a community and deliver content to that community without any impartiality or opinion on the account. A niche begins without a brand sentiment. Lurkers are more likely to follow a niche if they cannot see an ulterior motive connected to it. Contributors and creators will participate if they recognise an opportunity and a USP within the niche.

Examples of successful niches include:

- @Love_Food on Instagram – a food page which posts visually appealing content of mouth-watering food and has gained over six million followers.
- @BeFitMotivation on Twitter – posts motivational quotes, body image goals and gym wear to an audience of over 1.5 million fitness fans.
- @ProblemsAtUni on Twitter – is a student humour account revealing the pains of over 300,000 university residence dwellers all over the UK.

These niches thrive off sharing highly engaging content, usually curated from sources discovered all over the Web, and are typically run by people who are personally and passionately interested in the niche. As a result, these niches are regarded as genuine and informative. The pivotal element in creating a niche is to provide your audience with regular, relevant and high-value content.

Creating a hook

Viral content on social platforms thrives by using recurring hooks and concepts that can be applicable to a broad range of topics. When a new trend comes along, the same concept can be applied and the hook refreshed to be relevant. An example of a very successful and effective hook created on UK social media for a brand was the use of the 'RT to save a degree' campaign for RefME, a student referencing mobile app. The campaign was simple but highly effective and targeted towards student communities on Twitter. The content was simple. It consisted of three images showing how simple the process of referencing a book is by using the app. Supporting copy for the campaign focused on the theme 'RT to save a degree' and contained a direct link to the app store. The result of this campaign was many thousands of organic retweets and a large volume of app downloads. As a measure of the success of this campaign, RefME is now positioned as a referencing app of choice amongst UK students.

Trend awareness

Staying relevant on social media is key to becoming respected in your industry. If you can be aware of trends within your niche, you will be at the forefront of conversations. You can go further by taking trend awareness and translating it into engaging content. Trend awareness will also position you as a key influencer. Talking about trend awareness involves drawing in the latest conversations around your interests and being able to relay that to your audience in an engaging way past being a megaphone for the original content. If done correctly, huge audiences can be built purely off sharing the latest news and your opinion on that news.

Reputation management

Trust is an essential element of social media and should be embedded in all of your engagement and outreach activities. Trust in your brand is what makes someone confident to complete your calls-to-action, including purchasing. Trust also interacts with social capital in residing between individuals and brands and the individuals who represent brands (Valenzuela et al., 2009). Building brand engagement and increasing your social capital, as well as looking after and rewarding key influencers, all build trust and nurture communities. Trust takes a long time to establish but is easy to lose.

Based on the conformity concept, widely known in sociology, people tend to follow the lead of others. For example, in a study exploring online purchase decisions, it was found that the opinions of peers had a direct impact on the decision being made (Geber et al., 2019), because people wanted to be part of a group and wanted to take an informed decision. If your organisation can work with creators, your community can be encouraged to participate in low-level activities such as sharing feedback. Relevant networks such as Google Maps review, Trustpilot, TripAdvisor and others dependent on your niche all provide the mechanisms to engage your community and to encourage them to publicly articulate their trust in your organisation, its products and services, and its brands. Once you choose your preferred reviewing system, direct your customers to leave a review, in particular those who are enthusiastically positive about your service. Some of the most successful TripAdvisor organisations are not necessarily great in what they do, but they are great in encouraging their happy customers to share their reviews online. With any system that you choose, you must regularly monitor and reply to both negative as well as positive comments. Take note of common themes of complaint and genuinely act upon these with real resolutions and personalised comments. Do not be tempted to use websites which offer to generate positive reviews which are not genuine. These not only are unethical but are also easily identified as false signals. Prioritise encouraging genuine review processes in your organisation, including emailing your customers after a purchase and asking for a review.

Consider offering guidelines on how to create and to access review pages. Not all of your users are familiar with these systems.

Monitor your social media profiles regularly and have a team of people who would reply to complaints. It is generally accepted that a complaint is taken offline, since you do not really want to discuss the negative experience of your customers in front of others. Most people are reasonable and are happy to comply with your request to share a phone number for a private discussion of the issues being raised. However, in situations where unhappy customers are unreasonable and you feel that the case cannot be resolved offline, and you have tried reasonable ways of resolving an argument, you can explore the option of answering the complaint publicly as well as offering other community members the option to contribute to the same conversation. Whichever way you resolve complaints, it must be one of the entries in your risk register for monitoring and mitigation (see the discussion about project management in Chapter 5).

8.12 Summary

This chapter discusses some of the key principles of social media and its role in digital marketing. Social media is an increasingly important way to engage customers for any organisation that wants a successful digital presence. Strategic commitment to using social media platforms requires the allocation of tools and resources to the four areas of marketing, sales, operations and support.

Using social media tools and techniques such as netnography is a central way to understand your social media audience and to measure the success of your engagement with your buyer persona. You should also build social capital between your organisation and your buyer persona, which increases trust and brand value.

This chapter outlines many other reasons for using social media, including the creation of synergies for SEO and the multiple benefits of creating a blog.

The reasons for measuring social media activities will depend on your strategic and operational reasons for using these channels, but irrespective of the strategic aims you have, your organisation should monitor and measure its social media activities. Social media is broadly divided in this chapter into professional networks that are more focused on B2B industries and private networks used more for B2C interactions.

Social media cannot be controlled, nor should it be ignored. It is a powerful way to communicate with your buyer persona and achieve your strategic goals.

8.13 References

Ansari, S., Ansari, G., Ghori, M. U. and Kazi, A. G. (2019) Impact of brand awareness and social media content marketing on consumer purchase decision. *Journal of Public Value and Administration Insights*, 2(2), 5–10.

Batish, R. (2018) *Voicebot and chatbot design: Flexible conversational interfaces with Amazon Alexa, Google Home, and Facebook Messenger*. Birmingham: Packt Publishing Ltd.

Best, E. and Caylor, M. L. (2019) Risks and rewards of financial disclosure on Twitter: What CPAs and management should know. *The CPA Journal*, 89(6), 42–47.

Cofré-Bravo, G., Klerkx, L. and Engler, A. (2019) Combinations of bonding, bridging, and linking social capital for farm innovation: How farmers configure different support networks. *Journal of Rural Studies*, 69, 53–64.

Evans, M. M., Frissen, I. and Choo, C. W. (2019) The strength of trust over ties: Investigating the relationships between trustworthiness and tie-strength in effective knowledge sharing. *Electronic Journal of Knowledge Management*, 17(1).

Fenton, A. & Procter, C. (2019) Studying social media communities: Blending methods with netnography. *SAGE Research Methods Cases*. doi:10.4135/9781526468901

Ferneley, E., Heinze, A. and Child, P. (2009) Research 2.0: Encouraging engagement in online market research communities. In *European conference in information systems*, Verona, Italy.

Fueller, J., Schroll, R., Dennhardt, S. and Hutter, K. (2011) Social brand value and the value enhancing role of social media relationships for brands. In *Proceedings of the annual Hawaii international conference on system sciences*, pp. 3218–3227. ACM.

Geber, S., Baumann, E. and Klimmt, C. (2019) Where do norms come from? Peer communication as a factor in normative social influences on risk behavior. *Communication Research*, 46(5), 708–730.

González, F., Yu, Y., Figueroa, A., López, C. and Aragon, C. (2019). Global reactions to the Cambridge Analytica Scandal: A cross-language social media study. In *Companion Proceedings of the 2019 world wide web conference*, May, pp. 799–806. ACM.

Granovetter, M. S. (1973) The strength of weak ties. *American Journal of Sociology*, 78(6), 1360–1380.

Griffiths, M. and McLean, R. (2015) Unleashing corporate communications via social media: A UK study of brand management and conversations with customers. *Journal of Customer Behaviour*, 14(2), 147–162.

Groeger, L. and Buttle, F. (2014) Word-of-mouth marketing: Towards an improved understanding of multi-generational campaign reach. *European Journal of Marketing*, 48(7/8), 1186–1208.

Heinze, A., Ferneley, E. and Child, P. (2013) Ideal participants in online market research: Lessons from closed communities. *International Journal of Market Research*, 55(6), 769–789.

Jarman, M., Nowak, A., Borkowski, W., Serfass, D., Wong, A. and Vallacher, R. (2015) The critical few: Anticonformists at the crossroads of minority opinion survival and collapse. *Journal of Artificial Societies and Social Simulation*, 18(1), 6.

Kozinets, R. V. (2018) Netnography for management and business research. *The Sage handbook of qualitative business and management research methods*. London: Sage.

Lee, I. (2018) Social media analytics for enterprises: Typology, methods, and processes. *Business Horizons*, 61(2), 199–210.

Mawhinney, J. (2016) *37 Visual content marketing statistics you should know in 2016*. blog.hubspot.com/marketing/visual-content-marketing-strategy

Poor Rezaei, S. M. and Heinze, A. (2014) SME competitiveness through online brand communities: An exploration of brand loyalty. *Institute for Small Business and Entrepreneurship (ISBE) conference*, 5–6 Nov 2014, Manchester.

Valenzuela, S., Park, N. and Kee, K. (2009) Is there social capital in a social network site? Facebook use and college students' life satisfaction, trust, and participation. *Journal of Computer-Mediated Communication*, 14(4).

9 Content marketing

Sophie Iredale, Aleksej Heinze and Martin J Williams

9.0 Learning objectives

In this chapter you will learn how to:

- create content that will attract relevant and qualified online traffic;
- evaluate a range of strategies for building a positive brand reputation;
- engage with your buyer persona and encourage them to share your brand;
- generate high-quality inbound links; and
- encourage positive sentiment surrounding your brand that will generate a positive brand reputation.

9.1 The importance of content marketing

As mentioned in previous chapters, high-quality content is essential for branding and user experience (please refer to Chapter 6), for search engine optimisation (SEO) purposes (Chapter 7) and for pay-per-click (PPC) quality scores (Chapter 10).

Content marketing is the strategic process of creating and amplifying content for the purpose of informing, entertaining and/or building awareness of your brand, products or services within a target audience.

Content marketing is a cyclical process, which incorporates the following four stages informed by campaign management processes (see Chapter 5) for creating consistent content:

1 Plan: content planning and idea generation.
2 Act: content creation, development, implementation and amplification.
3 Observe: content tracking and monitoring.
4 Reflect: content evaluation.

Content marketing planning

The most crucial stage of a content marketing campaign is the planning process (Figure 9.1). The planning stage typically encompasses the following phases:

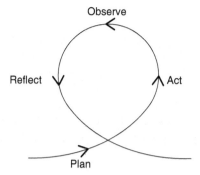

Figure 9.1 Content marketing cycle

- Goal setting.
- Defining your buyer persona.
- Resource management.
- Scheduling and editorial calendar creation.

Goal setting

Before any work can begin, it is vital you ask yourself what your content marketing purpose is. For example, is it to raise awareness of a service, an event or a product? Is it to entertain, inform or educate? Is it to increase referral traffic to your site? Is it to build your contact database? Is it being used to supplement marketing and/or PR activity? Without defining this in the early stages of your campaign, you will have nothing solid with which to align each stage of the content marketing process. Our recommendation is to think 'SMART' (for further detailed guidance on setting SMART goals, refer to Chapters 4 and 5).

Further explication of appropriate key performance indicators (KPIs) and performance metrics relevant to a content marketing campaign can be found in Section 9.5 of this chapter.

The big idea – how can you find an inspiration for your content? There are a number of inspiration points offline and online. Similar to your buyer persona development, *data-driven* or *creative-driven* strategies can be used to shape the ideas. Data-driven can be based on keyword research (Chapter 7), social media listening (Chapter 8) and other methods such as competitor content, what is topical in the news or industry research reports etc. For the creative side, brainstorming and identification of content areas in other industries that can be relevant for the pain points and the trust points of the buyer persona are key. Existing already-popular content – either on your digital profiles or published by your competitors – can be updated in a new and more engaging way so that it is repurposed.

The **Skyscraper content** (mentioned in Chapter 7 as part of SEO) is based on this principle of identifying what content works and developing similar content but better, more interactive and more colourful and therefore building an even greater presence and engagement with your buyer persona. Case Study 9.1 shows how a successful content marketing campaign was operationalised by Ad Rank in April 2016 for CruiseDeals.co.uk. However, not even a year later in January 2017 a competitor business also caught headlines with a twist on the same story "CRUISING for 52 weeks could cost a staggering £35,000 less than living in a city." PlanetCruise.com was seemingly inspired by their competitors and used the Skyscraper technique to generate similar levels of publicity with similar content.

Case Study 9.1   Is living in London more expensive than living on a cruise ship?

Content marketers working for CruiseDeals.co.uk have identified two common problems of high living costs in London and accessible prices of living on a cruise ship. This allowed work of PR teams, SEO teams and creatives to develop a story which is picked up by newspapers and social media communities (Ad Rank, 2019).

The SEO objective included building high-quality links back to the website as well as the PR objective of increasing brand awareness and brand engagement.

Having undertaken some original research into the cost of living comparison, the agency found that it was £7 per day cheaper to live on a cruise ship instead of living in London. This intriguing finding was attractive to a number of national and international press publishers as well as social media communities.

The results were also astonishing – over 200 publications from national and international publishers featured the story, and several of these linked back to a landing page which was hosted on the CruiseDeals.co.uk website. It featured the details of calculations and obviously it was just one click away from exploring the cruise deals to purchase.

The long-term positive impact of the gained links was the website traffic increase – over 30 per cent year on year which shows a cumulative benefit of a good content marketing activity.

Finding a hook is not a simple, straightforward process, and pre-campaign prospecting can help to refine the ideas to determine what is relevant for your buyer persona.

Ego Bait content is another creative source for inspiration when it comes to content that is going to be more likely sharable and attract links to your content (Foster, 2019). Unlike the Skyscraper technique that appeals to a wider audience, the Ego Bait technique targets specific influencers or website owners who would ideally link or engage with your organisation. The idea is based on a simple principle – if you say something positive about someone else, they are likely to reciprocate and mention you or your content to their network. By positively "stroking" someone else's ego you are winning a "friend" (Carnegie, 2010) and they are more likely to link to you in their own content. The main types of ego bait content are as follows:

1   Video and image infographics that mention individuals or content from those who you like to interact with.
2   Competitions where individuals are asked to say why they are the "best" and therefore can win a prize of just being recognised as a leader in a field.
3   Subject matter expert interviews – you are placing someone as an expert in a field and asking their views on a topic that is mutually helpful.
4   Key take-away summary post – following a public meeting, a networking event or a conference, this can be a post that mentions interview extracts from influencers in your area and you are simply comparing and contrasting their views.
5   Listicles. The idea of creating a directory of experts or best products can also lead to creating original content that attracts the attention of individuals mentioned in this list. Users are also finding lists that order and list things into league tables useful – it helps them to quickly make decisions.

Either Ego Bait or Skyscraper techniques have to be done within a strategic framework. The Buyer Persona Spring (see Chapter 3) serves as a guide to make decisions of what kind of content marketing ideas would be appropriate and which are not.

Defining your buyer persona

A full breakdown on how to create a buyer persona can be found in Chapter 3. Insight into your unique selling points (USPs) and key messaging, and how to identify the unique values of your brand, services and/or products (that will resonate with your buyer personas), can be found in Chapter 6. Once you have fully defined your USPs and key messages, you can start to build a content story around them.

Segmenting your target audience will allow you to create a composite breakdown of your buyer persona's interests, online behaviour and key demographics relevant to your brand. It will also allow you to think about where your buyer persona is within the buying cycle, so you can shape your content marketing strategy accordingly, assembling ideas, content types, channels and approaches to suit.

Resource management

At this stage, it is important to be clear about what budget and time you have allocated to your content marketing campaign.

Content marketing can be incredibly time consuming and, depending upon what content you want to create, expensive to produce. For example, a good blog post can take over a day to create, including time dedicated to researching the content, generating and sourcing unique data and quotes, outreaching the post and monitoring it. Even bigger pieces such as ebooks and videos can take much longer and require a whole host of designer and developer skills. However, if your content marketing campaign is executed correctly, the payoff is worth the investment.

Be sure to keep track of your time and budget in order to determine routes to optimising resources for future campaigns. Trello is a free time-management and tracking tool which can be used by multiple members of a content marketing team for full visibility on task lists and work completed. Further details about managing a campaign can be found in Chapter 5.

Scheduling and editorial calendar creation

Once you know who you are targeting and why, another important stage of the planning process is to look at your desired launch plan (see Chapter 5 for more details on operational planning). This is where seasonal trends must be considered to ensure you do not miss your optimum launch time and to give you enough time to strategically plan what resources you require and delegate tasks appropriately.

Suppose your aim is to raise awareness of a new flower shop and your campaign is to promote a bouquet giveaway for Mother's Day. You would need to ensure all relevant content has been created and launched and has given your target audience enough time to enter their personal details before Mother's Day (as well as allowing yourself time to send out the prize giveaway to those that have participated).

Google Trends is a recommended platform for planning your seasonal peaks and drops if your product or service is seasonally driven. For example, retailers selling ski wear would be mindful of peaks around winter and look to plan their promotions in line with winter ski seasons (Figure 9.2).

We also recommend you look at your historical website traffic in Google Analytics or other web analytics providers to determine average peaks and drops in activity.

In order to effectively synthesise your activity and allow transparency to all actors and stakeholders involved in the content marketing process, create a shared content marketing calendar (or an editorial calendar) that outlines your weekly, monthly, quarterly, biannual or annual campaign plans. It should ideally contain the following:

- Campaign description, key messages and themes.
- Related objectives.
- Task owners.
- Allocated budgets and time breakdowns.
- Launch dates.

As mentioned in the campaign project management chapter (Chapter 5), this stage of the planning process can take some time but is worth it from a project and resource management perspective.

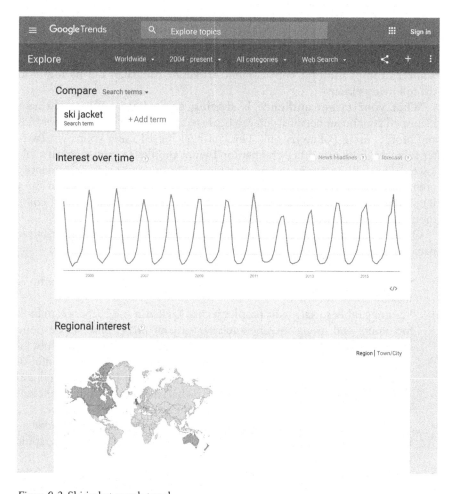

Figure 9.2 Ski jacket search trend

Source: Google Trends (www.google.com/trends)

9.2 The idea generation process

At this stage, you should have a good idea about who you want to target, when you want to target them and how much time and budget you have available to create your content. Taking into consideration these key learnings, this is when you can start the idea generation process.

Getting the 'idea' right at the beginning of your content marketing campaign is the most critical stage of the entire process. You want to choose an idea or a series of ideas that resonates with your buyer persona, giving them value whilst not pushing your sales proposition onto them. Contemporary marketing is subtle and not intrusive and acts as a natural step in the buyer persona's journey to conversion. It is not the end result.

Where to find content inspiration

Sources of inspiration for your content marketing campaign can be found in the following places:

What your target audience is sharing and where – When you have identified your buyer persona, you can begin to analyse their online Twitter bios and profiles using Followerwonk. This can be achieved using your own Twitter follower profile or other competitor Twitter profiles to cross-compare followers. This will help you to segment profiles by interests as well as identify other similar key influencers they are following. As a result, you open up a whole community of prospects, which allows you to better understand common interests and themes in the most popular content shared.

Other routes to identifying your target audience and segmenting your buyer persona could involve the following:

- Setting up Google Alerts for terms related to your brand to see who is sharing them and where.
- Scanning other social media profiles such as LinkedIn and Facebook to look for groups and group members relative to your niche. This can be done using the search bar for related terms to your product or service. Whilst an aim is to identify potential key influencers, you should also be mindful of what topics are being discussed, what type of content is being shared and where they are sharing the content from. This will help you build a picture of your buyer persona's interests and content consumption behaviour.
- You can also use Facebook Insights, YouTube Insights and Google Analytics to give you a deeper understanding of your audience's demographic data, such as geographic location, gender and age.
- Ask them! Suppose you already have a retained customer base, don't be afraid to send out a survey (or an interview, a focus group etc.) to ask them about their online preferences. This data can then be translated into something with deeper meaning to support the segmentation of your target audience.

Whilst auditing your target audience's preferences, be sure to pick up on subtle colloquialisms in their language, as this can help you with your key messaging and storytelling during the idea generation process. Though it is important to stay true to your brand's tone of voice, adopting nuances of your buyer persona can positively impact the engagement rate of your content.

What your competitors are promoting and where – Be sure to analyse competitor content to determine how successful historical creative campaigns have been. Analyse engagement metrics as well as quality links back to site with link analysis software such as Open Site Explorer. This will allow you to determine which pieces of content were the most popular (or not) and will provide a platform from which to develop your own ideas that build upon competitor successes.

Several networks allow you to monitor your competitors' social media profiles. In Facebook, for example, you can go to the Insights section setup and compare the performance of your page and posts with similar pages on Facebook.

At this point, it is important to note that it is copyright infringement if you copy the intellectual property of another without their explicit permission, so be careful where you decide to seek inspiration. The default for all content – text, images, video or sound – is that it is 'all rights reserved'. However, content under a Creative Commons licence (Creative Commons, 2019) identified by a CC logo usually offers some exceptions, where authors allow content to be shared without explicit permission as long as the rights of their licence are respected. Several content creators see CC as a way of allowing their message to be amplified and thus reach wider audiences compared to copyrighted content. The use of Creative Commons as a tactic in content marketing is a worthy consideration, particularly if the content is meant to 'go viral'.

Keyword research – Keyword research should not be the only source of inspiration for your content marketing campaign, but it offers a good source of ideas. Understanding what keyword is being targeted in your content allows you to gain maximum SEO value from your content marketing efforts and should be achieved through keyword-optimised digital content.

This is where you consider your keyword strategy – keywords related to your product or service that can be incorporated into your content in order to give the content its own ranking capabilities. We recommend that you target semantically driven search terms that answer a specific and relevant question your buyer persona might ask. Free content idea generators such as AnswerThePublic.com are a good place to start.

Further insight into keyword planning can be found in Chapter 7.

Identifying target publications – Identifying target publications relevant to your brand and to your persona's interests should give you some insight into current topics and popular content ideas.

For example, if you are interested in launching a content marketing campaign aimed at food wholesalers and suppliers, analysing the success of content on well-known fast moving consumer goods publications such as *The Grocer* might be of value to you. It can also give you an insight into what content topics have already been created to ensure you do not 'reinvent the wheel'.

Pre-campaign prospecting – Pre-campaign prospecting is the process of contacting key influencers, such as website owners, bloggers and journalists, to determine whether there are any pieces of topical content they would like to feature on their website.

Sometimes the best ideas are generated with the support of media specialists within your field. Seeking out key prospects for your content requires you to carry out various outreach tactics, which will be explained in Section 9.4 of this chapter.

A great way of sourcing content ideas and potential placements is to get in touch with journalists on websites such as HARO (Help A Reporter Out), which request specialist insight, personal experience and advice from individuals, groups or organisations across various industries, on a daily basis.

Alternative contact details of niche websites, journalists and bloggers can be sourced on Twitter using the hashtag #journorequest, as well as automated content marketing tools such as Ninja Outreach and BuzzStream.

Content aggregator sites – There are some automated campaign tools available to you, such as BuzzSumo, SocialMention.com and Ahrefs Content Explorer, which allow you to type in a specific keyword or target phrase/message to determine what content on related topics is being shared, where it is being shared and how successful it has been. This should give you ideas of where the content gaps are, as well as giving you insight into the types of relevant content.

Data sources – Data-driven content is beneficial, as it adds trust, unique value and reliability to your content messages. Data-driven content is especially useful for journalist pieces and press releases, which typically use data to help add gravity to newsworthy topics within the content.

Unique data can be generated through market research and customer relationship marketing (CRM) data. Should you undertake any market research to gain unique data, ensure your sample is of an appropriately large size to certify that your results are trustworthy (see Survey System, 2016). Many well-known publications will refuse to take your content if your data sources and sample sizes cannot be certified.

It is recommended that you try not to use statistics that are not your own, as they have likely been seen before and will lose impact. That being said, cross-comparing your data with existing data sources can give rigour to the point you are making. Free data sources such as the European Union Open Data Portal (EU ODP) can be mined for interesting data insights.

Existing content – Should you have a blog or media section on site, a recommended route to finding content ideas is to analyse historical posts and media to determine what content received a healthy level of traffic and engagement. This data can be found in Google Analytics. You can then look at possible routes to repurposing or repackaging content in a different way and relaunching the new content to a wider audience.

User-generated content (UGC) – UGC is any content that is created by contributors that are not employed directly by you or your brand. Content types usually comprise blogs, testimonials, reviews, videos and images – think 'Instagrammable' moments – and vlog reviews of your product/service. UGC can empower your users to become part of your campaign, which can build a perception of transparency and trust in your wider target audience. Content ideas can come directly from engaged users and assumes that other similar users will favour your UGC topics too. UGC can also save you production time costs, but it is important that all UGC is proofed and checked for duplicates to ensure that only quality content is added to your site so that it does not violate search engine quality guidelines (please refer to Chapter 7 for more details).

Offline activity – Offline activity such as PR stunts, experiential marketing and offers (in-store/restaurant/bar/supermarket) can be leveraged and amplified through online activity. This would require you to generate a trackable landing page for all related information and traffic generated via the offline PR and marketing activity.

For example, a charity event that is held by your organisation is a perfect opportunity to capture and generate new content. This could entail the following:

- Creation of a landing page with a data capture form to track potential event attendees. Details of who can be used in future outreach initiatives.
- Promotion of the event through your blog, external event promotions sites and your social channels.
- Live streaming of the event via live video transmission (now via YouTube and a number of other networks, which allow you this functionality).
- Creation of an event-specific hashtag, which could be used pre-event, during the event and post-event.
- As a way of prolonging the value of your event, you could capture high-quality photographs and upload images to your social networks to create a digital footprint of your event to allow your event visitors to engage with your content. As event organiser you could contribute to the discussion, amplify the positive content and reply in real time to your audience.
- Following the event, a press release detailing the amount of money generated through charitable donations could be syndicated across online and offline newspaper publications.

This integrated approach would generate opportunities for brand awareness, reputation building and inbound links.

The psychology behind viral content

When considering virality of content during the idea generation process, it is important to note that the vast majority of Internet users are passive – 'lurkers' – who simply consume content and do not engage with it (see Chapter 8 for more details). As such, whilst a viral campaign is the desired outcome of any content marketing campaign, the term can be considered ideological and there is no one strategy that will guarantee that your content goes viral.

However, there is one defining factor that unifies successful viral campaigns and that is emotion, such as empathy, surprise, excitement, sadness, joy and disgust. Generally, we make decisions based on emotion and justify them with logic at a later stage (Carnegie, 2010). Therefore, any content ideas you consider should ideally provoke an emotional response from your buyer persona.

As well as emotion, Berger (2013) observed that there are a number of factors that should be present in order to increase content virality and sharing. Berger's STEPPS model can be used as a guiding checkbox for content optimisation, in particular for larger budget content productions such as video.

S – Social currency – based on the assumption that what we talk about and share reflects how we are perceived. For example, does the content that your target buyer persona is sharing make them feel knowledgeable/witty/caring/cool?

T – Trigger – something that connects the audience to the story and how it resonates with your buyer persona. How will the person remember your content? What makes your content remarkable, memorable and mentionable? Is there an easily remembered song, slogan, strapline or hashtag?

E – Emotion – it moves the audience emotionally when we care about something. This is one of the most difficult aspects to achieve in content creation, as the interpretation of emotion is subjective. For example, humour is often used in content, but it is culturally and community dependent and can lead to misunderstanding. As previously discussed in this section, evoking an unexpected emotional response can set your content apart from other noise on the Internet.

Depending on what message you are trying to convey, overly emotive content could be less effective, whereas content that is too practical can be devoid of emotion.

P – Public – information should be publicly available. Keeping your content open in a public forum allows you to engage with a wider audience. Therefore, always consider whether your content really needs to sit behind a data capture form and make sure your content is optimised with social sharing buttons to encourage quick and accessible social sharing.

When putting your content on a public domain, always remember that people are increasingly aware of crowdsourcing and transparency of content creation. Is it possible to see that a number of other people have consumed your content (e.g. video viewers figures) and shared it (e.g. number of shares for a web page)? This public data adds to the logic of persuasion of your content. If the content is placed on a public social networking site, such as YouTube or Twitter, it is more likely to be amplified by your target audience when compared to a static brand-related web page.

P – Practical value – audiences can apply the lessons they have learned in practice. Informative content that educates and offers practical advice on your product and/or service, as well as offering guidance on topical issues relevant to your buyer persona, makes for highly downloadable and shareable pieces.

'How-to guides' are a common content piece with practical value. As mentioned earlier, tools such as AnswerThePublic.com offer suggestions for FAQ-style content.

S – Story – subtly and coercively generate a story through your content whilst still communicating your underlying content marketing message. Consumers do not like to be sold to as they peruse content. Too much of a sales pitch can put your target buyer off, and it is important you tread carefully with key messaging within your content.

The content mapping process

Once you have thoroughly researched your ideas and you can confirm they are relevant to your buyer persona, you can start to piece together your content ideas to begin visualising your content story. This is called content mapping or 'storyboarding'.

Ideally this process takes place within a team of marketers and creatives to allow full visibility of ideas, which act as talking points for potential content types and other related ideas that have not yet been addressed. It is recommended that the entire team behind the content mapping process is given a persona brief to ensure that this is at the forefront of everyone's mind when discussing ideas.

Content mapping should be tailored to your buyer persona, as discussed in Chapters 3 and 4. The process should allow you to see the relationships between content ideas, which could then offer potential for a content series or multi-method campaign that can be adapted for various content types and ideas. At this stage, you could also consider tying in other online and offline marketing events and activities to make your content marketing efforts more integrated.

Remember to have fun with the idea generation process, as this typically generates the best ideas. It all depends upon the type of content you want to create to fit your persona, whether its purpose is to inform, teach, entertain, trigger an emotional response such as empathy or grab attention through an unconventional PR stunt.

Be sure to document all ideas and do not throw any away, as they can be used at a later date.

Getting buy-in

A recommended final stage of this process is to ensure that the content ideas have been cross-checked with all relevant stakeholders so that content marketing plans can be achieved on time and within budget and that the idea is in keeping with the brand personality and brand guidelines.

If you have not already carried out pre-prospecting, then we also recommend you pitch your favourite ideas back to journalists and other influencers, including bloggers or vloggers, as well as media contacts, before content is created to ensure that there will be interest in your content before the process begins.

9.3 Content creation and development

Once you are confident in your idea and you have buy-in from all relevant stakeholders, you can commence your content creation.

Be sure to select a content type within budget and of relevance to your persona and content idea. For example, if you are wanting to launch a new and exciting hair product, a video demonstrating possible hairstyles might be better than an ebook or a white paper.

We have listed a series of potential content types that you could use to bring your content ideas to life. This is not an exhaustive list, but it contains some of the most commonly used content formats shared on the Internet.

- Blog post

  - What it is – Regular entries on your website that discuss industry updates, news, 'top 10' lists, how-to guides, case studies, award updates, etc. and can contain multimedia elements such as images, infographics and videos.
  - How to do it – Plan out your editorial content in advance and undertake research to ensure your content is unique and relevant. Good blog posts require high-quality specialist copywriting skills to ensure that copy is written in the style, language and tone relevant to the buyer persona. Try not to write just for search engines, although keyword targeting can be incorporated where applicable. Make sure the heading and URL are optimised and the page contains social sharing buttons, a comment box and other related links to encourage click-through to the rest of your site. Consider adding a trackable data capture form and ensure that all blog pages are being tracked in Google Analytics.
  - When to use it – Aim for weekly posts to keep your community engaged and to have fresh content continually added to the site. Therefore, if you say you will blog once a week you need to stick to it and make sure you always have enough to talk about. However, only write a blog post if there is something of value to write – writing for frequency and not for value will invariably affect quality and turn away readers, though consistency is key to encouraging a retained readership that knows when to expect content. Some of the main objectives of blogging are to position you and/or your brand as a specialist within your industry, as well as generating traffic and related keyword rankings. A blog can also be a strategic hub for all social media engagement activity and offers regular content for amplification on other social media profiles.

- Guest blogging

  - What it is – Guest blogs are typically opinion posts hosted on a website external to yours.
  - How to do it – Guest blogging requires time for sourcing appropriate, high-quality content placements with high engagement and high levels

of traffic. The aim is to drive social engagement and brand awareness, as well as generate quality inbound links and referral traffic back to your website. Good guest posts require quality copywriting from specialists within their field.

- When to use it – Utilise guest blogging only if the host website is relevant and active. A poor-quality guest blogging site will look like 'spam' and you risk a search engine penalty.

- Infographics
  - What it is – Infographics are a visualisation of data or other significant information.
  - How to do it – Good-quality infographics will require design time. Ensure that your content is eye-catching and legible and has a flow to it. Only place content into the infographic if it is meaningful.
  - When to use it – They are typically used in conjunction with blog posts to support and visualise key messages. Do not use infographics too often, as this can look like 'spam', which is not SEO best practice.

- Photographs/images
  - What it is – Taking your own photos or designing/illustrating your own images gives them the potential to be used by other blog writers and websites within content, as memes for example.
  - How to do it – Have a professional photographer at any of your events, or if this is not possible use your own smartphone camera to capture the moments which could be shared. When taking pictures of others, inform them in advance and ask permission to use the image as part of your marketing content. Keeping a bank of your own photos ready and searchable by optimising the images utilising SEO techniques (refer to image optimisation section within Chapter 7 for best practice guidelines) will make your photos easily accessible to others who may then request the use of your photos. Invite them to attribute a link back to your site as the original source of the photo if the host site is of a good quality. Consider sharing photos publicly on photosharing social networks such as www.flickr.com and www.instagram.com and setting them as a Creative Commons licence, such as Attribution 2.0 Generic (CC BY 2.0). You can also use images of others with permission or well-recognised meme generators such as https://imgflip.com/memegenerator.
  - When to use it – Images have high engagement rates when used as content on social media platforms. Use images when planning *Facebook, Twitter, Instagram, Pinterest* and *Snapchat* campaigns. There is no real limit to producing images, especially now that most smartphones have good photo camera functionality. Most importantly, ensure that your images are legal, unique and not duplicated from any other sources.

- Online video
    - What it is –Audiovisual content that can be streamed live or downloaded to the user's device. Video content includes vlogs, guides, interviews and adverts.
    - How to do it – Producing a good-quality video can be expensive. Ensure you have a good camera, ideally filming in high definition (HD) – most smartphones film in HD. Use a tripod – this will make sure your shots are steady. Have appropriate lighting so that your subjects are clearly visible and less effort is needed for post-production work. Use video editor software – these are becoming easily available, and even YouTube has its own built-in editor and animator if required. Video length will depend on a number of factors, but consider that most online videos will be watched on a mobile device and that data plans are quickly consumed with high-quality long videos. YouTube allows you to filter videos under 4 minutes (short) and over 20 minutes (long), so consider keeping it under 4 minutes or, if you are planning to create a long video, meet the search filter criteria. Online attention spans are short, so ideally videos should be under 1.5 minutes long, but it is wholly dependent upon the video purpose itself. Videos typically require storyboarding and a script, which need to resonate with your buyer persona.
    - When to use it – Video and in particular mobile video is one of the fastest-growing areas in digital marketing content according to the Internet Advertising Bureau 2019 statistics (IAB, 2019). In 2018, mobile advertising reached a new milestone in the UK, accounting for 51 per cent of total ad spending – from 47 per cent in 2017. Younger generations that grew up with constant access to the Internet are more likely to view video online compared to traditional TV (Smith, 2019). If you can ensure your video content is unique, there is no real limit to posting videos. Just ensure that the content is meaningful and relevant, as you will quickly find viewers will choose not to engage with your content if it has no point.
- Interactive content
    - What it is – Interactive content is any online material that lets the user actively engage with you. It can consist of interactive infographics, long-form articles, interactive videos, quizzes, surveys, etc.
    - How to do it – Good-quality interactive content typically requires design time and usually technical developer time to include the interactive functionality and moving elements. For example, a bank can create a mortgage calculator which is useful for providing quick advice to its buyer persona. Consider tracking interactive elements on the interactive content pages through Google Analytics or heat mapping software to understand how people are engaging with the content to inform future pieces of content.

- When to use it – Interactive content is expensive and should be used strategically to maximise budget and make the most out of an expensive activity.

- Free tools

  - What it is – Free tools can consist of downloadable templates, ebooks, white papers and software with the intention of helping the end user automate and/or optimise some of their existing work processes. As an example, this could be an Excel campaign planner.
  - How to do it – Depending on what free tools you create, this could require a developer, designer or someone proficient in Excel, as well as a skilled copywriter. Consider the pain points of your buyer persona in order to determine how you can save them time through using your tool. Ensure that downloads and tools are hidden behind trackable data capture forms to gather user data for future campaigns.
  - When to use it – Much like interactive content, free tools can take a lot of time to create; hence, these should be used for strategically important activities and can form part of a longer-term campaign.

- Podcasts

  - What it is – Podcasts are digital audio files that fulfil the same purpose as blog posts in that they are an audible way to discuss current events, news stories, interviews and opinion.
  - How to do it – Record an audio file and convert it into a podcast. You will need a good-quality microphone and solid editing skills. Consider branding this with theme music. Aim to get your podcast listed on iTunes or embed your podcast on your website or sound hosting platforms such as SoundCloud.
  - When to use it – Depending on your audience and your resources, consider adding podcasts on a weekly or a monthly basis for maximum pickup and engagement.

- Competitions

  - What it is – Competitions are giveaways of products, services and prizes, which can be relevant to your brand.
  - How to do it – Generating a landing page specifically for the competition details will give you an opportunity to easily share and track traffic to the page. Ensure that you integrate a data capture form and sharing buttons.
  - When to use it – If you choose to host competitions and giveaways regularly, ensure that the prize giveaway is of high value. Be sure that you do not regularly carry out competitions irrelevant to your brand, as you will find your database grows with individuals only interested in your prize giveaways and with no longer-term value.

- Press releases

  - What it is – Press releases are official statements typically detailing product and service launches, issued to industry-specific online and offline newspapers, magazines and general press to raise awareness to their readers.
  - How to do it – Press releases should follow a specific format, which requires a particular style of headline, opening statement, length, layout, quote and closing contact details. It is recommended that further research into press release styles and practice of press release writing is undertaken to fit with industry-specific journalists'/editors' exacting standards.
  - When to use it – Press releases are a PR activity and should be used in conjunction with content marketing strategy.

- Email campaigns

  - What it is – Emails campaigns are messages distributed to individuals within a targeted database containing images, newsletters and updates.
  - How to do it – Ensure that your email headline is attention grabbing and the content is personalised to the reader. Consider adding links back to your website to encourage referral traffic back to your website. Ideally, special mail automation management software is used. A number of free versions such as Mailchimp are available and can help you to trial this important and often underestimated strategy of communication. We also recommend the split a/b testing of email templates to test what drives the most interaction (mailchimp.com/help/best-practices-for-email-subject-lines/).
  - When to use it – Try not to send out too many emails unnecessarily, as the end reader could consider them 'spam'. Offer subscription options for monthly or weekly updates so that your audience can choose the frequency of communications. Make sure that you are only sending out truly relevant and targeted content. Be sure that you comply with opt-in and opt-out protocol and you are only sending your email content to those who are open to receiving it.

- User Generated Content (UGC)

  - What it is – User generated content (UGC) includes reviews, opinion posts, testimonials and content generated via social media channels.
  - How to do it – It is beneficial for creating natural content for your website, as well as other external sites, which can contain a link back to your website. It is also good for building brand reputation and user insight if managed correctly. Reviews are an essential trust-building process for your products and services. Actively

encouraging your customers to create reviews, in particular those customers who are delighted with your products and services, helps you to guide the opinions about your brand online. Make it simple for your customers to create and post reviews. UGC is also helpful for engagement through competitions, for example asking people to submit a photograph or video as part of a prize draw. My Starbucks Idea is a good example of an organisation encouraging the buyer persona to help innovate the business – crowdsourcing ideas for innovation.

- When to use it – There is no constraint on UGC; just ensure that it is well written, is not duplicated from any other sites and does not damage your brand reputation.

As mentioned in the SEO chapter, generating links is important for SEO, so avoid spam tactics when engaging in content marketing. For example, avoid adding your website to online directories unless they are very well known, such as dmoz.org and www.google.com/business/, as many directories are not compliant with Google's Penguin algorithm.

Using the right colours to convey the message

How you use colour in your content affects how your target audience engages with it. Colour helps you to convey your content messages and can guide your buyer persona towards key calls-to-action.

Your choice of colour also helps you to influence and emphasise attitudes and specific feelings towards your content, as each colour can trigger specific emotions. Interpretations of colours are likely to be subjective and can convey different messages based on the cultural background of the individual. For example:

Red communicates physical strength and warmth. It grabs your attention – that's why it is chosen for traffic lights all over the world. Whilst it is perceived as friendly, it can also be associated with aggression and danger.

Blue conveys intelligence, trust and efficiency. It is often used by politicians to convey their trustworthiness. However, it can be perceived as unemotional and unfriendly.

Yellow is associated with hope, positivity and optimism. Careful use of this colour in combination with others is advised, as it can trigger anxiety and depression.

Whilst the list above gives insight into emotional reactions related to the primary colours, lots of other colours and colour combinations can trigger specific reactions. As such, it is recommended that split a/b testing is carried out to determine which content style delivers the biggest impact.

Content tracking

It is important that you ensure you have proven and tested all elements of your content, such as data capture forms and social sharing buttons, before launching your content and sharing it with your audience. Poor content can put your audience off interacting with your brand and can make it hard to track how well your content marketing campaign has performed.

In order to track the progress of your content marketing campaign to ensure it is performing and to justify the budget for future content marketing campaigns, you should have tracked all elements of your content, such as 'clickable' elements and 'thank you' pages. More details on tracking are in Chapter 12.

Content tracking tools and KPIs will be explored in Section 9.5 of this chapter.

9.4 Content marketing implementation and delivery

Once you are happy that your content is fully integrated into your website or a website external to yours, and your tracking is correct, this is where you will look at sharing and amplifying your content to your buyer persona. The process of getting your content in front of your buyer persona is known as 'outreach'.

Research completed in stage one should have allowed you to construct a media list full of target publications, bloggers and key influencers who would be interested in hosting and sharing your content.

Outreach to contacts is a delicate, carefully considered process that requires a certain level of charisma to build a rapport and relationship with contacts in your media list. Remember that your contacts probably receive hundreds of requests per day, so ensure that your content pitch details the clear value and benefits of hosting or sharing your content. An automated email sent out to your list without any personalisation or thought will work against you and could sour the relationship for future content marketing campaigns.

To further amplify your content, we recommend the following distribution channels, though the most appropriate channels for your business are entirely dependent upon what content you have decided to create and which channels your target audience are using:

- YouTube/Vimeo – a video content platform that can be optimised to encourage ranking of video content in search engines.
- WeChat – a social network that is focusing on Chinese consumers and is mostly used by them inside and outside of China.
- Facebook – a social media platform that is typically used for informal content and networking. Good for business-to-consumer (B2C) and consumer-to-consumer (C2C) content marketing.
- Instagram – a photo- and video-sharing social media platform that is particularly useful for showcasing visual products such as clothing and cosmetics.

- Twitter – a content-sharing and networking platform. Consider using a hashtag for ease of tracking and consistency in branding.
- LinkedIn – a platform typically used by professionals and career-driven types. Good for business-to-business (B2B) content marketing.
- Email – free emailing platforms such as Mailchimp allow you to create email templates and track engagement rates.
- Paid media – paid-for content distribution channels such as PPC, display advertising and paid social advertising can be highly targeted and keyword-/interest-specific.

When planning your content marketing activities, it is helpful to consider what is happening currently by your organisation in terms of content creation and communication. Same analysis can be used to compare your competitors and to create future plans of desirable actions by your organisation in terms of content marketing. Table 9.1 shows an example of how to analyse the activity of a London-based florist who was introduced in the earlier chapters of this book (see Chapter 3).

Further details of social media marketing channels, platforms and tactics can be found in Chapter 8.

Be sure to keep track of outreach progress using free management tools such as Trello, Basecamp or Slack and ensure all correspondence is saved for future content marketing campaigns. If there is a team of you working on the outreach of your content marketing campaign, be sure to create a shared file of all contact made, related dates and status of communication to ensure there is no duplication of work and you are not continually disturbing your contacts. Should you be successful in placing your content, we also recommend that you request a link back to your website for SEO purposes and add this into your progress report. It is important to note that these inbound backlinks are a bonus of content marketing and not the driving motivation.

There are some automated tools to help you schedule your communication efforts such as Hootsuite and BuzzStream. The platforms also allow

Table 9.1 Content analysis table

Channel (Where will you publish it?)	Content (What are you publishing?)	Buyer persona (Who will benefit from this content?)	Value (How can you benefit?)
Facebook	Competitions and product development updates	Nigel Bloom	Engaging audience and learning about their preferences
LinkedIn	Top ten lists of wedding organisers in London	Lucy Bels	Awareness raising and attraction of best organisers to use our services

you to centralise your social marketing efforts by automatically tracking the pickup of your content.

We recommend that you continually test and optimise your outreach process (such as the time outreach occurred, key messages used in emails and tweets, which social profiles get the most traction – work or personal) to continually optimise and learn from your outreach and content marketing efforts.

9.5 Content marketing campaign evaluation

Assuming that you have been very clear about your goals set in the early stages of your content marketing campaign planning, this is the point at which you determine how well your campaign has performed against the common KPIs listed in Table 9.2.

Whilst return on investment (ROI) can be notoriously difficult to outline, you can split your conversions into primary and secondary sales metrics:

> **Primary sales metrics** – Those achieved through individuals landing directly on your website via your content landing page, a journey that is relatively

Table 9.2 Content marketing goals, metrics and tools

Goal	Metrics	Tool
Brand awareness	Traffic generated to content via referral, direct, paid and organic channels, traffic generated to website, click-through rate from content to rest of website, content views, time spent on content site/content	Google Analytics, using URL builder
Lead generation	Subscriptions and downloads	Google Analytics, using URL builder
Sales and ROI	Sales generated, conversion rate percentage	Google Analytics, using URL builder
Retention	Number of returning visitors	Google Analytics
Social engagement	Content views, shares, interactions, comments, followers (Followerwonk), time spent on content, in-page analytics, bounce rate	Twitter Analytics LinkedIn Analytics YouTube Analytics Google+ Platform Insights Facebook Analytics Simply Measured (for Instagram) Mailchimp reports (for Instagram) AdWords (for PPC)
Link building	Number of high-quality inbound links generated to content and website	Open Site Explorer, SEMrush, Linkdex

easy to follow should you have e-commerce and conversion tracking set up correctly, with a value assigned to each completed conversion.

Secondary sales metrics – As discussed in Chapter 1, the average consumer will come into contact with multiple content touchpoints over the duration of a campaign, which makes tracking the ROI of such journeys problematic. The recommended route adopted by various content marketers is to allocate an estimated monetary value to your marketing efforts, channels, goals and KPIs to build a clearer picture of how well your campaign has performed.

Free automated reporting platforms

Whilst it is recommended you monitor your Google Analytics and social media analytics profiles on a daily basis, there are free automated tracking and reporting tools such as Scoop.it (http://business.scoop.it/) and Buffer (https://buffer.com/) which remove some of the manual aspects of content marketing analysis from the reporting process.

Debrief

At the end of your content marketing campaign, we recommend that a full campaign debrief is undertaken with all members involved in the content marketing campaign in question. This will allow you to constructively assess which elements of the campaign worked and which elements could be improved upon for future campaigns. Key learnings can be used to streamline future processes, as well as contributing to a crisis communication management plan for the benefit of managing your brand reputation in future campaigns.

Case Study 9.2   Salford Business School UGC

The Salford Business School blog (Figure 9.3) was created to increase brand awareness of the Business School and to engage students, alumni and external organisations. The blog was launched in January 2014 and had the following four KPIs for the first year:

- Be updated once per week.
- Recruitment of ten bloggers.
- Get 10,000 views.
- Get at least one student to apply as a consequence of blog content.

The KPIs were modest for a new blog, as it was the first year, it was a trial project and there was no central marketing resource allocated

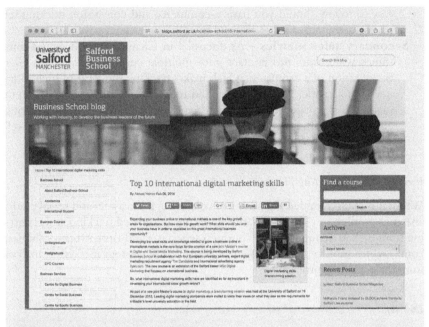

Figure 9.3 Salford Business School blog

Figure 9.4 Screenshot of Google Analytics for Salford Business School blog, 1 January 2014 to 1 January 2015

for this activity. As such, current students, business partners and academics were given the option to create UGC related to the Business School, as well as being encouraged to share and promote content via their preferred social channels.

For the students, content creation was part of their assignment brief. This assessment requirement encouraged blogging and enabled the development of content optimisation skills.

All the KPIs were met and superseded in the first year (Figure 9.4). Two distinctive days have been annotated on the Google Analytics time-line – 10 April 2014 and 24 July 2014 – which were when the student projects went live.

Source: http://blogs.salford.ac.uk/business-school/

9.6 Content creation and copywriting techniques and tips

Integrating your key messaging across platforms for brand consistency is not an easy task. You've defined who you are. Be it.

You'll have a mission statement or brand value proposition which captures your essence and which talks to your audience in a language they understand. A language that appeals, that builds proximity. So take that spirit and the language that represents it. Thread it through all your communications across all platforms, clearly and consistently.

As mentioned above, emotion is important in reaching out to your buyer persona and it is a key ingredient in making your content go viral. When Anton Chekhov (1860–1904) instructed his brother on how to write, he suggested to him to not directly tell the facts. Instead, he suggested that the impact of the fact should be described connecting with the reader on an emotional level (Chekhov, 1954).

It is important to appreciate the power of the six primary human emotions – anger, disgust, fear, happiness, sadness and surprise – as the driving force in eliciting a response to our writing. A seventh, often a component of the others, is yet more powerful still. More about that later, though.

Identifying both how your audience feels and how you want them to feel will dictate the language you choose to use. Here are some brief examples of language that you might use when appealing to the six primaries:

Happiness: Congratulations!
The best time you ever had?
Sadness: There's no easy way to say this.
For my daughter.
Disgust: This building smelt damp and had animal waste on the doorstep.
The stench of open sewers.
Anger: Please help us find the monster that took these beautiful puppies.
Widow cheated out of her life savings.
Fear: 48 hours to stop the next Chernobyl?
How would you cope with a tax office inspection?
Surprise: You don't need to be a millionaire to be treated like one.
Someone likes you!!!

That seventh emotion that keeps people hanging on your every word? Curiosity.

Tone of voice

A tone of voice represents your values, the reason you exist, what makes you different and the way you think.

Only once your values are clear (what you say) should you start to look at your vocabulary (how you say it) – the language you will need to express your values.

A good starting point is to look at the language your customers already use when they talk about your products and services.

Create a range of test writing and use it to identify what your tone is and, more importantly, what it is not. Use this comparative analysis to set tone-of-voice guidelines.

Be relevant

Deliver the right message to the right audience. Of course, you will want your content to have a fabulous aesthetic and to provide plenty of share options. But unless the writing talks to your audience about their lives, and unless it addresses the problems they face, offers solutions, scratches itches, informs, educates and entertains – unless it is laser guided – your content is going nowhere. Slowly.

Anatomy of a good blog post

To quote the classic David Ogilvy line about headlines: 'On average, five times as many people read the headline as read the body copy. When you have written your headline, you have spent eighty cents out of your dollar'.

Best make your headline as compelling as possible: a headline that provokes curiosity, conveys news or promises a benefit – ideally a combination of all three.

Your first paragraph should open with a bang, your conclusion even. Think inverted pyramid.

- Use short sentences.
- And short paragraphs.
- Make the copy easily scannable.
- An arresting image helps.
- Be interesting.
- Be interesting and fiercely relevant.

Content for multi-platform content marketing campaigns

Multi-platform copy is modular copy. In effect, the components of a single high-quality piece are split up and repurposed across platforms. That's not to say that the piece needs to even exist as a single entity before being carved up, though. It's the principles that count.

Make your headline and subheads into tweet copy. Write your Facebook updates to lure. Your high-impact intro paragraphs and your conclusions can all be enticing leads. Your body copy is the basis for a more in-depth, informative landing pages – they are the 'meat' on your social 'bones'.

If your ideas are strong and your copy supports with strength, with relevance, with humour, with empathy and with insight, you've already won.

9.7 Summary

This chapter focuses on the most important aspect of digital and social media marketing – content. Content comes in many formats – text, video, images – but one key message from this book is the need to understand the target audience and spend time identifying how they like to communicate and what is of interest to them. Only once the buyer persona is clearly understood is it possible to develop content that is relevant for them. The content is in the middle of the Buyer Persona Spring.

A range of processes and theoretical frameworks has been explored in this chapter, from viral marketing to the psychology related to the content types and formatting. All these considerations should be used when developing high-quality content. Once quality content has been produced, the amplification process commences and, here, effort and energy are invested to reach out to relevant stakeholders and influencers who can help to further amplify the content.

Content marketing implementation draws on all chapters of this book. The key challenge that you face when embracing content marketing is the ability to create high-quality content and having a sustainable routine of content creation and curation for community engagement which supports your strategic business objectives. Having a lot of views of your video is a good KPI, but what is important for your long-term strategy is how many of those individuals acted upon that content and whether you were able to get your message across – generating results for your campaign.

9.8 References

Ad Rank (2019) *Is living in London more expensive than living on a cruise ship?* www.ad-rank. com/our-work/cruisedeals-co-uk-online-pr-case-study/

Berger, J. (2013) *Contagious: Why things catch on.* New York, NY: Simon and Schuster.

Carnegie, D. (ed.) (2010) *How to win friends and influence people.* New York, NY: Pocket Books.

Chekhov (1954) *The unknown Chekhov: Stories and other writings hitherto.* Untranslated by Anton Chekhov, translated by Avrahm Yarmolinsky. New York: Noonday Press.

Creative Commons (2019) *Licenses.* creativecommons.org/about/

The European Union Open Data Portal (*EU* ODP) (2019) *Open data portal.* data.europa. eu/euodp/en/home

Foster, J. (2019) *How to use ego bait content to attract links & generate leads.* www.searchengine
journal.com/link-building-guide/ego-bait-content/

IAB (2019) *IAB/PwC study: Smartphone accounts for more than half of digital ad spend* www.
iabuk.com/news-article/smartphone-accounts-more-half-digital-ad-spend

Smith, K. T. (2019) Mobile advertising to digital natives: Preferences on content, style, per-
sonalization, and functionality. *Journal of Strategic Marketing*, 27(1), 67–80.

Survey System (2016) *Company website.* www.surveysystem.com/sscalc.htm

10 Paid advertising – search, social and affiliate

Rimantas Gatautis and Elena Vitkauskaitė

10.0 Learning objectives

In this chapter you will learn how to:

- understand the range of paid search, social and affiliate advertising opportunities;
- plan and implement paid digital advertising across multiple profiles; and
- evaluate and benchmark paid communications and affiliate advertising activities.

10.1 Paid advertising in context

In Chapter 7 you explored the benefits of working on the organic search engine optimisation (SEO) for your business. Here, we look at another way of directing traffic to your calls-to-action, either from external websites or via platforms such as search engines or social media networks – paid digital marketing communications.

Not only are paid digital marketing communications a way to have more control over the content and placement of your organisation's message, but, unlike organic SEO, they also offer instant results. As more users join social media platforms and spend increasingly longer periods of time socialising on them, paid social media marketing has become an increasingly important part of digital marketing.

But first, it is important to differentiate between 'paid display marketing' and 'paid search marketing', since the type of content and expectations on return on investment (ROI) tend to be different for each. Display marketing simply shows your ads when a user visits a certain website, which could be a social network site or a website that is taking part in the display advertising network. Display marketing provides more possibilities for advertisers to integrate their ads into the content of social communications between users and brands, as well as between users and other users. Although it is industry-dependent, display marketing is generally better placed for brand awareness communications. In contrast, search marketing tends to be closer to the purchase decision, since once someone is searching for your product or services, chances are they want to know more about them and might be keen to purchase these.

Although most platforms offering paid marketing solutions claim that they can set up and get ads running in no time, understanding how advertising works on each platform is essential in order to save time and costs by avoiding the most common mistakes. There are also potential benefits to running parallel paid and organic campaigns in order to increase the exposure of a campaign and thus obtain synergies for content reach to a level that individual channels could not achieve in isolation.

The increasing uses of ad-blocking software by browsers and through third-party offerings should be a factor into any planning for paid advertising. If your buyer persona can be identified as an adopter of these forms of technology then the benefits of paid advertising will significantly diminished.

10.2 Understanding paid advertising

Paid search marketing is also referred to as pay-per-click (PPC) search engine advertising or paid search, amongst other terms, and is part of search engine marketing. It differs from 'organic' or 'natural' SEO (discussed in Chapter 7) because it involves paid content placement.

In essence, search advertising is an advert that is triggered by a search engine user when they type a related keyword phrase into a search box. The ad copy is written by the advertiser and relates to their website offering in terms of what the user is searching for. Good ad copy will relay the benefits of the website to the user; if the ad is highly relevant to the search query, this should encourage the user to click the ad.

This ad is usually displayed on a search engine results page (SERP), either above the organic search results, below them or on the right-hand side (see Figure 10.1). The position of the ads always changes as search engines evolve. For example, Google removed its ads in early 2016 from the right-hand side of the desktop search results in a move to make its web pages more mobile-friendly. It is likely that other search engines such as Baidu, Bing and Yahoo! might follow this direction in due course. Descriptions of paid search marketing provided in this chapter are based largely on Google Ads, with details of the alternative systems covered separately later in the chapter.

A search engine's online advertising services might also provide the opportunity to place ads on third-party websites in their *display (content) networks*. Ads are posted on websites in relation to the content of those sites and relevance of these sites to the keywords defined by the advertiser. In this case the 'search' is conducted on behalf of the advertiser who wants to find a relevant platform for their content. Display advertising networks allow website owners to 'sell' space on their websites to display network management platforms such as Google AdSense. Display advertising is particularly popular amongst larger brands, but smaller organisations looking for targeted brand awareness can also reap the benefits of this method. Display advertising relies on creating message

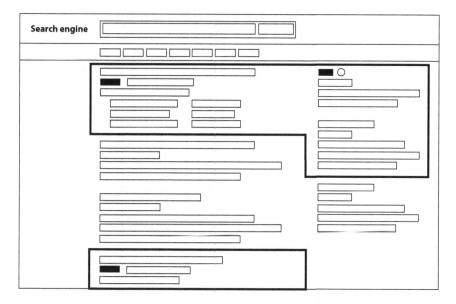

Figure 10.1 Paid search results on SERP

creative content such as images and video, which tend to be more labour-intensive and require more resources and skills. This is particularly important, since the organic content reach on major social network sites such as Facebook and Twitter is in decline.

Generally, ads can be paid for on a cost-per-click (CPC), cost-per-mille or cost-per-thousand impressions (CPM) or cost-per-action (CPA) basis. Ads can include images and video content, as well as text (Table 10.1).

Video and image ads tend to be display ad formats, since video and images don't tend to appear on search engines, but they do appear on social media search results pages of various social network sites such as YouTube. Search ads appear when the user makes a search. Display ads appear when a user fits an audience profile or through remarketing, without the need for the user to search. However, some search engines serve display ads on SERPs too.

How does PPC work?

The listing position of an ad in paid search results is decided through an *auction* that happens each time the ad is triggered by a keyword and other parameters (e.g. time of day, location of the user) that have been selected by the advertiser. Generally, the higher the ad position in SERPs, the more exposure it receives. As search engines strive to provide users with the most relevant search results, the maximum amount of the CPC bid is important, but is not

Table 10.1 Common types of paid advertisements

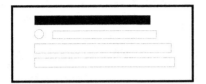

Figure 10.1.1 Text ads

Text ads
Contain only words. In Google Ads they are made of four lines visible to users: a headline of up to 25 characters long, 2 x 35 character-long descriptions and a displayed URL address no longer than 35 characters (online advertising services of other search engines have different character limits).

Text ads can also be enabled across the display networks – in other words, websites that are not owned by Google can also display your ads.

Image ads
Ads use static or interactive graphics. They allow advertisers to showcase their product or service in a visual way and to reach customers on websites in display networks.

With Google the ads can only be displayed across the Google Display Network. Some other search engines allow image ads on search results as well (e.g. mail.ru).

Figure 10.1.2 Image ads

Video ads
Online video advertising. Advertisers can run standalone video ads or insert them in streaming video content. These ads allow advertisers to deliver a rich and engaging experience to customers and to reach customers on websites in display networks.

In Google Ads such ads can only be displayed across the Google Display Network, as with image ads.

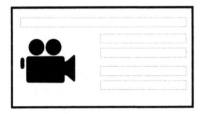

Figure 10.1.3 Video ads

Mobile phone ads
These are text or image ads for mobile phone devices. Usually, they have a smaller limit of characters to fit screens of non-smartphones.

They allow advertisers to connect with their customers on the go, targeting their ads based on customers' locations and offering different actions such as calling a phone number.

Figure 10.1.4 Mobile ads

Figure 10.1.5 Ad extensions

Ad extensions

Ad extensions are not full ads on their own. They extend other types of ads (mostly text ads) with more information, such as additional links to the website (site links), store address (location extension) or phone number (call extension) and others. Call extensions used in mobile ads enable users to make a call directly without visiting the page. In Google Ads, ad extensions usually appear across the Search Network. However, location extensions and call extensions may also appear across the Google Display Network.

Quality score

| 6/10 |

Learn more

Expected click-through rate: Average
Ad relevance: Average
Landing page experience: Average

Figure 10.2 Example of Google Ads Quality Score breakdown

the deciding factor in who wins the auction and is ranked in the top results. The relevance of the keyword is measured by another variable called Quality Score in Google Ads, which is equally as important a factor as the keyword bid amount in determining the outcome of the auction.

Google Ads introduced the Quality Score, and other search engines developed similar measures. Quality Score is defined as 'an estimate of the quality of your ads, keywords, and landing page' (Google Ads Help Centre).

In Google Ads, each keyword targeted gets the quality score – a number from 1 to 10 where 1 is low and 10 is high. It is also a number that is shared with the advertiser as a feedback mechanism to improve the quality of the ad (Figure 10.2).

This shows that Quality Score is measured based on the expected *click-through rate*, ad relevance to the keyword targeted and landing page experience, as well as on other indicators such as historical performance of the account, which Google does not fully disclose.

Generally, if a website is ranking number 1 in an organic listing for the same keyword term, it is going to have a positive effect on the paid ad quality score (Ayanso and Karimi, 2015). Therefore, coordinating keyword selection is helpful for synergies between paid search advertising and organic SEO.

For example, keywords clearly reflected in an ad copy, which match the keyword term query of the user and lead to a highly relevant landing page, would get a higher Quality Score. A higher Quality Score leads to lower costs for the advertiser and a higher ad listing position (*ad rank*). A lower Quality Score results in higher costs and a lower ad rank. Moreover, keywords that do not reach the minimum Quality Score would not trigger ads to be shown at all, no matter how high the bids offered by advertisers are.

How does remarketing work?

Whilst the above is a basic overview of paid ad strategies, there are also a number of more advanced, personalised ways to set up bidding options. All search engines continue to innovate to offer you the best way to reach your buyer persona. One of the more advanced options for paid search engine advertising is remarketing.

Remarketing works on the principle that once someone has visited your website they are more likely to interact with your website again because they are already aware of you. Technically this works by creating tags for your web pages, which are then placed in cookies on the computer of your visitor. Then, when the visitor browses a website that recognises the cookie, and if your remarketing settings are valid, the ad is displayed to the user.

Remarketing can be used successfully for users that have not completed the desired action such as a purchase and who will benefit from a reminder of your product or service. It can also be used for those who have made a purchase and might be interested in a repeat or additional purchase.

There are several remarketing formats. Google, for example, currently allows (as of March 2016) the following five options:

1   Mobile apps, targeting users of your mobile website or app when they view apps of others. Also, video remarketing targets those who viewed your video content.
2   Remarketing lists for search ads is the term used by Google for customising search ads campaigns.
3   Standard remarketing displays your ads to known visitors when they browse related display network websites and use display network apps.
4   Dynamic remarketing allows for the content of the exact product or service that was viewed to be shown to the user. The setting up of such methods does take more time, since each product has to be appropriately tagged, but the results are much more powerful since the user is offered the exact product or service they were interested in during the first interaction.
5   Last but not least is video remarketing – this format allows you to display ads to those who interacted with your YouTube channel or videos when they browse YouTube and visit display network websites, apps and videos.

When should you choose the CPM model?

Paid search ads tend to be well placed to trigger click actions related to sales or website traffic building. It is useful to bear in mind that for brand awareness campaigns, serving ads on a display network (and bidding based on CPM or cost-per-thousand impressions) is a more suitable option.

The CPM model provides a good suitable measure for campaign setting, where the advertising efforts are directly measured by thousands of impressions. The potential for fraud in CPM increases, since essentially all that the host of the ad has to do is prove that the page where your ad was placed was viewed. Therefore, regular monitoring of activities for CPM is important.

10.3 Differences in paid advertising on various search engines in Europe

Europeans mostly use the Google search engine for looking up information, with the popularity of other search engines lagging far behind (see Figure 10.3). On the other hand, Europe is not homogeneous, and popularity of search engines is not equally distributed across all countries. Therefore, it might be important to learn the peculiarities of advertising on different search engines popular in Europe, depending on the target markets that paid search marketing efforts are focused on. Reviewing these alternatives can offer potentially more cost-effective ways to reach out to your buyer persona, since the costs of ads can be cheaper when compared to Google Ads due to fewer advertisers competing for the same keywords.

Advertising on Yahoo! and Bing is currently done via Bing Ads. It gives advertisers access to advertising on both search engines, which together are called Yahoo! Bing Network. Therefore, the peculiarities of advertising on Google, Yahoo! Bing Network, Yandex, Mail.ru and Seznam are what we will now focus on.

Google

Google is the most popular search engine in all European countries, with more than a 90 per cent market share of the search engine market in most countries (StatCounter, July 2019). However, on a global scale there are exceptions and the market is in constant flux. For example, in China Google only has 3 per cent market share.

Advertising on the Google search engine is done by using the online advertising service Google Ads (https://ads.google.com), which provides advertisers

Figure 10.3 Grouping ads into ad groups

with access to place ads in the Google Search Network (a number of non-Google websites [like Ask.com], as well as Google Maps, Google Video and other Google sites), and in the Google Display Network (websites that show Google Ads). As most of the paid search marketing aspects discussed in this chapter are based on the Google Ads service, they are not repeated here.

Baidu advertising

For China, local search engines such as Baidu has over 75 per cent, Sogou over 10 per cent and Shenma over 4 per cent market share. Speaking the language and knowing the local culture would be the requirements for any brand wishing to venture out to Chinese consumers.

For any brand trying to reach simplified Chinese-speaking users, Baidu is the target search engine to approach. The process of setting up paid advertising is more elaborate compared to other search engines and will take time to process and might require you to make a substantial payment deposit as well as potential edits to your website. The process has to qualify you to be able to advertise before you can launch your campaigns. However, once you get approval the Baidu Tuiguang, Baidu's PPC management platform, is the interface which is somewhat similar to Google Ads, explained above.

Yahoo! Bing Network

Yahoo! Bing Network serves over 3 per cent of search queries in Europe overall (StatCounter, July 2019).

Advertising on Yahoo! Bing Network is done using the online advertising service Bing Ads (http://advertise.bingads.microsoft.com), which is similar to Google Ads and even enables importing Google Ads campaigns. The most significant differences listed in the Help section of the service relate to different targeting options and a different approach to calculating the Quality Score.

Yandex

The Russian search engine Yandex has lost its market share in several countries in Eastern Europe, most notably in Belarus and Ukraine and even in the Russian Federation. It might be an option for those advertisers targeting Russian speakers in Moldova, Estonia and Latvia, though the market share of this search engine does not exceed 5 per cent there. The international version of this engine also has a small search engine market share in Turkey (StatCounter, July 2019).

Online advertising service Yandex Direct (https://direct.yandex.com/) is used for search advertising on the Yandex search engine. Its major differences from Google Ads include fewer opportunities to structure campaigns; higher limits for number of characters in the ads; a different approach to auctions and bidding (advertisers can bid for specific listing positions on SERPs, and auction happens only for positions they have bid for); less sophisticated reporting of campaign effectiveness; requires minimum order size to start campaign; and offers discounts for large-scope campaigns.

Mail.ru

Mail.ru is another Russian search engine and could be an option for advertisers targeting Belarus, the Russian Federation, Ukraine, Moldova and Estonia.

The company owns a range of websites, their search engine being just one of many properties. Advertising on all those properties can be done using the online advertising service Target (https://target.mail.ru/). Significant differences between this and Google Ads include absence of text ads type (service mostly focuses on banner ads); ads are not related to keywords but placements; requires minimum order size to start a campaign; auctions depend on click-through-rate (CTR) and competition in same target market (in relation to targeting options); interface is only available in Russian; and offers advertising services directly.

Seznam

Established in 1996 as the first web portal in the Czech Republic, Seznam. cz was the most popular search service in the country for years. Currently, the search market in the country has been overtaken by Google, but Seznam is still the second largest search engine in the Czech Republic.

The company provides its Sklik service (www.sklik.cz/en/) to facilitate advertising on its properties. The service is similar to Google Ads and provides similar functionalities. On the other hand, these functionalities are more limited in comparison (for example, ad copy extensions are limited to site links), the interface is only available in the Czech language and the company offers campaign management services directly.

Even more search engines are available in European countries which do not have a critical mass of users at the time of writing, but might have become worthy of the attention of advertisers by the time you are reading this. Market shares of search engines can be checked on services like StatCounter Global Stats (http://gs.statcounter.com/).

10.4 Planning and managing paid search marketing

Since paid search advertising relies on the quality of the URL to which it is linked, it is recommended that the organic SEO of the web page, and ideally the entire website, be completed prior to commencing PPC experimentation. This will help in isolating the impact that paid search advertising has on the website and will reduce the potentially negative impact of poor user experience. This book encourages you to experiment. Only with a trial and error approach and evaluation of the results will you be able to determine whether paid search advertising works for your organisation.

The rapid nature of the paid search advertising setup process allows for quick experimentation and refinements of search engine marketing efforts, so it is essential to allocate regular times for monitoring paid search advertising activities. Unlike organic SEO, paid search advertising can very quickly use up a budget if not monitored closely, particularly if you are unfamiliar with the tools available to you. As with all other paid advertising options, there is a risk of fraud (where, say, your competitors click on your ads to run down your advertising budget). All search engines continuously work to reduce and mitigate click fraud but awareness of its ongoing impact must be incorporated into the planning and design of campaigns.

The following steps detail good practice and are grouped to cover ad targeting, budget and bid management, creative testing and campaign optimisation, analysis of campaign results and communications integration aspects of paid search marketing.

Structuring your account

Similarly to organic SEO, the paid search advertising account needs to be structured to reflect the structure of your website and particularly the products and services offered. Within Google Ads, you have the option to divide your account into campaigns, and within each of these campaigns you have several ad groups. The budgets and targeting are set at the campaign level, but the individual keywords to be targeted are defined in the ad groups. Learning about the effectiveness of different campaigns – for example, by targeting display networks or only search engine users – can give comparative data sets and offer evidence for future campaigns.

Account: Domestic appliances shop
Within this account a number of different product types could be advertised, for example:
Campaigns: Washing machines; Refrigerators; Cookers
Within each of the campaigns there are different ad groups that allow you to target different user needs with a shared set of keywords. For example, the one for refrigerators could have campaigns based on the type of refrigerator:
Ad groups: Refrigerators: Top Freezer Refrigerators; Compact Fridges; French Door Fridges

Within each ad group (Figure 10.3) you could have at least two ads which are interchangeably shared and constantly tested for their success. The ad rotation settings allow for optimising CTR or rotating evenly, which gives more feedback of a/b testing and data for identifying the more successful advertising creative. If manual bidding is set, make sure you review the results regularly.

When creating content for the display network, bear in mind that users are less likely to be in a research mindset, and therefore (similarly to social media network sites) the creative message should be less sales-focused. Monitor your ads' performance and revise, and if there is a theme related to a badly performing display network use the exclusion tool to refine where your ads appear. In the same way, review keywords and remove if a term is not performing – your aim is to only keep high-performing keywords.

Keyword alignment strategy

Overall organisational goals and business objectives can help in identifying specific ad groups. The number of keywords that are used to trigger a particular ad group depends on the granularity of the products and services being targeted. However, to make the ads relevant to what the user types into a search engine, using from 5 up to 15 keywords is a good benchmark to aim for and to keep to the lower numbers; otherwise the chance of your ad being irrelevant increases. Regular exclusion and deletion of keywords from ad groups can help to maintain a good Quality Score.

Around 20 per cent of keywords entered into a search engine are new and have not been used before – how can you capture these users? Using broad keyword match types allows your ad to be triggered when it contains a related term. But if you have a high-volume and high-value search term and are targeting it, then the exact keyword match type is more appropriate.

For websites where content related to their products and services is not updated daily, the Dynamic Search Ads can offer additional exposure. Unlike keyword targeting, these ads are based on content that has been indexed in organic search results. As an advertiser, you still have control of some of the aspects, but the headline and the URLs are being generated automatically by Google Ads.

Regular account maintenance requires identifying negative keywords, i.e. choosing those words which, should a user type them into a search engine, should not trigger your ad. Analysis of the search terms report and the Keyword Planner tool offers more insight into potential negative keywords for your Google Ads groups.

Budget and bid management

Developing a budget for paid search advertising should be based on the profitability and the return in the investment calculations. Ultimately, the results generated by paid search advertising are trackable and these should inform whether it is worth investing in paid search advertising and, if so, how much. Paid search marketing is ideal as support for organic SEO efforts. Test paid search advertising by entirely switching it off and then monitoring the impact. The management of daily budgets helps to control the overall spend, and understanding the buyer persona and the hours and days they are likely to benefit from your ad can increase conversion rates. Have time-specific campaigns if necessary.

The *ad rank* for an ad based on a targeted keyword changes dynamically as the advertiser competes with other advertisers. It is a number from 1 to 10 and is expressed as an average such as 3.4 to reflect how it varies with time. Always having your listing rank as 1 might be expensive because you might have to bid higher than every other advertiser. On the other hand, the lower positions usually do not yield good click-through rates, though they cost less. Therefore, it might be useful to have a balance in your keyword portfolio, with both high- and low-ranking terms.

Ongoing testing and optimisation

Ad creatives – in other words, text, images or video where relevant – are the only parts of a paid search campaign visible to searchers and therefore of great significance to the success of the campaign. Because of their relevance, it is important to incorporate your targeted keywords in the ad creatives. What makes your content different? Highlight your unique selling points (USPs). Continuously run three or four variations of ads and learn what makes the better-performing ads more appealing to your buyer persona.

Destination or landing pages are pages on your website where searchers land when they click on the ad. These pages have to be optimised for organic on-page SEO for the related search term. Using data from Google Analytics, regularly review whether the content of the page follows the AIDA model and offers the user what they were hoping for when they clicked on the ad. User experience testing can help to refine these landing pages.

Campaign review and optimisation is a structured approach to reviewing an existing campaign and improving the paid search advertising results. The review should take into account paid search marketing performance in relation to other channels, relative performance to historic time period, competitor activity, etc. These reviews can take place on a weekly or – if needed – daily basis, especially at the critical points of a campaign. Learn through this data about your buyer persona behaviour and, if necessary, share the results to inform activities on other channels.

Case Study 10.1   HIDROMOTAS

HIDROMOTAS (www.hidromotas.lt), a small Lithuanian company established in 1997, specialises in repairs and sales of power steering systems and hydraulic components. The company mainly serves clients from Vilnius city and its surroundings. In 2008 the economic crisis forced the company to look for more effective means to increase sales with a small budget.

Paid search marketing using Google Ads was the chosen trial campaign. By serving ads only to searchers located in Vilnius or in its vicinity, the traffic from regions that were not relevant to this organisation was avoided.

Using the insights gathered from Google Analytics, the keywords with high bounce rates and that were not converting to completed actions were removed from the list of keywords that trigger ads to appear.

As the company does not sell online, navigation to the Contact page was regarded as a conversion in this campaign.

With the initial budget of only 5 Lithuanian litas (approximately €1.45) per day for the Google Ads campaign, the company experienced a 25 per cent increase in sales and profit. The campaign optimisation efforts resulted in a bounce rate drop of only 8 per cent, and 38 per cent of website users visiting by clicking on paid search ads navigated to the Contact page.

Google Ads is especially attractive to small and medium-sized companies, as it allows tangible results to be achieved in a short time even with a very small budget. The campaign was regarded as a success according to Emilis Jarockis, HIDROMOTAS Google Ads account manager and digital marketing consultant at digital marketing agency Sinergija Verslui.

The HIDROMOTAS example illustrates the need to regularly review and refine keywords for a paid search advertising campaign. The non-performing keywords can be deleted or paused. Your preference should be to pause keywords to avoid the chance of their reactivation during the same campaign. By pausing a keyword and not deleting it, the campaign data is preserved and is available for future reference. Your keywords and campaigns must be regularly monitored. Depending on your daily budget, smaller campaigns should be reviewed daily, while larger budgets might be monitored hourly.

10.5 Paid social media marketing introduction

Social media marketing is an increasingly important part of digital marketing, as more users join social media platforms and are spending increasingly longer periods of time socialising on those platforms. Exactly because of this increase in using social media worldwide, it is no longer enough for organisations to rely on free organic engagement methods on social media. Organic content published by organisations on social media competes with ever-increasing numbers of contributions from other organisations and other users. Your content is not only competing with other content for the attention of followers. Social media platforms will filter content in order to only display what it regards as relevant material. Your content must also compete to pass through this filter.

Therefore, to reach the potential customers on social media, paid advertising (also called *paid social media marketing*, paid social media advertising and integrated social advertising) has gained increasing relevance, though organic engagement methods have lost none of their importance. Although paid social media marketing is used mostly to promote organic content, it is even more beneficial for organisations seeking to reach new potential customers from wider audiences rather than loyal customers who already follow the social media activities of the organisation.

Paid social media advertising is mostly related to content promotion, as mentioned above, and in this way it is similar to image or video ads used in paid search marketing. Despite this, it is important to discuss paid social media marketing separately from paid search marketing, as social media platforms provide more possibilities for advertisers to integrate their ads into the content of social communications between users and brands, as well as between users.

10.6 Overview of advertising on the most popular social media platforms in Europe

Facebook remains the most popular social media platform in Europe in 2019 (StatCounter, 2019). Unlike search engines, various social media platforms are used for different purposes (i.e. Facebook is used for private social networking and sharing with friends; LinkedIn is used for professional networking; reddit is used for sharing news) and by various audiences (for example, Pinterest is significantly more prevalent amongst women). Some users are more likely to actively use several social media platforms, unlike in the case of search engines, which are switched more by accident than intention. Therefore, awareness of the different paid social media marketing opportunities on various social media platforms is even more important than in the case of paid search marketing.

Facebook

Facebook is the social networking platform most popular worldwide. However, in Europe it is not applicable to all countries, for example in Belarus Pinterest is more popular and in the Russian Federation Vkontakte has significant popularity (StatCounter Global Stats, July 2019).

Paid advertising on Facebook can be done using a multitude of options. In the setup stage of an advertising campaign, Facebook leads advertisers through a sequence of ordered steps to create a campaign based on its objectives:

- *Page post engagement*: Promote page posts.
- *Page likes*: Get page likes to grow the audience and build the brand.
- *Clicks to websites*: Get people to visit a website.

- *Website conversions*: Get people to perform certain actions on a site (requires adding a Facebook pixel to the site).
- *App installs*: Get people to install a mobile or desktop app.
- *App engagement*: Get people to use a desktop app.
- *Local awareness*: Reach people who are nearby.
- *Event responses*: Increase attendance at an event.
- *Offer claims*: Create offers for people to redeem in the store.
- *Video views*: Get people to watch videos to raise awareness of the brand.
- *Lead generation*: Get lead information from people who are interested in the brand.

In the next step, Facebook would take the advertiser to their choice of location for placing the ads: Facebook desktop News Feed, the Facebook mobile News Feed or the Facebook right-hand column. The latest data at the time of writing shows that the broader choice of placements is more beneficial to advertisers than targeting exclusively desktop users or mobile users (see Table 10.2).

On Facebook, advertisers can target their audience based on location, age, gender, language and other common demographic characteristics, though the most valuable possibility is to target the audience based on interests and behaviours. For example, a pet hotel company could target the ad to people interested in birds and intending to travel soon. Therefore, Facebook provides organisations with opportunities to reach exactly the right audience for their products or services.

The advantages of advertising on Facebook for small and medium enterprises (SMEs) include more opportunities to increase brand awareness and reach of the message, increasing foot traffic to physical premises or increasing web traffic to the website.

Shewan (2014) suggests that organisations with the potential to produce a lot of imagery may benefit most from advertising on Facebook. When it comes to the type of content that is likely to result in high engagement rates, it tends to be of an emotional and philanthropic nature (Lee et al., 2018). This means that content that creates brand personality and shows information about social activities is more likely to result in activities when compared to product information, which tends to get negative engagement (op. cit.).

Table 10.2 Effectiveness of different placements of Facebook ads in Europe, fourth quarter 2014

	Desktop feed	Combined feed	Mobile feed
CPM	€2.13	€2.57	€2.81
CPC	€0.31	€0.14	€0.17
CTR	0.68%	1.86%	1.65%

Source: Salesforce, 2015

Twitter

Twitter is a microblogging service. There are six types of Twitter paid ads: Awareness, Tweet engagement, Followers, Website Clicks, App installs and Quick Promote (Twitter, 2019). Similarly to Facebook, Twitter ad campaigns can be categorised by objective (tweet engagement; website clicks or conversions; app installs or app engagement; video views; follower growth; and Twitter lead collection). Expected campaign costs will depend and vary greatly based on choices of objective.

On Twitter, advertisers can target their audience based on common demographic characteristics such as location, age, gender and language. The most valuable feature of targeting on Twitter is an opportunity to target the audience based on their networks. Twitter native advertising, where content appears as if it is just another message from a user, has the highest engagement rate when it is relevant to the buyer persona (Hayes et al., 2019).

The advantages of advertising on Twitter for SMEs include reaching a strong dedicated Twitter fan base who use it frequently, targeting the mobile market in a not overly intrusive way and extensively customisable targeting functionalities.

LinkedIn

LinkedIn is a social networking service for building and maintaining a professional network. Therefore, it is regarded as an important social media marketing channel in B2B, despite low popularity with the general public. The growing worldwide audience of LinkedIn offers a breadth of options for SMEs.

There are three main types of LinkedIn paid ads: Premium Display Ads, Email Marketing via Sponsored InMail and Direct Sponsored Updates.

Besides the opportunity to target ads based on common demographic characteristics, LinkedIn provides advertisers with more options to target based on business- and position-related features, such as industry, company size, job title, job position and seniority.

Case Study 10.2   Vaitiekūnų medelynas

Vaitiekūnų medelynas (www.vaitiekunumedelynas.com) is a Lithuanian family owned nursery-garden business that has been operating since 1990. Marketing of the company is carried out by the sole daughter of the family – Martyna Vaitiekūnaitė. This micro-business initiated its online marketing activities in 2013 by creating a website and a Facebook page (www.facebook.com/vaitiekunumedelynas).

The Facebook page fan base grew slowly but steadily over the years, with somewhat larger boosts of interest during the sweepstake contests organised during tree-planting seasons.

> By 17 February 2016, the Facebook page had 3,417 page likes with an average of four engaged page users per day. Martyna shared that day a link to the website with a promotion for an assortment of new saplings. After a few days she made the sapling offer a boosted post based on a recommendation by Facebook. She targeted Lithuanian 30- to 45-year-old female Facebook users interested in gardening or the home and garden. The post was boosted for a total period of 16 days at a total cost of €23.20.
>
> The boosted post was displayed 42,407 times and reached 26,740 unique people, of whom 1,016 engaged with the page or content on the page; 145 new page likes were made as a direct result of the boosted post (an increase of 4 per cent). However, during this period the average number of engaged page users increased to 99 per day, and the total number of page likes grew to 3,904 (an increase of 14 per cent).

The Vaitiekūnų medelynas example illustrates that even a small budget for a small organisation can have an impact on brand awareness. One of the examples illustrated here is that not all content should be boosted, but only that which shows signs of virality in its own right. A post which receives higher levels of natural engagement when compared to others that were not as active is likely to perform better when boosted through paid advertising. Therefore, don't boost every post, which can help you to make your budget go further.

10.7 Affiliate marketing

Affiliate marketing is a commission-based arrangement where referring sites receive a commission on sales or leads sent on to merchants' e-commerce sites. Commissions can be fixed per lead or action or an agreed-upon percentage of the purchase.

With the advent of paid search and social marketing, affiliate marketing is sometimes regarded as an outdated mode of paid advertising. However, in digital marketing, affiliate marketing is only as old as paid search marketing – both started in the mid-1990s. It can be regarded as another type of display advertising (together with image or video paid ads in paid search and social media). However, paid search and social ads could equally be regarded as a type of affiliate marketing. (Some affiliate marketing companies suggest dropping the word 'affiliate' and replacing it with 'performance', because of the negative attitude towards affiliate marketing by advertisers, who connect it to misleading, fraudulent, and 'making money online' sites that rip off advertisers and provide little, if any, return.)

Figure 10.4 The affiliate marketing process

An *affiliate* or publisher is a website that displays links (ads) to other web-sites, usually e-commerce ones, to its visitors. An affiliate network connects e-commerce websites (merchants) to affiliates.

Affiliate networks track and report all visitor activity to their clients (merchants) and usually make it available on their user interface. Visitor activities tracked include impressions, clicks, purchases, conversions, order value, shopping basket content and details of the referring publisher websites. Fees are charged for setting up a programme, a monthly licensing fee and a commission for successful sales. Figure 10.4 explains the basic affiliate marketing process.

Following standard rules, an affiliate gets a commission fee only if 1) a user browses to an affiliate's site, 2) the user clicks the affiliate's specially coded link to the merchant and 3) the user makes a purchase from the merchant (Edel-man, 2013). These performance-focused rules distinguish affiliate marketing from other forms of paid digital marketing.

Common types of affiliates include (PerformanceIN, 2015):

- *Cashback/loyalty websites.* Users receive money back on purchases made. Cashback can be in the form of money, points or another virtual 'currency'.
- *Comparison websites* enable users to compare products and prices online. The price comparison site publisher receives commission when a customer clicks through to the advertiser's site and makes a purchase.
- *Content websites.* Websites of this type include blogs, where the content is written by a company or an individual. However, any site which carries information could be classed as a content site.
- *Email providers.* These publishers specialise in advertising to users via email. Email affiliates generally own, or have access to, lists containing thousands

of email addresses. Merchants provide their creative materials that promote specific products and the publisher emails the promotion to their list(s).

- *Voucher code/discount websites.* Publishers hosting money-off deals capitalise on consumers who increasingly seek vouchers and discounts before making certain types of purchases. Merchants have become a little savvier when using voucher code affiliates to drive sales, as they begin to push high-margin items or end-of-range clearance items as a priority.
- *Mobile publishers.* There is a diverse range of mobile publishers that operate within the performance marketing space, from existing publishers who have increased their portfolio with an application, to mobile-specific specialists such as 'discovery' and 'review' applications who work to a cost-per-download metric. They all drive sales via a mobile app to an advertiser's mobile-optimised site or app.

10.8 Benchmarking and monitoring paid advertising activities

The simplest way to measure paid advertising activities is through the comparison of financial investment into these activities and the corresponding benefits in terms of completion of calls-to-action.

Dependent on the budgets invested, paid advertising activities can have devastating results if left unattended. Paid advertising services are set up for ease of use and spend, and if your ad is not relevant to the user it's possible for you to bid for it without gaining any financial benefit at all and, in fact, for this to be financially detrimental. The more times your ads are shown without a click-through by the user, the more expensive it will be for the same ad to appear next time, since it is a continuously dynamic calculations process. Therefore, ads should be reviewed regularly – ideally on a daily basis for a smaller-budget campaign; if the campaign is new and involves high budgets (e.g. over €500 per day), ad performance should be monitored on an hourly basis.

When considering key performance indicators (KPIs) for paid advertising, the same rules apply as for any other digital activities – the last click is not always the one that generated the customer's interest in your products or services, so wider awareness of metrics is useful to evaluate the branding and exposure generated by a channel (Table 10.3).

These are just some of the tools to help with a number of paid advertising benchmarking efforts, together with a quick overview of these tools and how they could be used:

- Google Analytics – offers a free powerful tool for tracking paid activities related to a website. Using the free URL builder allows an extension of Google Analytics where each campaign can be specifically tracked even by the smallest organisation, without the need for an external software budget. It integrates particularly well with Google Ads, where a paid search ad click can be tracked in terms of its conversions and revenue for e-commerce websites.

Table 10.3 Sample KPIs and monitoring tools for paid digital marketing

Paid marketing type	Examples of KPIs	Example tools
Paid search marketing	Quality score for individual keyword Click-through rate Cost-per-click Conversion rate Conversions Impressions generated by the ad	Native paid advertising management tools, e.g. Google Ads or Bing Ads KeywordSpy.com WordStream.com Weatherfit Google Analytics
Paid social media marketing	Post reach of content Engagement with your ad Cost-per-click Conversion rate Cost per lead/customer	Native paid advertising management tools, e.g. Facebook.com or Twitter.com WordStream.com SocialFlow Google Analytics
Affiliate marketing	Leads generated Conversions specific to your call-to-action Conversion rate Cost per acquisition Revenue Return on ad spend	Many affiliate network-specific tools such as AffiliateWindow, LinkShare and Zanox Google Analytics

- KeywordSpy – offers an overview of the average cost being paid for a keyword by some of your competitors targeting the same market. This tool offers some free information and, for a premium, more advanced analytics on paid advertising performance.
- WordStream – this advanced tool brings all your paid advertising accounts from Google Ads, Bing and Facebook into one place and offers paid advertising grading reports and landing page grading, as well as advice on how to optimise your efforts.
- SocialFlow – allows for managing and reporting on multiple social media platforms such as Facebook, Pinterest and Twitter campaigns.

10.9 Summary

This chapter has outlined the different paid advertising opportunities available within the digital marketing mix, focusing on search engines, social media and affiliate advertising.

When reaching out to the buyer persona, it's important to bear in mind that the customer journey to the online purchase can involve a number of different online profiles. By reaching out through paid channels, a brand can increase its presence and its opportunities to remind the buyer persona of its products and services. It is important to remember that users of social networking sites are in different mind-sets to those using search engines. When someone is searching for a product or a service on a search engine, they are more likely to make the decision to purchase; hence, the content of the ads should be focused on the purchase decision. On social media, ads should be less direct, since the user is less likely to be focused on purchasing the product or service at the time.

Although paid advertising is fast to set up when compared to organic optimisation of content, it has the obvious drawback of relying on financial resources to achieve presence. However, in addition to the main payment models such as PPC, which relies on payment for every visitor, the affiliate payment model is much more flexible and acceptable to those who are able to sell in volume and essentially pay a referral commission. On the other hand, the affiliate model has its own drawbacks, such as the need for a product or services that would be acceptable by the affiliate network and a longer setup process compared to paid search marketing.

As ever, experimenting with the most relevant options, carefully monitoring the impact of your paid digital advertising efforts and then adjusting them accordingly – and continuing to do so as a regular practice – is the best way to discover the models which will lead to the most rewarding results for your individual business.

10.10 References

Ayanso, A. and Karimi, A. (2015) The moderating effects of keyword competition on the determinants of ad position in sponsored search advertising. *Decision Support Systems*, 70, 42–59.

Edelman, E. (2013) The design of online advertising markets. In N.Vulkan, A. Roth and Z. Neeman (eds.), *The handbook of market design*. Oxford: Oxford University Press.

Hayes, J. L., Golan, G., Britt, B. and Applequist, J. (2019) How advertising relevance and consumer – Brand relationship strength limit disclosure effects of native ads on Twitter. *International Journal of Advertising*, 1–35.

Lee, D., Hosanagar, K. and Nair, H. S. (2018) Advertising content and consumer engagement on social media: Evidence from Facebook. *Management Science*, 64(11), 5105–5131.

PerformanceIN (2015) *Performance marketing guide 2015*. performancein.com/resource/performance-marketing-guide-2015/

Salesforce (2015) *Social.com advertising benchmark report*. www.salesforce.com/form/marketingcloud/socialcom-benchmark.jsp

Shewan, D. (2014) *Social media advertising: Which platform is right for your small business?* www.wordstream.com/blog/ws/2014/09/24/social-media-advertising

StatCounter (2019) *StatCounter global stats*. gs.statcounter.com/social-media-stats/all/europe

Twitter (2019) *Get started with Twitter ads*. business.twitter.com/en/solutions/twitter-ads.html

11 Mobile marketing

Bartłomiej Kurzyk, Tahir Rashid and Sayed Ali Hayder

11.0 Learning objectives

In this chapter you will learn how to:

- understand the impact of mobile marketing;
- recognise how mobile marketing is influenced by consumer behaviour;
- identify tactics to achieve maximum potential for your mobile marketing;
- enable online content to suit mobile advertising;
- acknowledge the importance of mobile commerce and its business value; and
- recognise the future of mobile marketing with the Internet of Things.

11.1 Introducing mobile marketing

Mobile marketing is marketing that involves the use of mobile devices, including smartphones, tablets and wearables as well as those technologies that incorporate voice interfaces such as Google Alexa and Baidu DuerOS. These devices are closely tied to a contemporary buyer persona who is technology-aware and expects continuous access to data networks no matter what the circumstances. Mobile devices are personal and are generally with an individual consumer at all times. These mobile devices also store personal and professional information and are used to communicate through social media, search for information, shop, pay and perform many other activities. In defining your contemporary technology-aware buyer persona, their use of mobile technologies should be considered an integral part of their life. For example, China is a world leader in mobile phone adoption, mobile advertising and mobile payments (Waugh, 2018). With 98 per cent of Chinese Internet traffic being mobile, it is more accurate to consider a mobile phone as not just a 'device' but as a multi-purpose tool.

The impact of mobile technology on the lives of consumers is significant. Prior to the widespread use of mobile devices, customers got product or service information through mass media or by physically visiting a store. With mobile devices, a buyer persona can walk into a restaurant, scan the QR code on their table to view the menu of the day, place their order and pay immediately through integrated mobile payment. Mobile marketing recognises that a buyer persona is engaged on many mobile devices and anticipates interacting with them across multiple devices. Using the data gained from mobile devices in the development of strategic plans (through analytics tools) introduces new market research opportunities and introduces more detailed understanding of consumer behaviour. Associating mobile data with social activities offers new ways for developing and promoting products and services as well as acquiring new customers and maintaining relationships with existing ones.

This chapter explains the uses of mobile marketing and its influence on the buyer persona. The focus of this chapter is on how to maintain a meaningful dialogue with buyer personas through multiple mobile devices on their buyer journey in ways that support your organisation's digital marketing strategy.

11.2 Understanding mobile consumer behaviour

Mobile technologies and the ways they integrate communication, information and entertainment have radically transformed the way consumers interact with products and services. The ubiquity of mobile technologies also provides consumers with more options and more control over their own buying behaviour. The continuous presence of devices with network access enables consumers to make highly informed decisions around immediate purchases irrespective of their location. Spur-of-the-moment purchases in a salesroom or supermarket can be deferred when better or cheaper products can be immediately identified online. Restaurant choices made in an unfamiliar location can be shaped by the opinion of others through reviews apps and the walking distance to alternative options revealed through GPS-enabled apps. These informed decisions can then, in turn, be shared with others in the same way.

Marketers used to have an upper hand over the purchasing behaviour of customers through their control of information flow. Mobile communication technologies represent a seamless bridge between the consumer's physical and virtual worlds (Müller et al., 2018), which removes the restrictions of a fixed place and enables direct access to context information with little or no mediation (Figure 11.1). Mobile connectivity allows consumers to receive information at any time, in any place and directly between one another. This ability is particularly evident during the Zero Moment of Truth (ZMOT) and the Second Moment of Truth (SMOT). At the ZMOT, a user could potentially ask the voice assistant on their phone for the location of a restaurant near them. The geolocation returned by the mobile device supports search engine results by offering places that are both close and have good reviews and ratings. At the SMOT, a user uses their device to take pictures and videos and shares this information to praise or complain about their experience. The ability to be a media producer and publisher has given the buyer persona the edge over marketers while also making them more proactive in their consumption decisions.

The features of mobile technology introduced by built-in sensors provides a more authentic and engaging experience to customers. Physical feedback through vibration and sounds, locational awareness and the ability to 'see' the

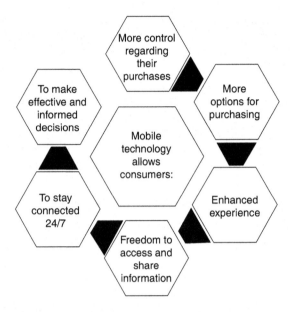

Figure 11.1 The impact of mobile technology on consumers

surrounding environment through the built-in camera all make the mobile experience more tangible and intimate than the more neutral desktop. These additional sensors embedded in mobile technology can also have negative implications. The ubiquity and traceability of mobile devices has seriously undermined consumer privacy. The habits of consumers can be more comprehensively traced through mobile devices, which while bringing some potential benefit to the consumer also has the potential to reveal personal information that the consumer may not prefer to have shared. With the increased capabilities of a mobile device, consumers may be unwittingly sharing their location, phone number, usage patterns and technical preferences by unwittingly agreeing to overly invasive terms and conditions when they download new apps.

A number of large organisations are reported to have designed their apps to capture significant amounts of data from their users (Whittaker, 2019). The data captured includes entire screenshots and the capability of replaying the clicks and navigation that a user took through the entire purchase cycle, including the entering of credit card details for a purchase. While this may be regarded as a thorough attempt to understand consumer behaviour, from a marketing perspective the practice also goes beyond what the majority of users would consider a fair or ethical examination of their activities.

The use of mobile devices does mean that consumers are spending more time with technology, and this exposure is showing evidence of changing social relations and behaviours. For example, the use of instant messaging between young adults is arguably limiting their ability to have real-time face-to-face conversations with other people. Social media channels that engender a 'fear of missing out' and the rise of influential 'YouTubers' all change the relationship that we have with one another. In this sense, mobile technologies may be defining new parameters for communications by altering the norms and expectations regarding how people and organisations interact with one another.

11.3 Responsive mobile websites and applications

As mobile devices have become the expected norm for accessing websites, this technical format should be the starting point for any design considerations. Applying more traditional approaches to creating a website with the assumption of a large screen might render content unusable on smaller mobile screens. A similar design consideration for the user of mobile device is the variability of their network access in different locations. Website content built with an assumption of a wired high-speed connection will very rapidly become a pain touchpoint to the majority of mobile users. Taking a 'mobile-first' approach to website design overcomes these potential sources of pain. One of the ranking factors that, for example, Google considers in the evaluation of a website is the speed and accessibility of it when rendered on a mobile device. This means that a website that works on a mobile device will rank above competitors who design firstly for a desktop user, assuming all other variables are equal.

Designers have three options for dealing with shifting consumer web habits.

Option 1 – *create two versions of the website*

One version is created for visitors using desktop computers. Another mobile version is designed for smaller screens. These websites might use two different URLs (desktop version: www.address.com; mobile version: m.address.com) but it is also possible to automatically use a small piece of code to automatically redirect visitors to the best possible experience based on the identification of their browsers. Users can also be offered the option to select the mobile or desktop version from a menu. Search engines offer technical guidelines on how to resolve the potential issue of offering duplicate content that might otherwise penalise your website's ranking if the pages are not clearly marked as being the same to search engines. This is significant because, from 1 July 2019, all new websites that are indexed by Google are evaluated using the mobile-first indexing (Google, 2019).

Option 2 – *use responsive web design standards*

Responsive web design refers to web design that enables content (including advertising) to resize, reformat, reorganise and reposition itself in real time so that it looks good based on whatever size screen is being used (Roth et al., 2018) (Figure 11.2). This approach has advantages for the designer, who only

Figure 11.2 A responsive website viewed on different devices

needs to create one version of the website. For the user, the automatic readjustment of the size means that all consumers see the same consistent content while still being able to read and navigate in the ways most suitable for their current device (Ricker and Roth, 2018).

Option 3 – build mobile applications

Mobile applications (or apps) are software applications designed specifically for smartphones and tablets. Apps can be downloaded through a mobile web browser, through centrally controlled distribution points such as Google Play or Apple's App Store, or they come pre-installed on a device. Apps can simply mirror the functionality of a normal website. Some apps provide an enhanced experience over what is offered on a website, which is enabled by the additional functionality of the built-in sensors of the device (Table 11.1).

Table 11.1 Differences between responsive websites and applications (apps)

Criteria	Responsive web design	Mobile web app
Versions	Single version – build the website and optimise across all mobile devices	Multiple versions – build one for website and another for each major mobile platform
User experience	Does not require users to install additional apps	Requires users to find and install app on their mobile device
	Limited or no interaction with smartphones' native functions – camera, calendar or GPS	Potential for advanced interaction with smartphones' native functions – camera, calendar or GPS
	Regular known navigation enabled from top to bottom by default. Non-standard navigation systems require customisation and modification in layout and code	Multiple methods of creating navigation and menus. Can cause confusion if the user is unfamiliar or the style does not mirror website-style navigation
Performance	Potential bandwidth issues when server sends larger media files than needed	Offline availability in areas with no wireless connectivity. Unseen bandwidth issues if the app requires regular contact with server
Ongoing maintenance	Low maintenance cost and effort	Medium maintenance
	Single version to maintain across all devices	Separate versions for website and each mobile platform
	Control and flexibility over updates and change. Update once change everywhere	Requires updates on each device for each new version. Risk of multiple versions with different content

Source: Adapted from Rapidvaluesolutions, 2018

The technical complexity and cost of building responsive websites has fallen to the point where this is an expected level of service from all designers except those offering the most heavily discounted service. Responsive design should be regarded as the baseline standard of design for any new website.

11.4 Mobile pay-per-click advertising

Mobile pay-per-click (PPC) is a paid online marketing model that advertisers are increasingly employing to engage consumers (Kotsier, 2018). In mobile PPC, an advertiser pays a search engine, app developer or website owner a certain amount of money each time their ad is clicked by the consumer. The advertisers pay for the keywords which are relevant to what they are selling and are more likely to be used by consumers when they are searching for their products and services. Mobile PPC ads are not limited to the traditional PPC of paid ads on search engine results pages (SERPs) and can include banner ads on news apps, video ads and other rich media embedded with content while also taking advantage of the technical abilities of mobile devices including GPS locating or using vibration to get the users attention. Location-sensitive advertising is particularly valuable for local businesses, as mobile consumers regularly use their devices to identify products and services while they are shopping.

Mobile PPC is different from traditional PPC advertising in various ways. For instance, the intent of consumers varies when they are on the move, at work or at home. Desktop consumers and those at home spend more time searching and comparing product information, while consumers are more interested in making instant purchase decisions when they are away from home and are likely to spend less time performing detailed research. Another difference of mobile PPC comes as a result of it still being considered a new technology. As a result, it is less costly than desktop PPC advertising and yields higher click-through rates. This difference, however, will be temporary as more organisations invest in their own mobile PPC campaigns (www.mobile marketer.com, 2019).

11.5 Mobile search engine optimisation

Alongside the rise of mobile device use is a continued growth in multi-screening, a behaviour where customers use multiple devices with different screen sizes at the same time to achieve their goals. Multi-screening is another important reason to invest in a single responsive version of your website as any key differences in your offer between different versions of a website will be spotted immediately (and shared). But the most important factor to push your mobile SEO strategy to the use of a response website comes from search engines. Both Google and Baidu now recommend responsive web design as their preferred choice for building mobile websites.

A responsive website may be difficult to implement for existing businesses. Older websites designed in a non-responsive way for a primarily desktop audience may have to be entirely rebuilt. Repurposing a website in this way can be a long and expensive process. New businesses, in contrast, have no such legacy and should use a mobile-first approach that invests in responsive web design from the start.

Other mobile SEO recommendations concentrate on the common errors that can hinder user experience within the mobile environment. Google (2019) published a list of common problems to avoid:

- Blocked JavaScript, CSS and image files
- Unplayable content (such as Flash)
- Faulty redirects (including irrelevant cross-links between desktop and mobile-friendly web pages)
- Mobile-only 404s (missing pages, dead links)
- App download interstitials (heavy promotion of the app version of the service that reduces the user's mobile web experience)
- Slow-loading mobile pages

Local and mobile SEO strategies also include a range of additional actions beyond traditional SEO advice:

- *Local profiles* – an organisation should claim and create a local profile, not just on Google My Business but also Yahoo! Local and Bing Places.
- *Citations* – a citation is any place online that uses your company name, address and phone number all on the same page; these details should be in the same format as your local listing to confirm and create trust with customers.
- *Address management* – using the same address format is important; it should be used on every page within the site (a repeating footer may be the best solution).
- *Reviews* – these are important on Google Places profiles but are also used on other websites and social media.
- *Metadata fields* – use your specific location in metadata tags and descriptions and within the content of your website.

11.6 M-commerce

With the greater use of mobile devices, it is inevitable that more people are also using mobile devices to make purchases. There are two phenomena that are closely linked with mobile shopping:

- ROPO (research online, purchase offline) – before making any purchase, customers find information about a product, finding deals, local suppliers, availability and potential alternative product options. Equipped with this information, they locate the physical supplier and complete the sale offline.
- Showrooming (research products offline, purchase online) – consumers visit shops and see products that they are researching. The consumer then goes online and purchases the product (usually for a lower price) at an online store.

Both scenarios contribute to the complex landscape of online and offline retailing. Both practices can be beneficial or harmful to different shops depending on a range of factors, including the similarity between online and offline prices. Other mixtures of the online and offline retail experience are also connected to the wide use of mobile devices:

- Consumers can research products and compare prices "on the go" using their mobile devices. There are apps that help consumers find the best deals by simply scanning the barcode of a product. This directly influences the purchasing process and can result in no sale for the retailer.
- Consumers can immediately purchase a product they see in a store window by using the digital twin of the shop and its mobile payment systems.

These effects all contribute to the growing importance of m-commerce, the act of shopping on a mobile device.

Case Study 11.1   Listonic's mobile shopping app benefits brands

Listonic is a Polish start-up that created a mobile shopping list app. Users can easily create, share and use shopping lists on the go. It is an easy solution for people to help them with their shopping, but it's also a great tool for advertisers to reach their prospective customers. Advertisers can:

- attach their recommendations non-intrusively within shopping lists (e.g. next to 'milk', users are presented with recommendations for a specific brand of milk) and
- run banner campaigns targeted at customers with specific products on their shopping lists and link the banners to landing pages with a direct response button such as 'add to shopping list'.

By using advertising options within the Listonic app, advertisers are able to show their message to prospective customers at the exact moment they are making a specific product purchase.

One such campaign was made with MobextPolska (Havas Media) for Durex (manufacturer of condoms and other mainstream sex-related products) in 2013 for Valentine's Day. On 14 February, users that had certain products (e.g. 'whipped cream') on their shopping lists were presented with additional context-based recommendations (e.g. 'for dessert, not only in the kitchen'). The campaign resulted in:

- 450,000 impressions of the banner ad with a CTR 0.69 per cent;
- 45,000 impressions of the context ad with a CTR 2.32 per cent;
- 1,162 per cent growth of month-to-month brand occurrences within shopping lists across all users; and
- 202 per cent growth of popularity of product category on shopping lists.

Source: tylkofmcg.pl/reklama-mobilna-durex-performax-intense-case-study/

On the Shopify platform – a one-click e-commerce solution – 79 per cent of the entire customer traffic and 69 per cent of sales orders come through mobile devices (Shopify, 2019). Traffic from mobile devices to sites like Shopify will continue to grow, making m-commerce channels an essential component for any organisation selling their products or services online.

As is the case with an organisational website, there are three approaches to creating an m-commerce offering:

- Design separate e-commerce and m-commerce versions.
- Design a single mobile-friendly online shop that uses responsive web design (there are numerous ready-to-use e-commerce platforms with m-commerce functionality that can be used as a solution).
- Design an m-commerce app that exploits native device functionality.

All three options allow the buyer persona to browse a selection of products using their mobile device. Another reason for the growth of m-commerce is the increased ease, growth of options and reduced risk for consumers using their mobile devices to complete their purchase. The success of payment providers such as Alipay is significant. As Alipay has become the preferred method of payment in China, the demand for its services is extending out into other countries driven by the increasing volume and prosperity of Chinese tourists. The importance of mobile devices for purchasing is also evidenced by the 2018 Cyber Monday retail event. On this day, 51 per cent of customers used their mobile devices to purchase products from both online and offline stores (Business Wire, 2018).

11.7 Mobile payment systems

Mobile payments (m-payments) bring different systems for exchanging money using mobile devices. With the majority of the systems, users can initiate, authorise and complete financial transactions to a payee. Since users generally have mobile devices with them almost all the time, there is a general expectation that mobile devices will act as a form of wallets with all the associated functions.

Organisations wanting to accept payments from mobile users have four options:

1   Mobile register apps – an integrated point of sale that uses mobile devices as a centre for the financial operations of a storefront. From the perspective of a customer, the transaction looks normal. From the perspective of a seller, a mobile integrated register app can provide significant benefits such as sales tracking, inventory management and financial data management, all synced to the cloud. To use it to its full potential, some investment is needed for additional mobile device compatible credit card readers, receipt printers and related products, such as those offered by squareup.com. This option is not a full m-payment system because, from the perspective of a customer, the transaction is performed in conventional way.

2   Near field communication (NFC) – in countries where PayPass and pay-Wave credit/debit cards are popular, mobile devices can be used as a credit card. More recent phones have the NFC chip already built in, but older

phones can also be enabled through a special sticker that can be placed on a mobile phone, which has an integrated microprocessor that acts as a normal NFC card. There are disadvantages with this approach that are primarily around compatibility with existing readers and payment systems.

3   Integrated mobile payment systems – in 2014 Apple introduced a similar concept to NFC under the name of Apple Pay. By using its own proprietary system of NFC terminals and Apple Pay, where users can keep their credit card data, users make payments using their iPhone, iPad or Apple Watch.

4   Mobile payment apps – a seller can choose to integrate payment options within its own application, by letting customer pre-store credit card information so that it is easy to choose as a payment method during mobile checkout. Alternatively, a pre-paid system can be used to finalise transactions on mobile devices, and users can use normal online payment methods to top up the balance on their accounts. An app can confirm transactions up to this balance. Three examples of this are:

- *WeChat Pay* – a widely used system for online and offline payment. It is available on mainland China but also internationally. Offline retailers can present a Quick pay QR code to scan by a user who can then use their mobile phone to make a payment. A brand can accept online sales transaction on their official WeChat shop – through payment integration built into the WeChat app. The reliance upon WeChat pay or Alipay is now so widespread in China that some consumers carry no credit cards or cash with them – all they need is their mobile phone.
- *Skycash* – a payment system operating in Poland where users can install the Skycash app on their mobile devices and pay for the tram, bus, rail tickets and parking.
- *Starbucks UK* – offers users a mobile device app that can be used for paying for orders using a pre-paid balance.

As with normal credit card transactions, these mobile payment systems usually operate by charging a fee for each transaction, which the seller must accept as the cost of meeting their customers' expectations of convenience.

11.8 2D and QR codes

The need to link the physical and digital worlds together, so that computers can interact with physical objects is an ongoing challenge for information technology.

One of the first solutions that went beyond the usual input devices of keyboards for touch screens that also gained widespread acceptance were barcodes. These simple printed labels were popularised in the 1970s and allowed products to be scanned quickly at store checkouts.

For its time, barcode scanning technology was a perfect solution for a very specific need. By placing barcodes on physical items, a computer could identify specific physical objects and link them to additional data, such as a product name or the current price.

The technology was cheap. The barcode is very simple, and you don't need very sophisticated image recognition technology to make it work. Placing barcodes on objects is also very easy – you just need to add an additional graphical element to the product packaging.

Barcodes are now ubiquitous but suffer from a limited data capacity. A typical barcode can only store 20 alphanumeric characters of data – a capacity that is sufficient to store a single unique count. This is enough to catalogue the products available at any given store or market but for any wider applications this is a severe limitation.

The answer to this data problem was the introduction of 2D codes in the 1980s and 1990s. With normal barcodes, information is coded only in one dimension. 2D codes use a coding method in two dimensions, allowing the storage of over 4,200 alphanumeric characters of data. Moreover, 2D codes can be read from any direction and can be recognised even when partially obscured or even destroyed. Depending on the error correction capacity level, up to 30 per cent of the information stored in a 2D code can be obscured while still remaining readable.

The invention of 2D codes was an evolution for barcodes, as it allowed for increased capacity without increasing the direct cost of 'tagging' physical objects. More advanced software is needed, but no more sophisticated image recognition system is required. Moreover, because of their shape and error correction, 2D codes are much easier for mobile phone cameras to read than standard barcodes.

There are two popular forms of 2D codes in use (Figure 11.3): QR (quick response) codes and data matrix codes. Although similar at first glance, the main key between the formats is the QR codes ability to embed kanji (Japanese characters) and other language character sets. Data matrix codes do not have

QR code

Data Matrix code

Figure 11.3 Encoding your messages

this functionality. The result is that QR codes have wider popularity, especially in Europe, where adoption rates continue to grow.

Since the 1990s, QR codes have evolved into many different types to serve a range of specific applications (Denso Wave Inc., 2016):

- Micro QR codes – this type of code can be printed in a smaller space.
- iQR codes – these can be printed as square or rectangular shapes.
- SQRC – these have reading restriction implemented, so they can be used to store secure information.
- LogoQ – these can incorporate logos, illustrations and letters in the code design.

In order to generate 2D codes, a special application is needed. However, since most of the common ways of encoding information in 2D codes use open standards, there are many free-to-use Internet applications that can be used to generate these codes for marketing purposes. Most of these applications can generate either QR or data matrix codes. Many of these applications also give users the option to generate either static or dynamic 2D codes.

For static 2D codes, the generator creates an image that contains the encoded data. If the 2D code includes a URL, scanning it will take the user directly to the desired landing page. As static codes, if something in the encoded information needs to be changed, such as the target URL, a new code must be generated.

With dynamic 2D codes, the image encodes a link to an intermediary site that then determines what the appropriate destination will be. If the dynamic code includes a URL, scanning it will link to a service which then redirects the user's browser to the correct web page. If the user wants to change something in the encoded data – the target URL, for example – they log into the service provider and update this information without the need to change the 2D code itself.

Dynamic 2D codes are provided by companies that offer not only 2D code generators, but also 2D code campaign management services. Using such a service usually allows:

- tracking of 2D code scans, allowing for analytics and campaign optimisation;
- dynamic changing of web pages linked to the 2D code;
- coupon code management; and
- multiple URLs encoded in a single 2D code.

The use of 2D codes for mobile marketing purposes is directly linked to the built-in camera capability of mobile devices.

There are two main barriers to the widespread use of 2D codes:

1 Use is limited to owners of smartphones with pre-installed 2D code reading apps. Not all smartphones have a 2D code reader pre-installed at the time of purchase.

2.   Although the codes are becoming more popular, there is still a substantial part of the population who do not know what 2D codes are and what to do with them.

Both types of 2D codes are used by organisations for marketing purposes. Typical areas of usage are the following:

*   Advertising – using 2D codes on promotional material such as posters, banners, printed ads and leaflets can help customers access additional content that is connected with the advertised brand. 2D codes can link to websites or social media profiles for the brand. Research shows that including a 2D code in an ad favourably changes the attitudes towards the advertisers.
*   Coupons – companies can distribute coupons with 2D codes that will offer customers benefits such as free products and discounts.
*   M-commerce – a company can use advertising or catalogues with 2D codes that link to its m-commerce shop, allowing for fast and easy purchase of the advertised products.
*   Enhanced shopping experience – retailers can display 2D codes beside the products in their store, where they can be scanned by customers who want additional information.
*   Product/service enhancements – museums and art galleries can display 2D codes next to exhibits to give visitors additional multimedia content.
*   Event experience enhancement – 2D codes can be used on invitations and name tags.

In order for the use of 2D codes to be successful, some consideration must be given to the purpose and experience that it generates for the intended buyer persona. Simply sticking a 2D code on everything is not a guarantee of success.

*   Scanning the code must give additional value to the buyer persona. Scanning a 2D code takes time; customers have to bring their phone out, load the application, position the phone in order to scan the code and wait for the linked content to load. In order to go through the process, customers should expect a high value.
*   Scanning the code should be easy and problem-free. Using the codes on billboards, vehicles or electronic displays, for example, may have limited success.
*   Linking a 2D code to a long URL creates denser and more complex images. Consider using a URL shortener service to reduce the amount of information encoded. This will make simpler looking codes with added benefit of being able to modify the link in the future without the need to change the 2D code. For example, once a campaign ends you could re-direct it to the home page of your website.
*   The resultant page that is seen after scanning a 2D code should be optimised for a mobile device experience. Scanning a code that links to a desktop or media-heavy web page will frustrate the buyer persona.

11.9 Internet of Things

Other more recent ways of linking the physical and digital worlds have fewer of the limitations that can be seen with 2D codes. The Internet of Things aims at getting rid of those limitations. In its conceptualisation it is a vast, invisible, global network in which nearly every product and physical object, including toasters, trees, milk cartons, shopping centre parking spaces, cars, roads, wristwatches and medical equipment, will be tagged with sensors that will gather and transmit data about their consumption, usage patterns and location.

The first phase of the Internet of Things is to enable Internet connectivity to various products that, as well as fulfilling their main function, also connect themselves to the Internet and transfer data about their usage. These types of products include wearables (such as watches and fitness trackers), security cameras, thermostats, smoke detectors and weights. This trend is becoming more and more prolific and profitable. The global IoT market was worth over $150 billion in 2018 and is expected to exceed $1.5 trillion by 2025 (IOT Analytics, 2019).

One such Internet of Things device is labelled the beacon. This device is a small sensor that detects when a mobile device has come within range and can, if suitably programmed, interact with that device. So far, the application of beacon technology is just starting. There are several companies producing beacons and publishing their software development kits to help application developers make use of them.

Similar to the situation with 2D codes, there are barriers for widespread beacon use as access is limited to owners of smartphones that are compliant with the Bluetooth low-energy standard. More significantly, in order for a mobile device to properly interpret beacon data and deliver the expected content and functionality, the customer has to install the appropriate customised app. A beacon interaction has to promise sufficient value to give their customers a genuine reason to install their apps, and then deliver on this expectation.

Some marketing uses for beacons have already been explored by a variety of organisations:

- Walk-by promotions – customers can get notifications about promotions and special offers when they walk into a store.
- Enhancing shopping experience – showing recommended routes, displaying ads and information on in-store monitors with displays targeted to specific customers, recommending additional products based on the customer's profile or the path taken in store.
- Coupons and loyalty programmes – customers can be identified automatically when in store by their mobile device app, without even actively using their phones. Loyalty benefits can be triggered not only by purchases but also by visits or by time spent in specific locations.
- Service enhancement – menu enhancement and museum guides. In comparison to 2D codes, beacons allow for a much more seamless user

experience. For example, in a museum, a visitor doesn't have to scan any code to get additional information on the exhibits – data is pushed to their mobile device as soon as the customer gets close to a device.

11.10 Wearable technology

Wearable technologies are devices that a user is able to wear on their body. Because of their proximity to the body and the smaller form that they take, wearables are generally more specialised in their functions than mobile devices such as phones.

There are many types of wearable technology gadgets trending in the market today in the form of watches, jewellery and skin patches. They come in a variety of shapes and forms and carry out various sensing functions simultaneously. The popularity of these gadgets can at least partially be explained by the way in which they connect the physical body with the virtual world. This enables a person-to-person connectivity that is built around competing against one another. Wearable data can also be used by employers, health care providers and medical insurers to better manage the health of their clients and provide them with quality health care at a reduced cost.

One of the most well-known wearables is the Apple Watch. With the Apple Watch, the user can take pictures, navigate, connect to the Internet or watch movies. In the context of marketing, an organisation can take advantage of the positive aspects of this device – such as the hands-free and motion signal features – to promote its products in new ways.

11.11 Voice strategies

Voice integration is an emerging technology that provides users with the opportunity to interact digitally by only using their voice. The potential of voice is not limited to basic tasks such as questions and answers, search, navigation, placing a call or playlist management. Voice activities also include shopping, email/calendar management and interactive games.

Google introduced voice integration in 2011. At that time the technology was in its infancy and considered a novelty. However, the use of cloud technology to handle the heavy processing coupled with improvements in speech recognition technology have drastically changed this position. For example, the latest research projects that 41 per cent of adults are already using voice interfaces at least once a day to interact with the Internet and soon 50 per cent of all searches will be carried out by through voice assistants such as Apple Siri, Amazon Alexa, Google Assistant or IBM Watson (www. dbswebsite.com).

Digital voice assistants allow users to stay connected online and do a range of activities without the need for any other interface. The compelling idea behind voice interfaces are that you can communicate as you would speak to your friend or family member to resolve your daily tasks. As the technology behind voice interface improves, there is increasingly an ability to anticipate your routines based on your previous interactions (Cnet.com, 2019).

11.12 Summary

Mobile technologies are already an integral part of consumers lives. From this point of view, the mobile sector has become a critical environment for marketing. With its rapid growth, it is crucial that marketers are fully aware of key mobile marketing concepts and differences discussed in this chapter. Knowledge and understanding of the increasing move towards mobile engagement and the increasing variety of physical/digital interfaces will ensure that your organisation stays up to date with new advancements that are emerging.

11.13 References

Business Wire (2018) *Adobe analytics data shows cyber Monday broke online sales record with $7.9 billion: Sales coming from smartphones hit all-time high with over $2 billion; buy online, pickup in-store up record 50 percent.* www.businesswire.com/news/home/20181126005829/en/Adobe-Analytics-Data-Shows-Cyber-Monday-Broke

Cnet.com (2019) *Alexa, google assistant and Siri will get smarter this year. Here's how.* www.cnet.com/news/alexa-vs-google-assistant-vs-siri-the-state-of-voice-after-google-io-and-wwdc-2019/

Denso Wave Inc. (2016) *Types of QR code.* www.qrcode.com/en/codes

Google (2019) *Common mistakes.* developers.google.com/webmasters/mobile-sites/mobile-seo/common-mistakes

IOT Analytics (2019) *State of the IoT 2018: Number of IoT devices now at 7B – Market accelerating.* iot-analytics.com/state-of-the-iot-update-q1-q2-2018-number-of-iot-devices-now-7b/

Kotsier, J. (2018) Mobile advertising will drive 75% of all digital ad spend in 2018: Here's what's changing. *Forbes,* 23rd February. www.forbes.com/sites/johnkoetsier/2018/02/23/mobile-advertising-will-drive-75-of-all-digital-ad-spend-in-2018-heres-whats-changing/ www.mobilemarketer.com

Kotsier, J. (2019). *10 key mobile pay-per-click fundamentals.* www.mobilemarketer.com/ex/mobilemarketer/cms/opinion/columns/12640.html

Müller, J., Pommeranz, B., Weisser, J. and Voigt, K. (2018) Digital, Social Media, and Mobile Marketing in industrial buying: Still in need of customer segmentation? Empirical evidence from Poland and Germany. *Industrial Marketing Management.* 10.1016/j.indmarman.2018.01.033.

Rapidvaluesolutions (2018) *The new design trend: Build a website; enable self-optimization across all mobile devices.* www.rapidvaluesolutions.com/wp-content/uploads/2013/04/Responsive-Web-Design-vs.-Mobile-Web-App-What-is-best-for-Enterprise-_Whitepaper-by-RapidValue-Solutions.pdf

Ricker, B. A. and Roth, R. E. (2018) Mobile maps and responsive design. *Geographic Information Science & Technology Body of Knowledge* [CV 40]. doi.org/10.22224/gistbok/2018.2.5.

Roth, R., Young, S., Nestel, C., Sack, C., Davidson, B., Janicki, J., ... Zhang, G. (2018) Global landscapes: Teaching globalization through responsive mobile map design. *The Professional Geographer,* 70(3), 395–411.

Shopify (2019) *Statistics and figures about Shopify: Posted by Thomas Holmes on December 07, 2016 and updated in.* www.shopifyandyou.com/blogs/news/statistics-about-shopify

Waugh, R. (2018) *How China is leading the world in tech innovation (and what the West can learn from it)*. www.telegraph.co.uk/connect/better-business/business-solutions/china-technology-innovation

Whittaker, Z. (2019) Many popular iPhone apps secretly record your screen without asking. *Tech-Crunch*, 6th February. techcrunch.com/2019/02/06/iphone-session-replay-screenshots/

12 Measuring brand awareness, campaign evaluation and web analytics

Alexander Christov, Verena Hausmann and Sue Williams

12.0 Learning objectives

In this chapter you will understand:

- why it is important to measure brand awareness;
- what indicators to use for campaign and brand evaluation;
- how to correlate indicators with business objectives in order to make decisions;
- web analytics and its relevant tools and concepts; and
- concepts of conversion.

12.1 Introduction

One of the key reasons that digital and social media marketing is gaining such popularity is that the data that can be obtained through digital campaigns is both rich and transparent. However, intelligent use of campaign data needs to go beyond simply the measurement of 'clicks' through websites or social media channels – it should associate these simple and readily obtainable metrics with the overall purpose and intent of the campaign, as well as the wider strategic position of digital marketing within organisations. This chapter advocates an approach to brand development and campaign management that is informed by evidence-based decision making.

The chapter will outline the main reasons and techniques for evaluating and tracking the online consumer journey and their connection to the effective use of business-specific key performance indicators (KPIs). The techniques discussed will cover those most commonly used, including tracking, physical response metrics, campaign reporting and user experience evaluation.

Understanding basic metrics and their correlations with business objectives will enable you to remain focused and purposeful in your decision making and actions. The exploration of paid, owned and earned KPIs shapes the discussion around the 'bigger' issues of building and maintaining brand awareness in European and international contexts and the development of sustainable conversion-orientated strategies.

12.2 Digital marketing = conversions + brand awareness

Measurement is an essential aspect of the marketing process. The measurement and assessment of the success of your marketing activities, including campaigns and brand building, is the feedback mechanism through which these activities can be improved. It's also how marketers learn and expand their practical knowledge. The more extreme view takes this statement even further to claim that marketing without measurement cannot be considered marketing at all. Although this claim may appear obvious to the more experienced marketer or overly clichéd to a student of the subject, it remains a truism for all forms of digital marketing.

In fact, digital marketing and its intimate link to the technologies of client/server systems – but especially web servers and browsers – provide access to far larger volumes of accurate and precise quantitative data at greater levels of detail than was ever possible within traditional marketing strategies. The ready availability of the right tools and the right data means there is little excuse for a lack of campaign measurement or a failure to assess the value of an activity. The challenge for a marketer when measuring the success of their actions, however, is to make sense of what can very quickly become a mountain of impenetrable 'big data'.

From the analytical perspective, the meaning and purpose of digital marketing can be practically broken down and understood as the sum of conversion and brand awareness activities. Both concepts themselves are the sum of many parts, and any judgement of marketing success may well not consider – or even need to consider – every single element that composes each of these concepts. Measurement and any evaluation of success that is extrapolated from the data received as a result of marketing activity must be done contextually with a holistic awareness of organisational and situational conditions. In optimal organisational situations, any evaluation of success will utilise mixed methods that consider both qualitative and quantitative inputs.

the push of conversion → ← the pull of brand

Brand awareness and conversion activities exert force on the consumer from two different directions. Brand awareness and reputation pull a consumer through a journey that results in a final concluding transaction. Conversion activities actively push consumers through the journey to a final transaction. Traditionally, these two processes are a powerful combination that, when done well, produce loyal regular consumers who act as advocates and perpetuate the success of a brand. However, in a digital economy organisations with little brand awareness can successfully compete with popular traditional brands by building a positive conversion experience, and for e-commerce organisations a brand can ultimately be built around this positive experience. Amazon's emergence as a recognisable global brand is at least in part due to its pioneering 'One Click' checkout system – itself an early but crude form of conversion tool.

Conversion

Conversion – in the most general sense – is a progression from a beginning action to a different, separate and concluding action. From a conventional e-commerce perspective, the most common form of conversion is based on pushing users who are prospective customers and visiting a website – the beginning action – through to a completed sale – the concluding action. This final action produces revenue for the business and brings a tangible bottom-line benefit as a result of this conversion. In e-commerce, it is also the conversion that can be most readily measured. A coarse conversion ratio can be derived by simply dividing the total value or volume of sales achieved over a period of time by the total number of website visits during the same time period.

More nuanced measurements employing additional tracking technologies can bring greater precision to calculating a conversion ratio when resources allow. This further sophistication will, for example, recognise and discard visits by web robots as well as duplicate visits. When a conversion progresses from action to action without any intervention of a third party – such as the marketer, peers or other external influences – the conversion can be regarded as 'natural'. When external forces – including those of the marketer – are required to push a consumer to undertake the final action, the conversion has required some form of interaction and can be described as a 'transacted' conversion. Natural conversions are a double-edged sword for the marketer, who is ever conscious of the importance of measurement to improve and refine their actions. Natural conversion occurs with no additional marketing action or direct costs, but these benefits in themselves result in a potentially restricted capacity to explain the reasons or motivations for a consumer's actions.

> Initial trigger action → final action (natural conversion)
> Initial trigger action → intersecting marketing action → final action (transacted conversion)

However, more sophisticated e-commerce operations that are conscious they are interacting with increasingly informed and discerning consumers have recognised the need to break down this coarse view of conversion into smaller and more refined units of conversion. This can minimise the number of conversions being identified as natural and potentially baffling and also enables the marketer to plan more precise and tightly focused interactions that promote conversion. In this way the consumer's journey to a final planned outcome is directed and guided through a series of small conversion activities in which the final action of one conversion becomes the trigger action for the next conversion activity.

> Initial trigger action → intersecting marketing action → concluding action (becomes) trigger action → intersecting marketing action → final action

There is a vast range of marketing actions that can move the consumer from an initial action to a final action. Retargeting is a good but controversial example of a technique that is increasingly used to convert a visitor – who is presumed to be a suspect through their actions – into a buyer after they have abandoned their initial visit to an e-commerce site. Amazon uses this technique, prompting its visitors to return to specific items by showing banner and block advertising on other websites that are visited after leaving the Amazon domain.

More precise understanding of the chain of conversion activities can also be used to iteratively improve the design of the user experience through each action. For the tangible properties such as websites and apps, this involves initial design testing followed by gathering ongoing feedback from consumers using the properties.

Brand awareness

Brand awareness encapsulates a more complex combination of factors than those represented by conversion. The concept and importance of brand is well documented and almost synonymous with the development of marketing as a discipline and as a professional practice. The promotion of brand and brand awareness has also been the focus and vehicle for much of traditional marketing practice. The result is that traditional marketing and the focus on brand primarily benefit larger organisations with the ability to invest significantly in traditional broadcast media advertising. This relationship of brand to large-scale advertising investment – and without necessarily direct measurement and consideration of success – has the self-fulfilling consequence of building brand awareness. However, it is essential to recognise that high levels of brand awareness do not always directly correlate with higher levels of conversion.

Digital marketing practice challenges the primacy of brand awareness and reflects the attitude that online businesses can compete with bigger 'brands' through a balance of good conversion tactics and engaging brand collateral. In fact, the influences of the 'social' and the 'open' in digital business act as a disincentive to being – or being perceived as – a big brand that has connotations of being impersonal, disconnected and solely motivated by achieving the next sale. These connotations also contrast with perceptions in some national markets – including the USA, the UK and Australia – that independent brands are better for their quality, service and attention to detail. In effect, this reversal in the relative perceptions of brands from the 1980s and 1990s is also a retreat from modernist concepts of the mass consumer and the associated positive principles of mass consumption techniques.

Brand awareness and brand perceptions shape the way in which a consumer is pulled towards a purchase. In extreme negative cases, the purchase may be made despite a resistance to the brand, for example, because the conversion process is so easy, the price is so low or the alternatives are so limited. In extreme positive examples of brand pull, the purchase is made irrespective of price, the complexities of a checkout system or a vast range of alternative options in the marketplace.

Building an appropriate and long-term sustainable brand takes time, requires investment and, above all, will only succeed when it is linked to the overall strategic direction of the business. These prerequisites towards building a brand – while arguably common sense – offer a significant explanation as to why small businesses have traditionally struggled to compete with larger businesses. More importantly, and obversely, it is not solely a lack of financial investment that prevents small businesses from competing – and this is where opportunity lies for small businesses. Increasingly customers expect a degree of transparency to be associated with a brand and a close integration and alignment between the claims of the brand and the actual conduct of its business. This is a relationship that traditional brands struggle with when they are still led by their brand and branding. Examples of this disconnection of brand and practice in traditional businesses can be seen in McDonald's high-calorie salad debacle. A small business with patience and strategic foresight that is prepared to be transparent and open can compete with the traditional brands.

12.3 Calculating return on investment and customer lifetime value

Just as brand building has traditionally been the form of marketing activity preferred by large businesses, so too do the preferred methods of calculating success differ between traditional businesses and digital businesses.

Return on investment (ROI) is regularly used for assessing a campaign against specific objectives. This approach favours large-scale brand-building techniques where a coarse measure of success can be readily obtained from calculating the total sales against the marketing investment over a given time period. The assumption implied by this approach is that all marketing investment will produce a positive consumer response that can be entirely captured and represented in the form of sales. Using ROI also presumes that there is a continuous level of marketing activity over a greater period of time than the one inspected by the ROI calculation that returns a consistent base level of positive consumer responses in the form of sales.

Customer lifetime value (CLV), as the title suggests, takes a longer-term and arguably more strategic view of a business's relationship with each individual customer. CLV calculates the average value of transaction from a customer over the period in which that customer continues to interact with the business. Because CLV measures the strength and value of long-term relationships, this tends to encourage focus on the widest parameters of service, extending beyond conversion tactics that produce a single immediate sale and instead aiming to convert the initial engagement of a prospect into them becoming a lifelong loyal brand advocate. This recognition of the need for vision to create a sustainable business is increasingly found in many truly digital businesses and contrasts with the traditional brand-building actions of businesses that have relied on broadcast media as part of their business strategy. Using CLV as a means of judging the impact of marketing activity enables recognition of the distinctiveness of customers and their different behaviours in relation to individual goods and services. This is acknowledged with varying values in the cost per acquisition and the varying duration of interaction with the customer, depending on the nature of goods or services. CLV can also introduce consideration of the effect of churn amongst customers (when existing customers stop doing business with you).

12.4 Web analytics

Why web analytics?

Web analytics has its origin in data mining (Cooley et al., 1997), which deals with the analysis of big data in order to find patterns and rules. Web analytics is specifically aimed at the 'objective tracking, collection, measurement, reporting, and analysis of quantitative Internet data to optimize websites and web marketing initiatives' (Digital Analytics Association, 2006).

Thus, the goal is to both understand and track what users or customers are doing while they are interacting with your digital profiles such as an app or a web page and then to use that intelligence to design effective websites which meet users' needs and also to shape or improve online marketing initiatives.

ROI in marketing initiatives is important for marketers. In many organisations, marketing is one of the single largest investments. Without some kind of analytics to assist in evaluating the effectiveness of online marketing initiatives, the outcome of this investment is often unclear. Web analytics can bring insight to this aspect of ROI. For example, the volumes of customers coming to a website as a direct consequence of a specific marketing campaign can be tracked and specific consumer groups can be identified. Web analytics also plays an important role in improving website design to improve customer satisfaction, for example, by making it easier to find information and generally improving the user experience.

How do we use web analytics?

The data we can obtain through web analytics does not itself tell a story. This data must be brought into context in order to provide transparency and assist in identifying, for example, marketing or website usage problems. The data which could lead to improving a website or campaigning or assisting in making business decisions requires skilled and sensitive analysis to enable interpretation and action taking (Chen, 2018). Using a web analytics tool is only one part of the process and must be complemented by effective analysis and interpretation in view of business objectives or those set out by a digital marketing campaign. Nevertheless, we need to understand the tools in order to get appropriate data for analysis. Therefore, the following section will give an overview of the web analytics market and its tools before an example for a web analytics implementation plan is outlined. Important measurables as well as reporting insights are given in the following sections.

Web analytics tool market

In the past, web analytics was usually achieved by analysing a website's log files, and it was only capable of capturing basic data such as the number of times a page was viewed. Today, a more common way for web analytics tools to collect data is to use the quantitative method of JavaScript tagging. When using JavaScript tagging, a short piece of JavaScript code must be included on the web page. With the help of this tagging code it is possible to capture a wide variety of data. Web analytics tools offer the possibility to log various user actions and events on websites. In addition, there are many tools which allow the tracking of social media actions. By analysing the logs, user interactions become observable and can be used for improvements in developing and maintaining a website, marketing campaigns, etc.

At the end of the 1990s the software tool WebTrends was one of the first commercial web analytics tools on the market. Since then, much has happened. Today, the number of different web analytics tools is enormous and at first glance it is difficult to distinguish amongst the different offerings, since they all cover similar development scenarios and are capable of tracking a wide range of similar things. The most obvious aspects for separation are the differences in where the data is stored, who has control of the data, whether the software is open source or commercial, whether the software is acquired as software as a service (SaaS) or an in-house installation and whether or not additional support is needed.

Even though many web analytics tools are available, only a few tools dominate the market (Datanyze, 2019). Looking globally, we can find that Google Analytics and its related Google offerings, Facebook Analytics, Snowplow, Hotjar and Matomo all have over 100k website domains using them. Google Analytics Standard, which was launched in 2005, is the most used web analytics tool in the world, counting more than 4.5 million registrations as indicated by Datanyze in 2019.

The following list includes some of the most widely used web analytics software products:

- Google Analytics
- Google Universal Analytics
- Google Global Site Tag
- Facebook Analytics
- Google Analytics Event Tracking
- Snowplow
- Hotjar
- Matomo
- MonsterInsights
- Baidu Analytics
- Adobe Analytics
- Yahoo Analytics
- Urchin
- Crazy Egg

Many companies are using more than one software tool at the same time and the market around web analytics is still growing, expanding in areas such as mobile and social analytics, targeted digital advertising and market automation.

How to design and implement a web analytics plan

Why do we need a plan for web analytics?

As with most tools and initiatives, web analytics is not just done by choosing a tool and implementing it. Web analytics should be seen as an ongoing programme including different phases, each of which should be carried out at different intervals. Goals need to be defined in order to be able to measure success and each output from web analytics can and should be used as input for another cycle.

What does a web analytics plan look like?

A web analytics process can be described in five different phases:

- Phase 1 – business requirements – the information needs should be analysed and an information architecture audit conducted in order to gain a clear understanding of the business needs.
- Phase 2 – planning for web analytics – includes the building of knowledge about web analytics metrics and analysis possibilities, as well as the identification of needs and the mapping to a suitable tool.
- Phase 3 – developing a data collection capability – contains the activities of implementing and setting up the selected tool so that the relevant data is kept.
- Phase 4 – generating value through web analytics – contains two activities and is the most important phase. First, the pattern analysis and reporting. In this activity statistics and reports are created and evaluated in order to gain an understanding of the website usage. The second activity is the action taking. Based on the results of the previous steps and bringing together web analytics aims and actual results, a clear pathway for possible changes as well as future measurements should be developed.
- Phase 5 – evaluation of actions – everything that has been done before should be evaluated and monitored. After several rounds of using the framework, it might be possible to benchmark metrics. This phase should help you to see whether the web analytics process has resulted in positive outcomes.

Figure 12.1 shows the web analytics framework, which includes the five phases described above, and further outlines the different process phases by dividing them into different actions and including questions to ask in each step.

At the beginning of each web analytics programme, you should ask yourself what you want to do with your website, what problems you currently have and what you look for within web analytics. Then you need to set clear objectives and goals for your programme. Furthermore, you need to identify the status quo of your website and your users in order to understand your business requirements (phase 1). For example, the design of a website normally undergoes a major review every 2 to 5 years and new technologies might be used, so this phase should be repeated each time a big change has happened.

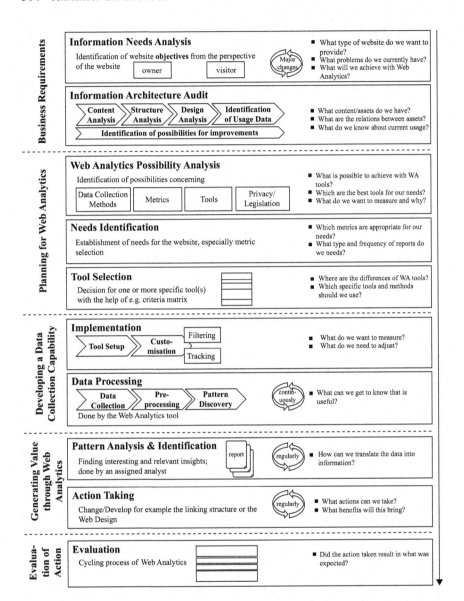

Figure 12.1 Web analytics framework

Source: (adapted from Hausmann et al., 2012)

Phase 2 centres around the requirements for the tools, the metrics that should be captured and on identifying the output you want, so that you can plan for web analytics and decide on a specific tool.

The implementation and customisation of the tool are the major activities in developing a data collection capability (phase 3). Only good data can help in improvements. In addition to the action taking, this can be seen as the most important action.

After the data is captured, we know nothing more than before. That's why the most important activity is to translate this data into usable information and generate reports for visualisation. Only when taking actions from the results is it possible to benefit from web analytics (phase 4).

In order to evaluate your initiatives – such as marketing campaigns, website developments or your web analytics programme itself – you should compare expectations with results and start the whole process again by identifying changes and setting a new goal for the next round.

12.5 KPIs for small and medium enterprises when using Google Analytics

Why KPIs?

The goal of web analytics is to get insights into the usage behaviour of your potential customers on websites and social platforms, so that you can then adapt your own digital offerings according to customer needs. Defined measurable attributes can be used to gain these insights. In web analytics these attributes are called metrics (Hassler, 2010), and the most important metrics for your organisation are called KPIs.

How do you find and use KPIs?

Your KPIs depend on the goals of your organisation, and they might change over time as your company changes or sets new goals. KPIs can and should be quite different depending on the kind of website you are looking at. For example, personal, commercial, organisational, informational and political websites all have different purposes in what they want to achieve (Crowder and Crowder, 2008). Most common for organisational marketing are organisational websites, where information about the organisation itself is given, and commercial websites, which include online shops and/or are set up to generate profit. For those websites, KPIs are often very financial in nature and take into account the revenue. Nevertheless, all organisations are asking the same challenging question:

What should be measured and how do you measure success?

By looking into the literature and testing different web analytics tools, you will find hundreds of different metrics. Very basic, well-known and commonly used metrics include the following:

- Page view: the number of times an individual page was visited.
- Most viewed page: most popular page.

- Visitors: number of people visiting the site; difference amongst total visitors, unique visitors and session and cookies.
- Visit duration: time spent on the website per visitor.
- Referrer: shows the source where user came from to visit the site.
- Entry and exit page: show the starting and the leaving page of a visit.
- Completion/order conversion rate: percentage that conducted a purchase.
- Path analysis: shows how a user clicked through the links on a site.

However, depending on the website type you will have more specific KPIs such as conversion rate, customer loyalty or bounce rate for commercial websites. The list of metrics is long, and the above only gives a sample. In addition, the names as well as the calculation of the different metrics vary according to the specific tools. However, as long as you understand what is included in the metrics, and as long as the numbers you compare over time are from the same tool, this does not really matter.

In order to give more details on how to use KPIs, we will concentrate on Google Analytics. Why Google Analytics? As outlined before, Google Analytics is the most used web analytics tool in the world. It is free of charge and thus easy to use for small and medium enterprises (SMEs), for whom financial resources are often limited. It is not the aim of this chapter to outline all available KPIs for web analytics, but instead to offer an impression of how you can find out which metrics are available and work out which are best for you.

General information and support for Google Analytics can be found on the Google Support page (support.google.com/analytics). When starting web analytics with Google Analytics (GA), you will get first measurements directly after you have registered and placed the snipped code onto your website and the first users have visited your website.

Note: Dependent on your website content management systems (CMS), this process could be as simple as pasting your GA code into a Google Analytics setup on your system. For example, a commonly used CMS is WordPress, and to enable Google Analytics on it is simply a case of pasting the GA number, which updates the code on each web page.

You will then have the possibility to customise your own dashboard and/or use the predefined structured metrics and reports:

- Audience – who is looking at your site?
- Behaviour – how are they browsing?
- Acquisition – where did your users come from?

If, later, you have defined website conversion goals, etc. you can find them within the section Conversions. All sections are customisable. Figure 12.2 shows an example of the standard Google Analytics layout and menu, and Figure 12.3 shows a behaviour flow of an example website.

When using Google Analytics, you will come across Universal Analytics as well. Universal Analytics enables you to gather customer data across multiple

Figure 12.2 Google Analytics design

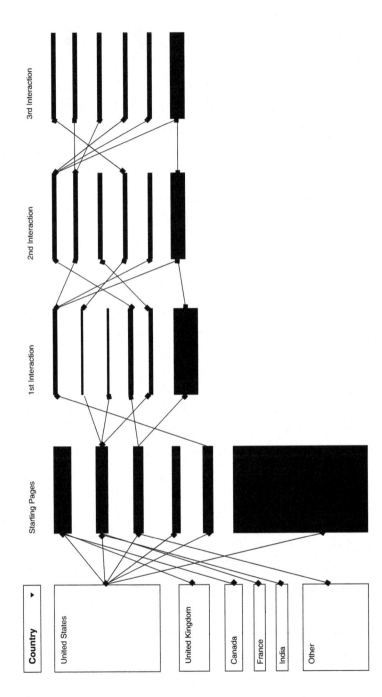

Figure 12.3 Behaviour flow

platforms and devices, and it increases the possibilities for metrics. However, all data is imported into your Google Analytics accounts, which by now are completely integrated with each other.

When defining KPIs, there are a few general things which should be kept in mind:

- KPIs are quantitative and often have a monetary value, e.g. turnover.
- As long as you are not comparing to your own historical data, try to avoid absolute numbers; KPIs should be ratios or percentages.
- KPIs should be time-based.
- Different stakeholders might be interested in different KPIs, e.g. e-commerce, webmaster, customer support.
- The KPIs should be aligned to your business goals.
- KPIs should meet the following characteristics: relevant, well defined, understandable, usable, comparable, testable, cost effective and efficient.

12.6 Designing web analytics reports that meet business needs

Case Study 12.1   Enterprise 2.0 uses web analytics to redesign starting page

The website www.e20cases.org is a platform which presents case studies around the topic Enterprise 2.0. The publishers and editors of the site are various groups from universities within Austria, Germany and Switzerland. The goal of the website is to document case studies in which social software is used in organisations in order to transfer and enrich the developed knowledge into research and across and between interested organisations.

The website is an informational website and has no commercial aims. It is set up with the open source CMS WordPress. Even though web analytics was running on the site for a while, no one was examining the data until a student project took over responsibility for the web analytics data.

By analysing the gathered data, it became obvious through an in-page analysis that many links on the starting page were not used at all, and the ones which were used often were further down the page. In order to provide a better overview, and to better show which topics are included on the page, a restructured starting page was designed and tested for 2 months.

The data collected in the testing phase of the new design of the web-site was then compared to the previous collected data in order to see the differences. Two significant results were found: 1) within the testing period several links were used which previously had not been clicked on for the 2 years that analytics was tracking the site and 2) the descent rate was reduced by 12.63 per cent.

Source: www.e20cases.org

12.7 Meaningful reporting and campaign tracking

Nowadays, businesses use digital media advertising in order to increase the awareness of their brand. It is vital to track those campaigns in order to understand whether the resources invested in a particular digital campaign are having efficient results and are contributing towards the realisation of business goals.

The first aspect to be considered is having proper campaign tracking and reporting. Without this, it is impossible to accurately collect campaign data that will allow the occurrence of analysis and optimisation. Beginning to use campaign tracking across the entire organisation will provide significantly better data about the age, gender, cultural background, needs and wants and opinions of potential customers, as well as how many people click on the particular digital marketing page. In order to achieve this, some KPIs that could be established include search engine ranking, site traffic, new/returning traffic and mobile traffic (Rowles, 2015).

There are various tools available for campaign tracking. One of these is Google Analytics, which provides audience demographics to referral sources and gives you a solid breakdown of how people are finding the particular website, what's getting the most attention and the amount of time they spend on your website. Google Analytics even tracks the traffic patterns people take within the website.

Another popular tool is Facebook Insights. This monitors how many people view particular social media posts, the number of clicks each post receives and how many times people are sharing the posts with others. It also gives a breakdown of the different demographics of the page's Facebook network (Rowles, 2015). Similar popular tools include LinkedIn Insights, YouTube Analytics and Hootsuite.

Proper campaign tracking will give the company reports about its most valuable networks, how much social media contributes to the overall visits of the website and information about landing pages, which will allow the company to gain significant knowledge of the market and build a competitive advantage (Linnell, 2011).

12.8 Digital campaign tracking – UTM codes

Urchin Tracking Module (UTM) parameters (UTM codes) are short texts which are added to the end of a URL in order to depict and track the success of particular marketing campaign content on the Web. There are five parameters of UTM:

- Campaign (utm_campaign): identifies a specific promotion or a strategic campaign and groups all of the content from one campaign in your analytics.
- Source (utm_source): which website is the source of the traffic (e.g. search engines, newsletters).
- Medium (utm_medium): the type of marketing medium that the link is used in.
- Content (utm_content): used to track the different types of content that point to the same URL from the same campaign, source and medium codes. Often used in pay-per-click (PPC) or with two identical links on the same page.
- Term (utm_term): used to identify the keywords you've paid for in a PPC ad.

Once a particular link is clicked, the tags are sent to different tracking tools. Using these codes allows companies to assess the effectiveness of digital campaigns and identify how to increase the number of visitors to the website. For example, UTM parameters can be used to see how much traffic came from a particular Facebook post rather than the general website traffic. On a particular Twitter account, the companies can tag the tweets and compare these to the overall website referrals.

However, UTM parameters have some drawbacks, one of which is parameter order. The UTM URL has to come before any additional tracking parameters, and if the order is mixed up the performance will not be properly accessed. Another disadvantage is 301 redirects. These can strip the particular tracking of URL and categorises PPC into organic or direct (Polivka, 2014).

Regardless of the drawbacks, UTM codes are irreplaceable in tracking digital marketing campaigns and provide sufficient information about minimising costs on advertising and reducing time spent on campaigns (Ellsworth, 2013).

Useful tips and tools to consider are as follows:

- Google Analytics – if the content appears on your own website, ensure that all content is tracked using Google Analytics to be able to easily and effectively monitor traffic sources and volumes, as well as bounce rates and time spent on the site.
- Event tracking/thank you pages – ensure your link elements have been tracked with event tracking and that any thank you pages have tracking on them also.
- UTM tracking – you can generate custom campaign parameters for your URLs to easily isolate your campaigns in Google Analytics.

12.9 Ethical dilemmas in marketing research and data collection

Marketing research, measurement and evaluation in the digital environment raise even more sharply the issue of ethics, related to the interaction between the communicator and consumer. Now companies and organisations possess new and developed tools both for data collection and marketing research, and some of them are definitely not ethical and at the very least can be seen as controversial. Therefore, the constantly developing practices in this field need to be structured, and some limitations should be implemented – this is usually done by professional associations in digital marketing and/or in marketing research on a country level.

The ethical considerations in digital marketing research are closely related to the concept of privacy – currently the hottest issue when talking about consumer protection in the digital environment. In order not only to protect the interests of people from misuse of their personal data but also to motivate them to engage and interact online, it is becoming even more important for digital marketers to follow ethical behaviour and to protect consumer privacy. Therefore, four aspects of information exchange (interactions) between marketers and consumers where ethical dilemmas can arise can be highlighted (Milne, 2000):

- Information requests and disclosure statements: made by marketers – explicitly asking for information by registration and others.
- Information provision and marketing contact: volunteered information exchange by consumers with subsequent contact by marketers – filling in surveys, participation in campaigns, etc.
- Information capturing without consent: observed information gathered by marketers that is not volunteered by consumers – collecting information for visits and online behaviour, including leaving cookies.
- Information practices: uses of information by both marketers and consumers – personalisation software and others.

To summarise, consumer privacy can be seen as enhanced when consumers are aware of information practices and given a choice over information provision and use. On the contrary, consumer privacy can be seen as decreased and ethical issues emerge when there is unwanted marketing contact of information gathering without consent.

The ethical dilemmas in marketing research, like all ethical dilemmas in marketing, are being solved based on the professionalism and personal attitude of marketing or research specialists. However, to contribute to this process, three main aspects can be outlined – informed consent, access and data protection. Consumers and respondents should be properly informed about everything that might influence their decision to get involved. Regarding the access, it is clear that digital marketing research tools provide more opportunities to get involved in a particular study or campaign. However, it should not be discriminative or designed in such a way as to give preferences to people with better access than others. And finally, data protection is perhaps the biggest ethical consideration to be taken into account. The researcher should ensure that everything is password-protected and encrypted, so as to avoid misuse of information.

12.10 Quantitative data analysis methods

Moving forward from the point where marketers have their hands on the data collected through web analytics, it is of high importance to understand the several statistical methods that can be used in order to interpret such massive amounts of quantitative data. Nevertheless, even with the big amounts of data collected through analytics, the limitations of quantitative data analysis are still sufficient to prevent one from properly understanding the buyer, and this is why extra qualitative approaches are required. To this end, this subsection will focus on quantitative methods and topics, while the next will present several qualitative methods that can be used to triangulate with the quantitative methods in order to lead to more accurate buyer-related observations/facts.

Regression analysis

Regression analysis is divided into two categories: linear and multiple regression. Linear regression analysis is used to identify the value of a variable while the value of the other variable is known (example: identify the effect of buyer preference for a specific buyer age group). Multiple regression analysis is used to identify the value of a variable when two or more other variables are known (also called predictors). To achieve this, a hypothesis for the type of relationship is made, and proximate values are assessed in relation to the parameters in order to establish an estimated regression equation. The multiple regression equation can be tested using the coefficient of determination (r^2), which always ranges between 0 and 1 (Lind et al., 2010).

Correlation analysis

Correlation analysis is a technique that examines whether two variables are related to each other and to what extent they are related. To examine this, the correlation coefficient (r) is used. The value of (r) represents the strength of the relationship (i.e. -0.1 to 0.1 means there is no relationship or the relationship is very weak). However, it should be noted that the correlation coefficient only measures linear relationships between variables (Lind et al., 2010).

Sample size

Sample size refers to the individual units of data collected in a survey. It is crucial to determine the accuracy and reliability of a survey's outcomes (Anderson et al., 2010). However, the sample size can never reflect the real values unless a census of the population is conducted. This is not just expensive but also impossible. Therefore, surveys are usually based on a small proportion of the population, which makes them less reliable. This is called sampling error. Non-sampling errors occur when due to systematic or random factors (i.e. selection bias) the outcomes do not reflect the 'true' value for the entire population (Anderson et al., 2010). Nevertheless, in the case of web analytics, the sample size is generally large and thus this should not be considered a primary area of concern.

Hypothesis testing

Hypothesis testing is a statistical process for determining whether a null hypothesis should be accepted or rejected in comparison to an alternative hypothesis related to a survey or test result (Aczel, 2009). In order to determine the significance level of the test, the null hypothesis is tested at 5 per cent. If null hypothesis is rejected at 5 per cent, the test moves to 1 per cent. If the null hypothesis is still rejected, then the result is 'highly significant'; if it is not rejected, the test result is 'significant'. If the null hypothesis is rejected at 5 per cent, the test moves to 10 per cent, and if it is still rejected, then the result of the test is 'weakly significant'; if not, the test result is 'not significant' (Aczel, 2009).

12.11 Qualitative data analysis methods

Focus groups

Focus groups refer to groups of individuals who are assembled to provide feedback on the plausibility of a product, service or campaign. Although this might be effective in some cases, it may also not reflect the opinion of the larger target population (Onwuegbuzie et al., 2009). However, focus groups may be used as an option to validate (from an expert's point of view) the findings of quantitative analysis of web analytics, for example.

Interviews

Interviewing includes asking questions and receiving responses from the participants in a survey. Interviews can be structured, semi-structured or not structured and can be either face-to-face individual or group interviewing or via other communication channels. Although interviews can lead to extracting valuable amounts of information, the quality of the responses can be questionable, as participants might offer responses they consider the interviewer will appreciate. This is called 'the interviewer effect' (Edwards and Holland, 2013). However, as with focus groups, this technique can prove useful to cross-validate quantitative findings.

Online ethnography – netnography

Netnography refers to the adaptation of ethnographic methods to the research and analysis of the communities and cultures created through computer-mediated social interaction. This was discussed in detail in Chapter 8. There are several methods to conduct cyber-ethnography, including observation, field diary, participatory choices, storing conversations and content and discourse analysis (Kozinets, 2018). This can prove useful to cross-check quantitative findings; however, such a technique might be biased towards the attitudes/opinions of the researcher, as with any other qualitative research methods.

12.12 Summary

This chapter has highlighted the wealth of data about your customers that is now available through evaluating and tracking the online consumer journey. By understanding basic metrics and their correlations with business objectives, by using the techniques discussed above and by taking action to apply them to your business, SMEs are now in an ideal position to develop successful brands and campaigns that are constantly evolving and improving in line with their customers' needs and expectations. To the same extent, adopting, in an ethical manner, research methodologies and practices towards analysing/tracking consumer behaviour is also presented as a core objective of today's digital marketers.

12.13 References

Aczel, Amir D. (ed.) (2009) *Complete business statistics.* New York, NY: McGraw-Hill Higher Education.

Anderson, D., Sweeney, D. and Williams-Rochester, T. (eds.) (2010) *Statistics for business and economics.* Mason, OH: South-Western Cengage Learning.

Chen, M. (2018) Improving website structure through reducing information overload. *Decision Support Systems,* 110, 84–94.

Cooley, R., Mobasher, B. and Srivastava, J. (1997) *Web mining: Information and pattern discovery on the world wide web.* In Proceedings Ninth IEEE International Conference on Tools with Artificial Intelligence, 3–8 Nov, Newport Beach, CA.

Crowder, P. and Crowder, D. A. (2008) *Creating web sites bible.* Indianapolis, IN: Wiley Publishing.

Datanyze (2019) *Market share category: Web analytics.* www.datanyze.com/market-share/web-analytics

Digital Analytics Association (2006) *Description.* www.digitalanalyticsassociation.org/mission-vision

Edwards, R. and Holland, J. (2013) *What is qualitative interviewing?* Graham Crow: University of Edinburgh.

Ellsworth, J. (2013) *Marketing on the internet.* Hoboken, NY: John Wiley & Sons, Inc:.

Google Support (2019) support.google.com/analytics/

Hassler, M. (2010) *Web analytics: Metriken auswerten, Besucherverhalten verstehen, Webseiten optimieren.* Frechen, Germany: MITP-Verlags GmbH & Co.

Hausmann, V., Williams, S. P. and Schubert, P. (2012) *Developing a framework for web analytics.* aisel.aisnet.org/bled2012/11

Kozinets, R.V. (2018) Netnography for management and business research. *The Sage handbook of qualitative business and management research methods.* London: Sage.

Lind, D., Marchal, W. and Wathen, S. (eds.) (2010) *Statistical techniques in business and economics.* New York, NY: McGraw-Hill Higher Education.

Linnell, N. (2011) *Campaign tracking: A vital analytics tool for marketers.* www.searchengine watch.com/2011/11/08/campaign-tracking-a-vital-analytics-tool-for-marketers/

Milne, G. (2000) Privacy and ethical issues in database/interactive marketing and public policy: A research framework and overview of the special issue. *Journal of Public Policy and Marketing*, 19(1), 1–6.

Onwuegbuzie, A. J., Dickinson, W., Leech, N. and Zoran, A. (2009) A qualitative framework for collecting and analyzing data in focus group research. *International Journal of Qualitative Methods*, 8(3), 1–21.

Polivka, J. (2014) *Introduction to UTM parameters and best practices.* The Hangar. blog.rafflecop ter.com/2014/04/utm-parameters-best-practices/.

Rowles, D. (2015) *Digital marketing toolkit, target internet.* www.targetinternet.com/resources/ DigitalMarketingToolkit.pdf

13 Future users, content and marketing

Gordon Fletcher and Alexander Christov

13.0 Learning objectives

In this chapter you will learn how to:

- consider the future of digital business;
- recognise activities in an organisation that will make them become fully digital;
- understand future trends; and
- recognise future business models that will respond to future trends.

13.1 Introduction

In this chapter we explore the future of digital marketing with a discussion of the Digital Business Maturity Model. This model can be applied to any organisation and any of its operations.

Positioning an organisation within the Digital Business Maturity Model recognises its current levels of digital activities – including marketing – as well as its future potential. Identifying an organisation's current digital business maturity in relation to its current strategic position also offers a clear understanding of the progression route required to achieve even greater levels of digital maturity. Digital maturity should itself be considered a desirable, if not essential, development trajectory for any organisation. The relationship that the Digital Business Maturity Model introduces between strategic perspectives and the combined threats and opportunities of digital technologies for an organisation is significant. Holding and maintaining a strategic understanding of your current situation is as much a challenge for many organisations as keeping pace with technological change. However, in a world that is increasingly digital, a strategic perspective will serve the combined beneficial purposes of avoiding short-term decision making and preventing fire-fighting approaches to the day-to-day management of your organisation. Being strategic also lifts your perspective above a desire to just 'use' the current, favourite social media channel or newest technological devices towards a recognition of the need to continuously engage your buyer persona through digital channels. Overall, the

Digital Business Maturity Model presents the need for greater integrated use of technology within your organisation as part of wider, more systemic change to processes and management. In the long term, this approach will give you new efficiencies, redefine your employees' roles (if you have any) and present your entire organisation as an engaged component of the global digital economy.

13.2 The Digital Business Maturity Model

Informally, your digital maturity can be measured through the regularity with which your actions and your organisation's functions – including marketing – are prefixed with a label indicating that they are 'digital' (or 'e', 'i' or even 'cyber'). As a rule of thumb, the greater the digital maturity of an organisation, the less often a special case needs to be made for being digital. An extreme example of this can be experienced when friends or colleagues insist on using the term 'electronic mail' rather than 'email' or even 'mail', which shows how the process of embedding technology within an organisation occurs over time. Positioning your organisation's strategy for greater levels of digital maturity also allows for management reflection. More specifically, this reflection can reveal how far your organisation's digital maturity is ahead of your current buyer persona. This reflection will, in turn, assist in explaining why an organisation cannot always immediately reap the rewards of its current investment in technology or its commitment to organisational change. Organisations that are lagging behind the experience, knowledge and expectations of their current buyer persona risk losing to more dynamic, newer and potentially more aggressive competitors.

There are five stages of the Digital Business Maturity Model (Figure 13.1). At the base of the model there is no digital activity or engagement. The organisation is effectively off the Web, cannot be found through social media and does not conduct any of its functions through digital channels. A proxy for these organisations having their own web presence can be found in online directories that are analogous with the traditional Yellow Pages. But, as with this older form of print media, online directories are of little value to these organisations. These presentations are automatically created for organisations through common simple templates that primarily benefit the business creating the directories rather than those being represented. In many cases, these businesses have only minimal involvement in the creation of their own entry, further reducing the benefits of any messaging. The business of online directories currently exploits organisations that are at this base level of digital maturity. As more organisations leave this level of digital maturity behind, the value of the business model of online directories will also fall away. However, with up to 50 per cent of small businesses still offline in the UK – and higher proportions elsewhere – the demise of online directories as a proxy for web presence is still many years away.

The next stage of digital maturity sees an organisation become visible online through, for example, a website, a blog or a Facebook page. This second stage of the Digital Business Maturity Model is described as having 'presence'. At the core of presence activity is a 'broadcast' view of the relationship between an

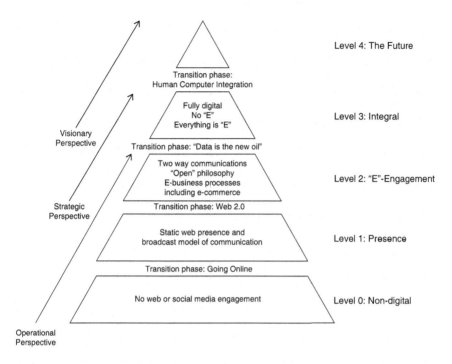

Figure 13.1 The Digital Business Maturity Model

organisation and the buyer persona. Broadcast modes of communication involve sending messages out to the world with only minimal differentiation or consideration for the differences that exist amongst the many types of customers and prospects. In the Buyer Persona Spring, organisations at this level of maturity equate the buyer persona with all users. If some knowledge and understanding of customers *does* exist within the organisation, there is no differentiation in the messages being broadcast.

The limited capability and capacity of early information and communications technologies (ICTs) was originally a barrier for creating and managing differentiated engagement with multiple buyer personas. The earliest movers in digital business, who now have a presence that stretches from the 1990s, had to recognise these early limitations and worked around them or produced innovations as a response. However, both the technology of the Internet and those early adopters have now moved on significantly from these early and tentative starting points. Conventional web presence and mobile applications can now be supplemented by more recent technologies, blockchain, artificial intelligence powered chatbots, including the use of quick response (QR) codes – presented as static devices on printed media that link consumers to an online presence and primarily equivalent in purpose to a printed URL.

More commonly within level 1 of the Digital Business Maturity Model there are many examples of traditional methods of brand building being translated into a digital realm. For example, Google AdWords, with its obvious and direct analogy to traditional display advertising in broadcast and print media, is a hallmark of a broadcast-focused web presence. Facebook's advertising model also conceptually exploits this same business model. The advantage of Google and Facebook advertising is the built-in capacity to target prospective customers with a greater degree of accuracy and to produce reports that are more accurate than traditional forms of advertising.

All these forms of technology enhance straightforward presence without extending the form of interactions. A solely broadcast presence simply amplifies the reach of your content. Organisations that recognise the limitations of a broadcast presence and the low level of engagement with the buyer persona that conventional advertising brings are also organisations that are ready to progress to higher levels of digital maturity. In contrast to straightforward broadcasting techniques are those technologies that can be added to a current web presence and can extend the type and volume of interaction with the buyer persona. At the same time, moving towards two-way conversation and engagement is a hallmark of an organisation's move to the next level of digital maturity.

The third level of the Digital Business Maturity Model consciously designs and embeds two-way interactions between the organisation and its buyer persona. The organisation is also engaging with more of its stakeholders, including suppliers, regulatory bodies and potentially competitors, through digital communications, even if this engagement may initially be confined to emails. Interaction between the buyer persona and the organisation at this stage of digital maturity is most commonly recognised as a form of e-commerce – it is also regularly described in technology terms as Web 2.0 – with the conscious 'designing in' of engagement with a clearly defined buyer persona. The key step forward at this stage of digital maturity is epitomised by the difference between a Facebook page that solely communicates information and a constantly staffed Twitter account through which two-way (and three-way) communications happen rapidly and openly with genuine, trusted responses from the organisation.

At this stage of digital maturity, there is at least some recognition that 'the digital' in the form of different ICTs has had a significant impact on all aspects of the organisation. The buyer persona is increasingly regarded as an active participant in the organisation's activities and not solely a passive consumer. This level of digital maturity also brings an awareness of, if not full engagement with, an 'open' business philosophy and the practices of co-creation and coproduction at the overall level of the brand, as well as through individual goods and services. Considering this definition, it is evident that many organisations have a level of digital maturity that sits between simple presence and genuine engagement. Having recognised the limitations of only maintaining a presence, these organisations must build their capacity and alter their view to fully enter the engagement level of digital maturity.

There is a challenge to becoming a fully engaged digital business and it is not without its hazards. For many organisations there is a tendency to drift back to 'old ways'. Traditional multinational brands that have already attempted to engage customers through co-creation have shown a tendency to reduce the process to familiar marketing techniques and to present the process as, for example, a superficial time-limited competition. Walker's Crisps in the UK have regularly run large-scale television advertising and social media campaigns to promote a competition that allows customers to design their own flavour of crisps. The 2014 winner received £1 million for proposing 'pulled pork in a sticky BBQ sauce'. However, there are indications that the process is not one of co-creation. The corporate website that announced the winner prevented cutting and pasting content and featured a large warning announcing that the website's content is copyright protected. These are not the sentiments of a company open to adopting an engagement level of digital maturity.

There is also a tendency to regard businesses built entirely around an e-commerce model as being fully engaged digital organisations. For example, Amazon, Spreadshirt and Etsy have all been described in terms which suggest they are to be regarded as fully engaged digital businesses. However, this misleads other organisations seeking engagement and their buyer persona as a co-creator. For each of these aforementioned businesses, the mechanism that enables customer customisation and co-creation occurs through a model of structural franchising. Amazon stores take advantage of both the technical infrastructure and the brand the company has built up in order to present goods within the systematised Amazon framework. Amazon stores are, in effect, tenants in an online shopping centre, and so how, or whether, Amazon engages with their customers will vary from experience to experience, though everything is mediated by the Amazon system, which requires a certain level of service that is monitored through feedback services.

Apparel company Spreadshirt also offers a technical infrastructure that allows individuals and small businesses to present their own products. However, this means that the mechanisms for customer engagement and co-creation are entirely mediated by the predefined infrastructure of the Spreadshirt system. Etsy, too, works on a similar model, except that the franchise holders of Etsy create their own products.

In contrast, organisations that understand that co-creation is a more comprehensive and longer-term relationship with customers and suppliers take advantage of external stakeholders to reach the next stage of the Digital Business Maturity Model. Examples of genuine engagement of customers by small organisations can readily be identified. Many of these examples – perhaps unsurprisingly – are based around a social enterprise or charitable mission. This engagement necessitates that the customer is actively involved in the functions of the organisation in a way that goes beyond their participation in a single straightforward purchase.

The Moss Cider Project (http://themossciderproject.org/) in the south Manchester suburb of Moss Side brews cider from apples gathered from across Manchester by future customers. Those who bring in apples or help with the production process are rewarded with credits against the final products – either apple juice or brewed cider. Customers and local residents are engaged through a dedicated website and Facebook presence, and the project has received considerable amounts of local press coverage. Importantly, the project web pages include statements asserting openness about the ingredients and process used to produce the cider. The project requires a digital model to function, as the number of apples required to produce viable quantities of juice or cider requires a vast geographic range for gathering raw ingredients that extends beyond what more traditional methods of community communications could achieve.

The fourth level of the Digital Business Maturity Model embraces the adage that 'data is the new oil'. The recognition in this statement is that all interactions with internal and external stakeholders are opportunities to accumulate and aggregate data. This level of digitally mature business attempts to extract intelligence and actively learn from the volumes of data that are being gathered. This 'integrated' stage of the Digital Business Maturity Model finds and stores data from every interaction and engagement and regards this data – irrespective of its current meaning and understanding – as being valuable to the organisation. The large-scale collection of data can already be evidenced in many organisations, where it precedes the recognition or understanding of the value of what is being gathered. Early examples of data-driven business actions are the various supermarket loyalty card schemes, particularly schemes that span multiple businesses such as the Nectar card in the UK. However, these schemes are themselves not representative of this level of digital maturity, but instead should be considered an early vanguard towards complete business integration and awareness.

Examples of organisations that have recognised the importance of data and its flow between traditionally separate business functions are more difficult to recognise when these organisations are small or the data they manipulate has a degree of sensitivity, e.g. if it is primarily personal data. St Patrick's College in London (www.st-patricks.ac.uk/) is a small private college of further and higher education that has operated for many years. The UK Government heavily regulates private education providers and places significant data-gathering and management requirements upon each of these colleges to track and monitor individual students. The significant administrative burden that this places on what are generally small business operations has contributed to the demise of many providers.

St Patrick's is noteworthy in that it expanded in a period of heavy scrutiny. This expansion was due, in part, to an early recognition of the pivotal importance of data in day-to-day operations. Data was everywhere at St Patrick's, including the student registry, learning managements systems and external-facing web and social media presences. As a result, St Patrick's utilises a fully integrated business and information system, where prospective students making an enquiry through the website have their data stored in the same system from their initial point of enquiry through attendance monitoring until they become alumni. This not only brings efficiencies for the college in its registration and monitoring processes but also enables the potential for comprehensive reporting about any individual student from the date and time of their individual enquiry through to the day they arrived at the college, the grades they received for individual assessment items and the award with which they left.

In recognising the way that data flows continuously throughout the organisation, the organisation at this level of digital maturity has moved far beyond straightforward transactional relationships. Communication between stakeholders is integrated with the systems that require the data, and systems that were intended for external customers might now also be deployed for internal use – and vice versa. St Patrick's College is again an indicative example of the conceptual breakdown in what were traditionally separate business functions and the decoupling of an individual business function from a specific mechanism for that function. For the college, all online enquiries flow through a single web portal. Prospective students, current students, prospective lecturers and other business enquiries all utilise the same contact point, which is then routed through the college's system to the most appropriate respondent. Other examples of this blurring of intended usage and application include the use of wiki systems for corporate knowledge management or microblogging systems for internal business communications. The popularity of WordPress as a platform for content management systems (CMSs) for small businesses also breaks down the distinction between external and internal communications and information needs. An organisation with this degree of digital maturity will inevitably be affected by organisational change. The results are seen in changes in employee role and in management hierarchy, as well as efficiencies, both planned and unexpected, being recognised and embraced by the organisation.

There are inevitably negative impacts in this development of digital maturity, too. The negative impacts of digital maturity can be seen within the human factors of an organisation and specifically within the change in business culture that such a business – one that has progressed through the earlier stages of digital maturity – must experience. Effective business systems can reduce the need for tasks currently completed by employees, but they can equally raise the need for other, new and higher-level tasks. The impact of digital maturity will require some employees to re-skill or re-train entirely. More challenging within a business is the need for employees to give up existing practice and the certainty of regularised work patterns and well-defined regular work outputs in exchange for degrees of flexibility and, consequently, uncertainty.

13.3 Future work

Greenhill and Fletcher (2013) describe the difference between the demands and expectations of semantic and syntactic labour. Syntactic labour is the regularised, repeated work that is best represented by factory work, but can be seen in many work environments. The digitally mature business has released the need for human labour to complete day-to-day syntactic labour tasks. In place of this work comes the requirement for additional semantic labour – the processing of complex and incomplete data to a conclusion. Digital technology can deliver incomplete information and potentially even recognise this data as being incomplete, but the ability for a system to efficiently manage this incompleteness is limited and requires human intervention. This changing requirement reflects the need for new job roles and also offers at least a preliminary explanation as to why call centres are rightly and increasingly described as the factories of the digital era.

With the Internet of Things, the need for humans to complete syntactic labour is further reduced, as inanimate objects autonomously interrelate with systems and aggregate the data of an organisation in the same way that people can retrieve business intelligence. From an organisational perspective, the Internet of Things is not simply reduced, for example, to a smart light bulb. The Internet of Things enables simple two-way communication and a range of interactions directly between different things, as well as between individual things and employees or your buyer persona. The future prospect is that these relationships with things will reach a form of transparency allowing two-, three- and more-way engagements between connected things and connected people.

An example of this prospect is the driverless delivery van that will directly communicate with a customer's house and the business's warehouse to facilitate delivery arrangements. The planned delivery might be interrupted in transit by a sudden change in the client's diary that now requires alternative delivery arrangements to be made to their home instead of to their place of work. Similarly, in a domestic setting, a dinner meeting might be moved back 30 minutes to allow the host to visit a virtual wine shop and arrange immediate delivery, as the home cellar has reported that there are no suitable bottles of wine available for the planned menu. The integrated stage of digital maturity still remains at least partially speculative on a day-to-day level.

The greatest challenge to the achievement of this level of digital maturity is the twinned preparedness by an organisation to reduce the constraints created by current practices and processes and equally to avoid 'cargo cult' responses to the observable activities of competitors. The theory of constraints paradigm identifies that an organisational constraint within the existing system can be turned into an opportunity that can be exploited to gain competitive advantage. Cargo cult thinking, in contrast, acts as a warning, particularly to smaller organisations, to avoid assuming that imitating external observable factors and readily identifiable features of success in another organisation will automatically impart the same levels of success in their own. Small businesses are particularly prone to this combination of allowing existing constraints to override their ability to innovate and change and of assuming that copying the practices of others will bring tangible benefits to themselves. For example, a local corner store in Salford brands itself in blue and red and is named Tecco in an obvious imitation of the more familiar international Tesco brand. Another overly simple example of this combined tension is the race amongst more digitally conscious small businesses to have their own 'app', even though the strategic purpose or immediate benefits of an app may be of marginal advantage at best. Here, cargo cult thinking is used as a substitute for having a clear strategy.

Beyond the integrated third level of the Digital Business Maturity Model – with its incorporation of the exploitation of the Internet of Things – the model becomes more speculative. The final stage of the Digital Business Maturity Model represents the visionary future of an organisation with still greater degrees of uncertainty. If we extrapolate from the current trajectories of technology development, it points to closer human–computer integration, with the prospect of an Internet of connected humans and, more speculatively, a completely clickable world.

At this final level of digital maturity, a range of technologies will offer new opportunities, including:

- virtual reality;
- augmented reality;
- wearables and implantables; and
- telepathic technologies.

All of these technologies will first fire the imagination of games developers before having a more nuanced impact on business functions and operations. Already, the expectation of young people born into our digital age is that everything is responsive to the clicks or swipes pioneered through current touchscreen interfaces and that all 'things' will necessarily respond positively to this type of regularised interaction. These current trajectories of development will increasingly have a significant impact on marketing strategy. Marketing will become ever more personalised through algorithms and data matching, a trend that has first been explored through cookies and retargeting in web-based interactions. The true personalisation of the customer experience will be focused around individual preferences rather than – as is currently the case – the accumulated histories and cookies stored on each connected device or through the stored actions of logged-in users.

To manage the complexity of buyer persona behaviours, their traits and behaviours will be classified around typical and atypical actions. This is a subtle but pivotal distinction between current marketing and future marketing. Technology still remains a limiting factor in fully engaging with customers when each of their potentially many devices are disconnected and disjointed from one another. Ultimately, the behaviour of the buyer persona is, for the moment, a best guess of actions conducted on a range of separate devices.

Marketing, as a particular set of online practices, will become more closely allied with co-production. This will be distinct from the broader association that it currently has with sales and public relations. Individuals will be capable of designing their own goods and services to such an extent that individual businesses will only offer the templates and frameworks within which individualised production can safely and functionally operate. Perhaps unsurprisingly, software engineering has already recognised the advantages of this approach, with object-oriented methodologies, design patterns and reusable code libraries all providing robust building blocks for high-level customisation.

The approach has developed still further with the wide availability of public application programming interfaces (APIs) for a range of services including Facebook, Google and Twitter. The result is that at least some of the success of all these services can be connected to the preparedness of these businesses to release some control over the way in which the services are presented to customers in favour of enabling other businesses to re-package and re-present their data in multiple different ways. Some 3D design and printing services already hint at this potential for fully customisable consumer products in relation to physical objects, by presenting catalogues of functional designs that can be customised in at least some way by the consumer before final print production.

In this newly emerging environment of digital business, some functions will be reduced to the process of data transfer and will require data manipulation without any direct human intervention. With this resultant shift in organisational processes and functions, new roles will emerge for employees that could be described as information curation tasks – the necessary addition of human semantic context as meaning making onto data sets in order to create information. The key change for an organisation, irrespective of its size, will be the degree of preparedness that exists internally to give up control of some of its business processes and functions. Control in this sense is not the action of outsourcing a function – the control relationship in this case is simply regularised, reduced and systematised into a contractual or service-level agreement. More importantly, it is control that is released towards the consumer and, more broadly, all external stakeholders. This release of control can only be satisfactorily achieved when there is clear strategy and a clarity around the relationship of this strategy to a vision that directs and drives the organisation. Those operational processes and functions of the organisation that do not now contribute to creating a pathway towards the vision are superfluous. The functions of the business that do build the pathway to the vision require close and careful management. The aspects of the organisation that already represent part of the vision are prime opportunities to release control, but only to the extent that their manipulation does not distort the purpose and intent of the final vision.

Despite these many radical changes, a fully mature digital organisation of the present is (simply) what all organisations will look like in the future.

13.4 Future marketing ethics

Being digital and being a digital organisation is also transforming ethics. The most significant ethical issue for digital businesses will be the management, control and security of personal data. Despite the discussions throughout this book about needing to connect more closely with your buyer persona, one of the main challenges for any organisation is overcoming the dehumanising aspect of technology and avoiding the temptation to reduce your buyer persona to a data set that can be manipulated, measured and even experimented upon. The relationship between face-to-face interactions and computer-mediated interactions is not simple. In the early era of digital communications much time was spent arguing for its effect of distancing individuals from one another. However, computer-mediated communications increasingly draw people together as much as other forms of interaction. In this context, several important trends for future marketing ethics can be outlined.

Attention, authenticity and truth

Since your buyer persona's attention is becoming a dynamic variable and the competitive environment is increasing, organisations are being forced to act faster and more efficiently. This pressure produces a tendency for shortened and louder messaging. This pressure equally places a challenge on the organisation to remain fair and authentic. Expressing the truth, keeping a high informational value in each message and respecting the data privacy of consumers require time and space. In a high-pressure environment, you should make even more effort to remain efficient and ethical. In order to maintain the prevalent advertising business model of the Internet, your marketing strategy must remain resolutely respectful and consider the experience of your buyer persona rather than viewing online activity as the achievement of a marketing strategy (Quigley, 2015).

Privacy and requests for consent

Increasing interaction online will continually raise the issue of user privacy. Gaining consent from your buyer persona to make two- and three-way interactions possible will become an increasingly important aspect of your strategy, campaigns and tactics. Content will remain 'king', but without consent your content will be heavily lopsided and appear very broadcast-orientated – and ultimately be damaging to your authenticity.

Extreme opinion and user-generated content

The means to publish opinions, thoughts and streams of consciousness is now in the hands of any user. Web 2.0, the Interactive Web or the User Web – whichever term you prefer – encourages user-generated content. This content can represent a major challenge in the context of your owned channels – you cannot control this, but you must manage it. Various social media channels have also become a forum for expressing extreme opinions, including those directed to specific organisations. These opinions can spread virally. The ethical challenge for your organisation now, and in the future, will be to manage opinion. This will be achieved, in part, by maintaining a consistent image while remaining fair and transparent.

13.5 Interactive everything and the Internet of Things

The digital landscape presents a culture of interaction between people and between organisations. The tools for this interaction continue to expand in form, e.g. watches, phones and embedded devices. Simultaneously the forms of interaction also expand, e.g. car sharing, dating and room rental. The range of mechanisms, channels and forms of potential interaction will continue to expand outwards.

This expansion of channels and devices will create an exponential increase in the structured data that is captured from all online activities. The 'everything of everything' is now being created, as a network of structured data is leading to 'everything' being connected to 'everything' else. Google is increasingly a multimedia engine by indexing images, videos, apps, tweets and Facebook pages. While you cannot predict the future, using structured data for content publishing can prepare your organisation to move into the future without significant legacy problems.

The Internet of Things presents a very near future in which the objects of everyday life will be digital and able to communicate with one another, with your organisation and with your buyer persona. The Internet of Things will make marketing and interaction ever more immersive and pervasive. By enabling access and interaction with a wide variety of devices such as, for instance, home appliances, surveillance cameras, monitoring sensors, actuators, displays and vehicles, new services will emerge (Zanella et al., 2014). Undertaken correctly, the Internet of Things will improve our quality of life.

This is both a challenge and an opportunity for your organisation and your marketing strategy (Patel, 2015):

- On-demand services will be expected everywhere.
- New relationships will develop through improved data-driven decision making.
- Nothing will remain unmarketable.

The Internet of Things will shape the near future of your organisation, your buyer persona and your digital strategy.

13.6 Future business models and structures

As data becomes the new oil in an increasing number of organisations, the management and structure of the business will increasingly be informed and directed by its data. For the majority of organisations, data will become the most important asset. For some, data has already become their primary asset, but they are yet to recognise this pivotal fact and yet to base their strategies upon this recognition.

The framework for a future information strategy (Figure 13.2) does not explicitly identify marketing functions. This is, in part, because what are currently labelled as marketing processes and functions permeate the entire model.

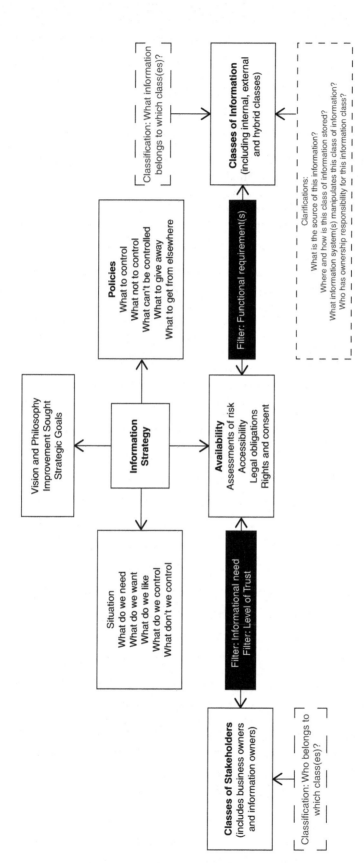

Figure 13.2 A model for a future information strategy

The future information strategy also removes the assumption that your organisation is both large and structurally divided into discrete departments with hierarchical management structures.

Management in small businesses can also defy neat mapping in a meaningful two-dimensional organisation chart. The challenge of being small in the era of digital business is to gain the understanding and perspective of larger brands and businesses without committing to the requirement for a long evolution through the Digital Business Maturity Model from pre-digital to higher levels. No organisation of any size wants to become involved in massive infrastructure purchases or become tied to syntactic labour processes that can be undertaken through outsourcing or be completely automated. Smaller organisations have the additional incentive and advantage of becoming a digital business, as they are less encumbered by burdensome commitments to particular technology contracts or large-scale investment in rapidly aging infrastructure. Building an information strategy also provides a smaller organisation with the tools to 'design in' their digital maturity and circumvent long and slow development phases.

From a governance perspective, the interactions amongst availability, accessibility and rights to specific classes of information will be regarded as the points at which information can be controlled in relation to specific classes of stakeholders. A marketing perspective on the same information and stakeholders would regard these same points of interaction as key touchpoints. What information is drawn from which classes of information and what mechanisms are employed to interact with consumers – who are a specific form of external stakeholder – become the primary questions for any business function, whether it is marketing, accounting, human resources or strategic management. This framework for an integrated information strategy also embeds internal marketing as an interchange that exists between people – internal stakeholders – and information, and is of equal importance to external interactions.

Just as the Digital Business Maturity Model acknowledges the imminent demise of digital as a primary point of distinction within organisations (Evans and Wurster, 1997), so too can a fully articulated and comprehensive information strategy be regarded as a perfectly functional business strategy – at the broadest level. The need to identify and manage the interactions between classes of information and classes of stakeholders, and, by implication, the definition of who belongs to which classes, takes an organisation into a strategic, if not visionary, perspective and moves it away from day-to-day operational and reactive decision making. The advantage of a strategic perspective is often recognised in small businesses but difficult to realise against the backdrop of day-to-day operational necessity. An 'information strategy first' approach – bringing together this book's emphasis on marketing strategy and data – shifts the place and perspective of information in an organisation and, in doing so, offers a mechanism for achieving an always strategic approach.

Clear vision and visionary management are pivotal to the success of an information strategy. The key to a vision of a digitally mature business is to not be bound by current technologies but rather to be informed by what is currently possible.

New business models will be shaped by well-articulated visions of transparent information flows within the organisation. The information strategy of the organisation will be the realisation of a vision that permeates all aspects of a digitally mature business. The most challenging and exciting example of a new business model that takes up this perspective is described as decentralised organisations (DOs) and decentralised autonomous organisations (DAOs). The latter concept has found particular favour amongst cryptocurrency advocates, particularly Bitcoin evangelists. This is largely due to the fact that the backbone of existing Bitcoin technology, the blockchain, provides an underlying solution to the financial and, by extension, contractual arrangements required in a DAO, where the operations are primarily conducted as functions of autonomous artificial intelligence. The exchanges between autonomous (computing) agents in the DAO are conducted technically through the blockchain network and are built on codified business rules and logic. In the fully realised DAO, human interaction with the organisation is primarily as external stakeholders – with the single exception of shareholders. The organisation conducts its business functions entirely through computing power and the application of artificial intelligence. It is possible to envision a future for DAOs in which higher and higher levels of business functions become reduced to effectively syntactic tasks for artificial intelligence. In a DO, people still figure within the organisational structure for their labour contribution. The distinction between syntactic and semantic labour offers a clear explanation as to why and when this contribution will be required, but at the same time increased processing speed and computing ability have the potential to shift currently semantic (higher-level interpretative) tasks to syntactic (mundane and repetitive) work. The analogy here is with the utopian claims of 1960s office automation, which attempted to engineer the paperless office – a vision never fully realised despite the ability of technology to enable the prospect. Similarly, the future vision of a humanless office is also extreme because, despite the prospect that technology will enable this capability, there will be at least residual social and cultural reluctance to fully accept this seemingly dystopian prospect.

From the perspective of digital marketing, DAOs represent a challenge to existing marketing thinking and concepts. The DAO removes much of the emotive aspects of decision making to exchanges formed as a contract and visible on the blockchain. Digital marketing of the future will need to engage with autonomous agents and things – as part of the Internet of Things – alongside the shareholders and developers of these systems. But as this digital maturity evolves, the systems employed for marketing will themselves become more automatic. Many marketing actions will be reduced to syntactic labour functions completed through artificial intelligence and codified business rules and managed by the blockchain as part of a distributed autonomous organisation.

The information strategy first approach (Figure 13.2) commences with interrogation of the vision and philosophy for the use of information within the organisation. Businesses with a digital maturity will position data as their primary asset, and questions of vision are consequently questions regarding the organisational mission and purpose. These 'big' questions are necessary to ensure that strategic viewpoints overarch and drive operational necessity. Within the information strategy, by asking questions of classification and clarification regarding the stakeholders and information within the system – effectively the entire organisation – the operational reality of business can then be recognised and incorporated into a forward-thinking approach that can respond to changing circumstances, including new technologies, without the organisation itself becoming unviable.

The future of business is entirely digital. The future of marketing is entirely digital. These observations build on the recognition that we will inevitably interact with each other through the mediation of technology, including the rise of smart machines. This is not a new observation. Neanderthals communicate to us with cave paintings and Egyptian pharaohs communicate with us through their tombs. What is constantly changing is the speed and amplification of our communications, made possible through newer, more sophisticated technologies. To manage and keep pace with this change we must ourselves inevitably make use of the same new technologies – in whatever forms they eventually take.

13.7 Summary

This chapter provided insights into the future through discussion and development of the five-staged Digital Business Maturity Model, as well as a model information strategy. Both models can be applied to any organisation and encourage the application of a consistently strategic perspective.

Positioning an organisation within the Digital Business Maturity Model recognises its current levels of digital activities – including marketing – as well as its future potential. Identifying an organisation's current digital business maturity in relation to its current strategic position also offers a clear understanding of the progression route required to achieve even greater levels of digital maturity. The Digital Business Maturity Model provides a mechanism for measuring an organisation's current and future prospects for participating in the global digital economy.

An information strategy takes digital marketing to a holistic position by embedding it within a single data-oriented view of the organisation. The marketing function is everywhere in the organisation and an integral part of every action – as are all business functions and processes.

13.8 References

Evans, P. and Wurster, T. (1997) Strategy and the new economics of information. *Harvard Business Review*, 75(5) (September–October), 70–82. hbr.org/1997/09/strategy-and-the-new-economics-of-information

Greenhill, A. and Fletcher, G. (2013) Labouring online: Are there any 'new' labour processes within virtual worlds? *Journal for the Association of Information Systems (JAIS)*, 14(11).

Patel, N. (2015) *How the Internet of Things is changing online marketing.* www.forbes.com/sites/neilpatel/2015/12/10/how-the-internet-of-things-is-changing-online-marketing/#690d55456e2f

Quigley, C. (2015) The ethics of attention and the inevitable future of digital advertising. *WallBlog.* wallblog.co.uk/2015/11/13/the-ethics-of-attention-and-the-inevitable-future-of-digital-advertising/#ixzz3ycFhMRri

Zanella, A., Nicola, B., Angelo, C., Lorenzo, V. and Michele, Z. (2014) Internet of things for smart cities. *IEEE Internet of Things Journal,* 1(1), 22–32.

Index

Printed in the United States
by Baker & Taylor Publisher Services